CW00351035

exploring
*I*RELAND

Published by The Automobile Association,
Fanum House, Basingstoke, Hampshire RG21 2EA

exploring
IRELAND

Written and researched by Sean Callery
Edited by Emma Callery

Published by The Automobile
Association, Fanum House, Basingstoke,
Hampshire RG21 2EA

© The Automobile Association 1992

Maps © The Automobile Association

All rights reserved. No part of this
publication may be reproduced, stored in
a retrieval system, or transmitted in any
form or by any means – electronic,
mechanical, photocopying, recording or
otherwise – unless the written
permission of the Publishers has been
given beforehand.

A catalogue record for this book is
available from the British Library

ISBN 0 7495 0523 0

Filmset by Servis Filmsetting Ltd,
Manchester
Colour reproduction by Daylight Colour
Art Pte Ltd, Singapore
Printed by Butler and Tanner Ltd, Frome

Set in 8/9½pt Garamond

The contents of this publication are
believed correct at the time of printing.
Nevertheless, the Publishers cannot
accept responsibility for errors or
omissions, or for changes in details given.
They would welcome information to
help keep the book up to date.

*Photograph page 1: an informative
signpost on the Ring of Kerry.*

*Photograph pages 2–3: Merrion Row,
Dublin.*

*Photograph pages 4–5 (these pages):
the promontory fort of Dun Beag, near
Ventry on the Dingle Peninsula.*

CONTENTS

INTRODUCTION

Visiting Ireland is a joy, for it offers superb and varied scenery, dotted with fascinating historic sites, and some beautiful cities. Pervading it all is a relaxed and fun-loving attitude to life, together with deep religious sentiment and a strong sense of the past. Sometimes referred to as 'the Emerald Isle', Ireland is rich in greenery, but its landscape is also filled with majestic mountains, mysterious bogs, and verdant valleys, culminating in a wild and beautiful coast. Another attraction is that most of it is quite unspoilt by the influx of tourism, which provides a welcome boost to a struggling rural economy: a warm welcome is part of the charm of the country.

This book explores Ireland by taking each of its four provinces in turn, beginning with an overall description and a county-by-county briefing. This is followed by a comprehensive gazetteer giving descriptions of the most interesting and important places to visit. With each entry is a map reference allowing the reader to find the place described with ease.

To help the visitor get the most out of a trip to Ireland, the book starts with text giving general useful information, advice on where to stay, guidance for the motorist, and a brief history of the country which will enhance an understanding of much that you will see. There is also a four-page atlas and, within the gazetteer, plans of the major cities of Dublin and Belfast.

The beautiful, and very Irish, Errigal Mountain in Donegal.

KEY TO ATLAS

♦

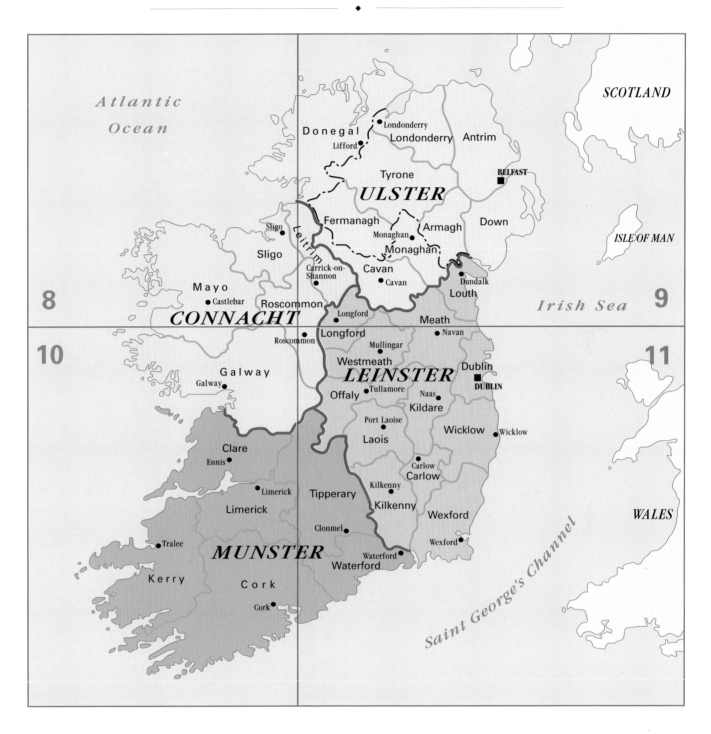

Atlantic Ocean

SCOTLAND

Donegal

• Londonderry
Londonderry   Antrim

Lifford •

Tyrone

ULSTER

BELFAST ■

Fermanagh

Down

Sligo •

Monaghan •

Armagh

ISLE OF MAN

Leitrim

Sligo

Monaghan

Carrick-on-Shannon •

Cavan

Mayo

Cavan •

Dundalk •

Louth

Castlebar •

Roscommon

Irish Sea

CONNACHT

Longford •

Meath

8   9

Roscommon •

Longford

Navan •

10   11

Mullingar •

Galway

Westmeath

Dublin

LEINSTER

DUBLIN ■

Galway •

Offaly

Tullamore •

Naas •

Kildare

Port Laoise •

Clare

Laois

Wicklow

Ennis •

Wicklow •

Carlow •
Carlow

Limerick •

Tipperary

Kilkenny •

Limerick

Kilkenny

Wexford

Clonmel •

Tralee •

MUNSTER

Wexford •

Waterford •
Waterford

WALES

Kerry

Cork

Saint George's Channel

Cork •

MUNSTER		LEINSTER		CONNACHT	ULSTER	
Clare		Carlow	Offaly	Galway	Antrim	Londonderry
Cork		Dublin	Westmeath	Leitrim	Armagh	Monaghan
Kerry		Kildare	Wexford	Mayo	Cavan	Tyrone
Limerick		Kilkenny	Wicklow	Roscommon	Donegal	
Tipperary		Laois		Sligo	Down	
Waterford		Longford			Fermanagh	
		Louth				
		Meath				

Abbeydorney G2
Abbeyfeale G2
Abbeyleix G4
Adamstown G4
Adare G2
Adrigole H2
Ahascragh F3
Ahoghill D5
Allihies H1
Anascaul H1
Annalong E5
Annestown H4
Antrim D5
Ardagh G2
Ardara D3
Ardcath F5
Ardee E4
Ardfert G2
Ardfinnan G3
Ardglass E5
Ardgroom H1
Arklow G5
Arless G4
Armagh D4
Armoy C5
Arthurstown H4
Arvagh E4
Ashbourne F4
Ashford F5
Askeaton G2
Athboy E4
Athea G2
Athenry F3
Athleague F3
Athlone F3
Athy F4
Augher E4
Aughnacloy D4
Aughrim G5
Avoca G5

Bailieborough E4
Balbriggan F5
Balla E2
Ballacolla G4
Ballaghaderreen E3
Ballina G3
Ballina E2
Ballinafad E3
Ballinagh E4
Ballinakill G4
Ballinalee E3
Ballinamallard D4
Ballinamore F3
Ballinamore E3
Ballinascarty H2
Ballinasloe F3
Ballindine E2
Ballineen H2
Ballingarry G3
Ballingarry G2
Ballingeary H2
(Beal Atha an Ghaorfthaidh)
Ballinhassig H3
Ballinlough E3
Ballinrobe E2
Ballinspittle H2
Ballintober E3
Ballintra D3
Ballivor F4
Ballon G4
Ballybaun F3
Ballybay E4
Ballybofey D3
Ballybunion G2
Ballycanew G5
Ballycarry D5
Ballycastle D2
Ballycastle C5
Ballyclare D5
Ballyconneely F1

Ballycotton H3
Ballycumber F3
Ballydehob J2
Ballydesmond H2
Ballyduff H3
Ballyduff G2
Ballyfarnan E3
Ballygalley D5
Ballygar F3
Ballygawley D4
Ballygowan D5
Ballyhaise E4
Ballyhale G4
Ballyhaunis E3
Ballyhean E2
Ballyheige G1
Ballyjamesduff F3
Ballykeeran F3
Ballylanders G3
Ballylongford G2
Ballylooby G3
Ballylynan G4
Ballymahon F3
Ballymakeery H2
Ballymaloe H3
Ballymena D5
Ballymoe E3
Ballymoney C4
Ballymore E3
Ballymore Eustace F4
Ballymote E3
Ballynure D5
Ballyragget G4
Ballyroan G4
Ballysadare E3
Ballyshannon D3
Ballyvaughan F2
Ballywalter D5
Balrothery F5
Baltimore J2
Baltinglass G4
Banagher F3
Banbridge D5
Bandon H2
Bangor D5
Bangor Erris E2
Bansha G3
Banteer H2
Bantry H2
Barryporeen H3
Beaufort H2
Belcoo D3
Belfast D5
Belgooly H3
Bellaghy D4
Belleek D3
Belmullet D2
(Beal an Mhuirhead)
Belturbet E4
Benburb D4
Bennetsbridge G4
Beragh D4
Birr F3
Blacklion D3
Blackwater G5
Blarney H3
Blessington F4
Boherbue H2
Borris G4
Borris-in-Ossory G3
Borrisokane F3
Borrisoleigh G3
Boyle E3
Bracknagh F4
Bray F5
Bridgetown H4
Brittas F4
Broadford G3
Broadford G2

Broughshane D5
Bruff G3
Bruree G3
Bunclody G4
Buncrana C4
Bundoran D3
Bunnahowen D2
Bunnyconnellan E2
Bushmills C4
Butler's Bridge E4
Buttevant G3

Cadamstown F3
Caherconlish G3
Caherdaniel H1
Cahir G3
Cahirciveen H1
Caledon D4
Callan G4
Caltra F3
Camolin G4
Camp G1
Cappagh White G3
Cappamore G3
Cappoquin H3
Carlanstown E4
Carlingford E5
Carlow G4
Carndonagh C4
Carnew G4
Carnlough C5
Carracastle E3
Carrick D3
(Ah Charraig)
Carrickfergus D5
Carrickmacross E4
Carrickmore D4
Carrick-on-Shannon E3
Carrick-on-Suir G4
Carrigahorig F3
Carrigaline H3
Carrigallen F3
Carriganimmy H2
Carrigans C4
Carrowkeel C4
Carryduff D5
Cashel G3
Castlebar E2
Castlebellingham E5
Castleblayney E4
Castlebridge G4
Castlecomer G4
Castle Cove H1
Castlederg D4
Castledermot G4
Castleisland G2
Castlemaine H2
Castlemartyr H3
Castleplunkett E3
Castlepollard E4
Castlerea E3
Castlerock D4
Castleshane E4
Castletown F4
Castletownbere H1
Castletownroche H3
Castletownshend J2
Castlewellan E5
Causeway G2
Cavan E4
Ceanannus Mor (Kells) E4
Celbridge F4
Charlestown E3
Clady D4
Clane F4
Clara F3
Clarecastle G2
Claremorris E2
Clarinbridge F2
Clashmore H3

Claudy C4
Clifden F1
Clifden F1
Cliffony D3
Cloghan F3
Clogh G4
Clogheen H3
Clogher D4
Clohamon G4
Clonakilty H2
Clonard F4
Clonaslee F4
Clonbulloge F4
Clonbur (An Fhairche) E2
Clondalkin F4
Clonmany C4
Clonmel G3
Clonmellon F4
Clonmore G5
Clonony F3
Clonoulty G3
Clonroche G4
Clontibret E4
Cloobannin H2
Cloondara E3
Cloonkeen E3
Cloonlara G3
Clough D5
Cloughjordan F3
Cloyne H3
Coagh D4
Coalisland D4
Cobh H3
Coleraine C4
Collinstown E4
Collon E4
Collooney E3
Comber D5
Conna H3
Cookstown D4
Coole E4
Cooraclare G2
Cootehill E4
Cork H3
Cork Airport H3
Comamona F2
Corofin F2
Courtmacsherry H2
Courtown Harbour G5
Craigavon D5
Craughwell F3
Creggs E3
Creeslough C3
Croagh G2
Crolly (Croithli) C3
Crookedwood E4
Crookhaven J1
Crookstown H2
Croom G2
Crossakeel E4
Cross Barry H2
Crosshaven H3
Crossmaglen E4
Crossmolina E2
Crumlin D5
Crusheen F2
Culdaff C4
Culleybackey D5
Curracloe G5
Curraghboy F3
Curry E3
Cushendall C5

Daingean F4
Delvin E4
Derrygonnelly D3
Derrylin E4
Dervock C4
Dingle (An Daingean) H1
Doagh D5

Donaghadee D5
Donaghmore G3
Donegal D3
Doneraile H3
Doonbeg G2
Douglad H3
Downpatrick D5
Dowra E3
Draperstown D4
Drimoleague H2
Dripsey H2
Drogheda E5
Droichead Nua F4
(Newbridge)
Dromahair D3
Dromcolliher G2
Dromore D5
Dromore E4
Dromore West D2
Drum E4
Drumconrath E4
Drumkeeran E3
Drumlish E3
Drumod E3
Drumquin D4
Drumshanbo E3
Drumsna D3
Duagh G2
Dublin F5
Duleek E4
Dunboyne F4
Duncormick H4
Dundalk E5
Dunderrow H2
Dundrum E5
Dunfanaghy C3
Dungannon D4
Dungarvan H3
Dungarvan G4
Dungiven C4
Dungloe C3
Dungourney H3
Dunkineely D3
Dun Laoghaire F5
Dunlavin F4
Dunleer E4
Dunloy C5
Dunmanway H2
Dunmore E3
Dunmore East H4
Dunmurry D5
Dunshauglin F4
Durrow G4
Durrus H2

Easky D2
Edenderry F4
Edgeworthstown E3
Eglinton C4
Elphin E3
Emyvale D4
Enfield F4
Ennis G2
Enniscorthy G4
Enniscrone D2
Enniskean H2
Enniskillen D4
Ennistymon F2
Eyrecourt F3

Farnaught E3
Farranfore H2
Feakle F3
Fenagh E3
Fermoy H3
Ferns G4
Fethard H4
Fethard G3
Finnea E4
Fintona D4
Fivemiletown D4

Fontstown F4
Foulkesmills G4
Foxford E2
Foynes G2
Freemount G2
Frenchpark E3
Freshford G3
Fuerty E3

Galbally G3
Galway F2
Garrison D3
Garvagh C4
Geashill F4
Gilford D5
Glandore J2
Glanmire H3
Glanworth H3
Glaslough D4
Glassan F3
Glenamaddy E3
Glenarm C5
Glenavy D5
Glenbeigh H1
Glencolumbkille D3
(Gleam Cholm Cille)
Glendalough F5
Glenealy G5
Glenfarne D3
Glengarriff H2
Glenmore G4
Glenties D3
Glenville H3
Glin G2
Glinsk F3
(Glinsce)
Golden G3
Goleen J1
Goresbridge G4
Gorey G5
Gort F2
Gortin D4
Gowran G4
Craiguenamanagh G4
Grallagh G3
Granard E4
Grange D3
Greencastle E5
Greyabbey D5
Greystones F5
Gulladuff D4

Hackettstown G4
Headford F2
Herbertstown G3
Hillsborough D5
Hilltown E5
Hospital G3
Holycross G3
Holywood D5
Howth F5

Inch H1
Inchigeelagh H2
Inishannon H2

Johnstown G3

Kanturk H2
Keadue E3
Keady E4
Keel E1
Keenagh E3
Kells D5
Kenmare H2
Kesh D3
Kilbeggan F4
Kilberry E4
Kilbrittain H2
Kilcar D3
(Cill Charthaigh)
Leap J2

Kilcock F4
Kilcolgan F2
Kilconnell F3
Kilconnell F2
Kilcoole F5
Kilcormac F3
Kilcullen F4
Kilcurry E4
Kildare F4
Kildavin G4
Kildorrey H3
Kildress D4
Kilfenora F2
Kilfinnane G3
Kilgarvan H2
Kilkee E5
Kilkeel E5
Kilkelly E2
Kilkenny G4
Kilkieran F2
(Cill Ciarain)
Kilkinlea G2
Kill H4
Killadysert G2
Killala E2
Killaloe G3
Killarney H2
Killashandra E4
Killashee E3
Killeagh H3
Killeigh F4
Killenaule G3
Killimer G2
Killimor F3
Killiney F5
Killinick H4
Killorglin H1
Killough E5
Killucan F4
Killybegs D3
Killyleagh D5
Kilmacanoge F5
Kilmacrenan C3
Kilmacthomas H4
Kilmaganny G4
Kilmaine E2
Kilmallock G3
Kilmanagh G4
Kilmanahan G3
Kilmeaden H4
Kilmeage F4
Kilmeedy G2
Kilmichael H2
Kilmore Quay H4
Kilnaleck E4
Kilrea C4
Kilrush G2
Kilsheelan G3
Kiltealy G4
Kiltegan G4
Kiltimagh E2
Kiltoom F3
Kingscourt E4
Kinlough D3
Kinnegad F4
Kinnitty F3
Kinsale H3
Kinvarra F2
Kircubbin D5
Knock E2
Knockcroghery E3
Knocklofty G3
Knockmahon H4
Knocktopher G4

Lahinch F2
Lanesborough E3
Laragh F5
Lauragh H1
Laurencetown F3
Leap J2

Leenane E2
Leighlinbridge G4
Leitrim E3
Leixlip F4
Lemybrien H3
Letterfrack E2
Letterkenny C3
Lifford D4
Limavady C4
Limerick G3
Lisbellaw D4
Lisburn D5
Liscarroll G2
Lisdoonvarna F2
Lismore H3
Lisnaskea D4
Lisryan E4
Listowel G2
Loghill G2
Londonderry C4
Longford E3
Loughbrickland D5
Loughgall D4
Loughglinn E3
Loughrea F3
Louisburgh E2
Lucan F4
Lurgan D5
Lusk F5

Macroom H2
Maghera E5
Maghera D4
Magherafelt D4
Maguiresbridge D4
Malahide F5
Malin C4
Malin More D3
Mallow H2
Manorhamilton D3
Markethill D4
Maynooth F4
Maze D5
Middletown D4
Midleton H3
Milford C4
Millstreet H2
Milltown H2
Milltown Malbay G2
Mitchelstown H3
Moate F3
Mohill E3
Molls Gap H2
Monaghan E4
Monasterevin F4
Moneygall G3
Moneymore D4
Monivea F3
Mooncoin H4
Moorfields D5
Mount Bellew F3
Mount Charles D3
Mountmellick F4
Mountrath F4
Mountshannon F3
Mourne Abbey H3

Moville C4
Moy D4
Moylett E4
Moynalty E4
Moyvore F3
Muckross H2
Muff C4
Muine Bheag G4
Mullabohy G4
Mullagh H4
Mullinavat G4
Mullingar F4
Myshall G4

Naas F4
Nad H2
Naul F5
Navan E4
Neale E2
Nenagh G3
Newbliss E4
Newcastle E5
Newcastle West G2
Newinn G3
Newmarket H2
Newmarket-on-Fer[gus]
Newport G3
Newport E2
New Ross G4
Newry E4
Newtown G4
Newtownabbey D5
Newtownards D5
Newtown Butler E4
Newtown Forbes E3
Newtownhamilton E4
Newtown Mount Kennedy
Newtownstewart D4
Nobber E4

Oilgate G4
Oldcastle E4
Omagh D4

C
D
E
1
2

Aran Island
Gweebar[ra]

Rossan Point
Malin More
Glencolumbkille (Gleann Cholm Cille)
Glencolumbkille Folk Museum 1972
SLIEVE LEAGUE
Carrick (An Charra)
Kilcar (Cill Charthaigh) Killyb[egs]
St John's Point

Inishmurray
D o n e g a l
R279
Grange 1722
Lissadell House BENB[ULBEN]
Rosses Point N15
Sligo Bay

Erris Head Broad Haven
Downpatrick Head
Ballycastle Killala Bay Easky Rosses Point
Dromore West Strandhill R292 S[ligo]
Belmullet (Béal an Mhuirhead) R314 Killala Enniscrone
Bunnahowen Carrowmore Lough R315 Colloney Ballys[adare]
Inishkea Bangor Erris R313 N59 Bunnyconnellan Tobercurry R206
Duvillaun More Blacksod Bay Crossmolina Ballina OX MTS
2369 Connaught Regional Airport N17
2204 SLIEVE MORE Keel 2646 NEPHIN Curry Charlestown Carracastle N5
Achill Head Lough Feeagh Foxford Swinford Ballaghaderre[en]
Achill Island R319 R312 R320 Kilkelly R325 N17 Frenchpark
Clare Newport R311 Turlough N5 Castlebar Kiltimagh R293 R325
Clew Bay Westport R335 N60 Ballyhean Knock Loughglinn Castlerea
Louisburgh CROAGH PATRICK 2510 Westport Zoo Balla Ballyhaunis Ballinlough
Caher R330 N84 Claremorris R327
Inishturk Partry Ballindine R327
Inishbofin Ballinrobe Kilmaine R333 Dunmore Glenamaddy
Inishark Cruagh 2239 Neale R345 Cregga
Leenene Letterfrack R344 Clonbur

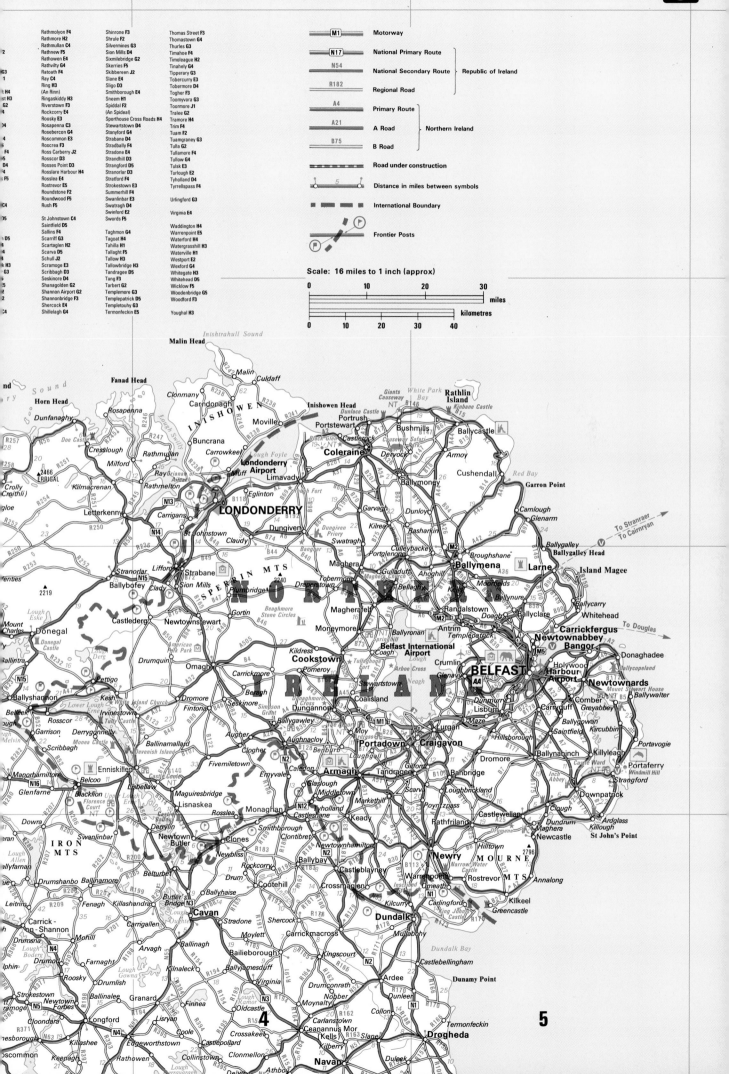

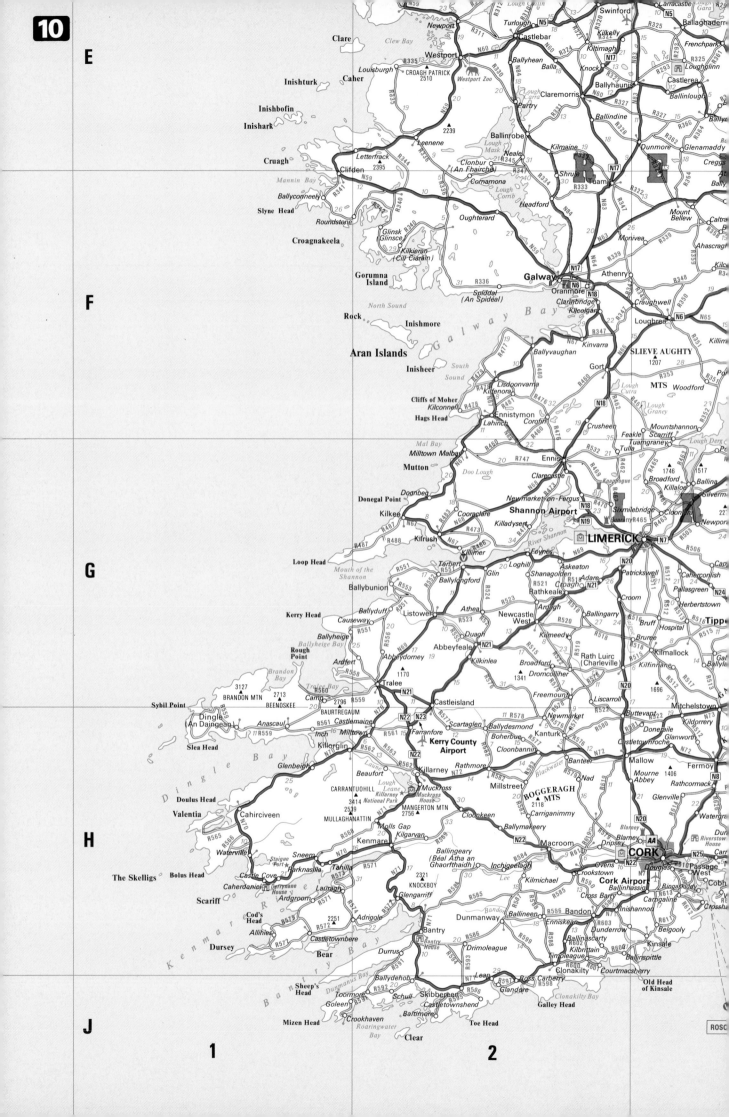

GENERAL
*I*NFORMATION

DOCUMENTS

British nationals can enter and stay for any length of time in both Northern Ireland and the Republic without a passport. Visitors from other countries will require one, which entitles them to stay for three months (extendable on application to the Department of Justice in Dublin). It is important to take some form of identification – and a passport is the most convincing – for cashing travellers' cheques and in case you need to use the medical services.

HEALTH

No inoculations are required before visiting Ireland. Britons have their normal right to treatment in Northern Ireland, and to claim this in the Republic they must have a certificate of entitlement. Details of this are given in leaflet SA40, which is available from the Department of Health and Social Security, and which contains an application for Form E111, which is the certificate. If you do require treatment in the Republic, make it clear immediately that you wish to be treated under the social security arrangements of the European Community, otherwise you are likely to have to pay in full. Other EC citizens may have these rights too: check before you travel.

INSURANCE

It is sensible to take out insurance to cover vehicles, travel and health before your journey.

MONEY

In Northern Ireland, the currency is pounds sterling, and all the major British banks are represented. In the Republic, it is the Irish pound, or punt, which is divided into 100 pence, but is worth slightly less than the British pound. Many shops will accept the more valuable British pound, but without reducing their prices. You can change some money in advance for immediate expenses, and take the rest in the more secure form of travellers' cheques or Eurocheques, which can be changed at banks, larger tourist offices and bureaux de change. It is worth changing money while in a large town before going to a remote area where the banks may only open for a few days a week. There is no limit on the money you can take into the Republic, but you cannot leave with more than IR£150, or with foreign currency notes above IR£1200 in value.

Wherever you travel, you are rarely far from water, which creates views such as this one at Glenveagh.

To	From	Operator	Journey time (hrs)
Belfast	Liverpool	Belfast Car Ferries	9
Cork	Swansea	Swansea –Cork Ferries	10
Dublin	Holyhead	B + I, Sealink	3.5
	Liverpool	B + I	9
Larne	Cairnryan	P&O	2
Larne	Stranraer	Sealink	2.5
Rosslare	Fishguard	Sealink	3.5

Sailings to some destinations are also possible from the French ports Le Havre, Cherbourg, and Roscoff.

CREDIT/CHARGE CARDS

Access/Mastercard and Visa/Barclaycard are accepted in large shops, hotels and upmarket restaurants both sides of the border, though Diners' Club and American Express are not as widely recognized. The same applies at major petrol stations, but you may not be able to use cards to pay for petrol in rural areas.

TRAVEL

Air Flying is rapidly replacing the ferry as the cheapest and most convenient way to reach Ireland. However, motorists will then have to hire a car at one of the most expensive rates in Europe. Among the airlines flying regularly to Ireland are the country's own Aer Lingus and Ryanair. Flights are offered to Dublin or the regional airports, though you sometimes have to change at Dublin for these, which are at Belfast, Cork, Derry, Dublin, Galway, Kerry, Knock, Shannon, Sligo and Waterford.

Sea crossings This is the only way to get to Ireland with your own car, but it is not cheap, and some sailings can take up to ten hours. It is worth considering your best option and whether to cross overnight or lose a day by travelling in daylight. The following table shows the main routes and carriers.

Rail Combined sea/rail tickets can be purchased from local stations in Great Britain. Once in Ireland, the rail network fans out from Dublin and is fast but not comprehensive or cheap. Irish Rail sells a Rambler Ticket which allows unlimited rail travel on eight days out of 15, or 15 out of 30. There is also an unlimited ticket for rail and buses.

Coach and bus Coach fares from Britain to Ireland are low, but the journey takes about 12 hours, and once in the country the same characteristics of good value but slow travelling speeds apply. As with rail,

there are some tickets giving unlimited travel over a set period. It makes sense to buy a timetable at a major bus station as some remote areas are only visited by bus twice a week.

Car hire One option worth exploring, particularly as air travel can be relatively cheap and quick, is of hiring a car in Ireland. There are hire car firms at all airports and major cities, but they are notoriously expensive in the Republic. Smaller firms are likely to be cheaper, but they may not be flexible enough to allow you to drop off the car in a different location to where you picked it up. Booking ahead will allow you to shop around for special deals – which often come in the form of fly-drive or rail-ferry-drive packages. Some companies may only hire out to drivers who have held a full, valid and endorsement-free driving licence for two years, and the general age limit is over 23. You should inform the hire company if you intend to enter or leave the Republic.

Disabled travellers If you or one of your party are disabled, tell your travel agent of any special requirements you have. Airlines, ferry companies and most hotels will make provision for those who cannot walk.

OBTAINING INFORMATION
Information about Ireland is available from the Irish Tourist Board (Bord Failte) and the Northern Ireland Tourist Board (NITB). Their addresses are: Bord Failte, Ireland House, 150 New Bond Street, London W1Y 0AQ, telephone 071–493 3201; it has its head office at 16 Nassau Street, Dublin 2, telephone 01–679 1977. The NITB is at 11 Berkeley Street, London W1, telephone 0800–282662, or 071–493 0601, with a head office at St Anne's Court, North Street, Belfast, telephone 0232–231221. The Irish Consulate in Great Britain is at 17 Grosvenor Place, London SW1X 7HR, telephone 071–235 2171. In the country itself, there are tourist offices in most places of interest, identified by a white letter 'i' on a green background.

SECURITY AND THE POLICE
The police force in the Republic is called the Garda or Gardai, and its members wear black and blue uniforms. In Northern Ireland policing is by the green-uniformed Royal Ulster Constabulary, and in large settlements you may also see some of the British army. Representatives of both may stop you, and obviously it pays to be as polite and cooperative as possible. It is imperative that you use official border crossing points between the North and South, and these are well signposted and marked on all up-to-date maps. There are security zones in many large settlements in the north, where it is illegal to leave your car unattended. It is also against the law to photograph police barracks and army installations.

Ireland has a number of charming seaside towns which succeed in retaining a sense of the past, as here at Dawkey in County Dublin.

In the North, there are no left luggage facilities, and bags must never be left unattended. South of the border, most bus and train stations have left luggage facilities. If all this seems a little daunting, in reality you are as safe, probably safer, in Ireland as in any other part of Europe.

BANKING AND SHOPPING HOURS
In the Republic, banks open on weekdays from 10am to 3pm, closing for an hour from 12.30pm, while many are open until 5pm on Thursdays. In the North, the hours are 10am to 3.30pm, still with the lunch hour but not staying open later on Thursdays. In both cases, outside the cities, some banks are open only on certain days. Shop hours are generally 9am to 5.30pm, Monday to Saturday, with some half days and some late opening. Trading hours are a good deal more flexible in the rural south, especially as many of the village stores are also pubs.

RECLAIMING VAT
If you buy goods in Ireland to take home with you, and leave within two months of the purchase, you may be able to claim a refund on the sales tax (Value Added Tax, or VAT). This does not apply to British visitors to Northern Ireland. If you are from an EC country, this applies to more expensive items and is dependant on the shop operating a refund scheme. If you are from a non-EC country, you can reclaim the VAT regardless of the cost of the item, provided the shop operates a refund scheme. You will need a passport or some other form of identification to show in the shop.

USING THE GAZETTEER
The gazetter lists places of interest in alphabetical order, province by province. The place name is followed by its county in brackets, and a map reference follows. Any Gaelic name for the site is given in italics, and English translations are provided wherever possible.

PUBLIC HOLIDAYS
The public holidays are (R = Republic only, N = Northern Ireland only):
1 January New Year's Day; 17 March St Patrick's Day; Good Friday; Easter Monday; First Monday in May (May Day); Last Monday in May, Spring Bank Holiday (N); First Monday in June (R); 12 July, Orange Day (N); First Monday in August; Last Monday in August (N); Last Monday in October (R); 25 and 26 December, Christmas Day and St Stephen's, or Boxing, Day.

ACCESS TO SITES
Most of the sites described in this book are open to the public. In some cases, visitors will be directed to pick up the necessary keys from a local guardian. Most museums and tourist sites close for one day a week, and many are shut between October and March. Consult the local tourist office.

TELEPHONES
As usual, it is always cheaper to use a public callbox than a hotel room phone. The ringing tone is two short tones repeated at regular intervals, while long tones with short pauses mean the line is busy.

Service	Republic	NI
Operator	10	100
Directory enquiries	190	192
Long distance calls	10	100
International calls	114	155
Telegrams	115	190/195

CUSTOMS
The standard EC customs regulations apply when travelling between the Republic and Northern Ireland, and into either from another EC country. Visitors may import or export goods for their personal use up to certain limits depending on whether the goods were bought in ordinary shops (tax paid) or duty-free shops. On leaving the Republic, a departure tax of £5 is charged, which is usually paid when you buy your ticket.

ELECTRICITY
Plugs are British-style three square pins, although there are a few two-pin round wall types left. In the Republic, 220 volts AC is standard, in Northern Ireland it is 240 volts AC – both of which are compatible with British appliances.

WHERE TO STAY

HOTELS

There are upmarket hotels in most major cities, and some establishments in rural areas which offer very good value. Hotels offer food to residents and non-residents alike. A number are listed by the Irish Hotels Federation in an annual booklet. Many have been inspected and approved by the AA, in which case they will display their AA classification. These are:

1-star: Generally small-scale and with good furnishing and facilities.

2-star: Offering a higher standard of accommodation, and with 20% private bathrooms or showers.

3-star: Well-appointed and with private bathrooms or showers in two-thirds of the bedrooms.

4-star: Very well-appointed, with high standards of comfort and service, and private bathrooms or showers in all rooms.

5-star: Meeting the best international standards. In provincial areas, some services may, however, be provided on a more informal and restricted basis.

GUESTHOUSES

Some of these are much the same as small hotels, but with more limited facilities. They provide clean, comfortable accommodation in homely surroundings. They must have a minimum of six bedrooms, and there should be a general bathroom and general toilet for each six bedrooms without private facilities. There will also be parking close by.

TOWN AND COUNTRY HOMES

Available only in the Republic, these are similar to guesthouses not usually smaller, family-run concerns. They must have at least four bedrooms and a general bathroom and toilet. Many are period homes (some are even castles) run in country house style, so that, for example, breakfasts and dinners are eaten at a communal table.

FARMHOUSES

These are family homes on a working farm, offering bed and breakfast accommodation. They are often particularly popular with children who enjoy seeing the daily life of animals on the farm. Some form loose associations – one grouping consists of organic farm guesthouses.

SELF-CATERING

There is plenty of self-catering accommodation available, especially in rural areas. You may be able to rent a traditional Irish cottage with a turf-burning fire. In some

*I*reland has a wide variety of accommodation to offer, from luxury hotels to bed and breakfast in a farmhouse. Whatever kind you choose, book ahead. July and August are often booked up well in advance, and if a festival is due to take place, rooms can be hard to find. Dublin in particular can get very booked up. Some establishments charge lower rates out of season, or special package deals, but others close for six months of the year. You should expect to pay a supplement for single occupancy.

A number of booklets listing different kinds of accommodation in town and

Spectacular Mount Stewart House is not a hotel, but you might find accommodation in such grand settings.

country have been produced by the Irish Tourist Board in the Republic. Look for their 'Bord Failte Approved' sign outside some premises, and also, of course, the AA Classification signs that good premises display. For Northern Ireland, consult the Northern Ireland Tourist Board, which also produces a booklet on accommodation. Bed and breakfast accommodation is a little more scarce in the North than in the Republic; booking ahead is advisable.

IRISH FESTIVALS

The following list of regular festivals will help alert you to possible shortages of accommodation in the area you intend to visit – and give you the opportunity to enjoy them too, provided you book your room in advance.

February: Cavan International Song Contest.

March: Belfast Music Festival.

17 March: St Patrick's Day – festivities for several days in large cities.

April: Irish Grand National – major horse race held at Fairyhouse (Meath).

April/May: Cork International Choral and Folk Dance Festival – internationally recognized.

May: Killarney Pan Celtic Week – traditional sports and music.
Irish FA Cup Final – held in Dublin.
An Fleadh Nua – a three-day festival of music, song and dance at Ennis (Clare).
Music festival in Ballywalter (Down).

June: Sea angling festival, Westport (Mayo).
Irish music festival, Monaghan.
Irish Derby – one of many big race meetings in Kildare at the Curragh.

July: Cobh International Folk Dance Festival.
Glens of Antrim Feis, Glenariff – music, dancing, sports.
Festival of Humour, Shannon.

August: Rose of Tralee International Festival (Kerry). Galway race week.
Fleadh Cheoil na Eirann – the biggest traditional music festival, which is held at venues around the country.
Kilkenny International Arts Week – drawn, written and spoken art.

September: Lisdoonvarna Matchmaking Festival – a famous date for lonely hearts

from around the world.
All Ireland Hurling Final – Dublin
Oyster Festival – opens the oyster season, held at Clarinridge on Galway Bay.

September/October: Cork Jazz and Film Festivals – these are separate and prestigious events which sometimes overlap.

October: Castlebar Song Festival – an international event held at Castlebar (Mayo).
Wexford Opera Festival – a friendly event which is world famous among opera cognoscenti.

---

tourist areas there are also a number of purpose-built 'villages', and some country estates have cottages to let.

CAMPING, CARAVANNING AND RIVER CRUISING

There are a number of camping and caravanning sites throughout Ireland which, like many of the rooms, get booked up for July and August. Both tourist boards have lists of caravan and camping parks. There are package deals including car ferry and caravan hire. In rural areas many farmers will be happy to let you stay in a field for a small fee, and sometimes for nothing. Horsedrawn caravans can be hired through CIE Tours International.

You can rent cruisers and sometimes narrow boats on the Shannon, the Grand Canal and the River Barrow, and in the North, on Lough Erne.

The only drawback of this life in the open is that the Irish climate is unpredictable and you may suffer constant rain if you are unlucky. If you are using paraffin or gas for heating and cooking, make sure you stock up in a large town as it may prove elusive in remote areas.

HOSTELS

There are a number of chains of hostels offering basic accommodation which appeals to the young or anyone holidaying on a very tight budget.

DISABLED VISITORS

The Irish Tourist Board has an accommodation guide for disabled people, which is published in conjunction with the National Rehabilitation Board, 24–25 Clyde Road, Ballsbridge, Dublin 2. This organization has also published an access guide to Dublin and offers advice and help to disabled visitors. Wheelchairs can be hired from the Irish Wheelchair Association, Blackheath Drive, Clontarf, Dublin 3.

Useful addresses for disabled travellers in Northern Ireland include the Northern Ireland Council on Disability, 2 Annadale Avenue, Belfast BT7 3JR, and the British Red Cross Society, 1st Floor, University Street, Belfast BT7 1HP.

IRELAND FOR THE MOTORIST

*I*t pays to take a relaxed attitude when driving in Ireland. Apart from helping you enjoy the scenery, this will ease the strain of the inevitable delays caused by some very poor roads, and the slow pace of some rural traffic. The main AA offices are at Rockhill, Blackrock, Dublin (tel 01–283 3555), 12 Emmet Place, Cork (tel 021–276922) and Fanum House, 108–110 Grt Victoria Street, Belfast (tel 0232–328924). They will be happy to answer any queries you have about motoring in Ireland.

ACCIDENTS

If you have an accident you must stop and use your hazard warning lights or a warning triangle. The emergency services can be called by dialling 999.

BREAKDOWN

If your vehicle breaks down, try to move it somewhere where it will not cause obstruction. Use the hazard warning lights and/or warning triangle. If the car is rented, contact the rental company. If it is your own car, and you are a member of the Automobile Association or one of the AIT (Alliance International de Tourisme) driving clubs, you can call on the AA rescue service, which operates in Northern Ireland and the Republic. The RAC operates a similar service only in Northern Ireland. If you go to a garage for a repair, it should display a list of its charges, and any invoice should detail separately the costs of labour, parts etc. You should recover any parts which have been replaced.

Your journeys are likely to be short and frequent – because the best way to enjoy scenery such as these mountain views between Kenmare and Glengarrif is by stopping and getting out of the car.

DOCUMENTS

You will need a valid driving licence (with an English-language translation if you wish to hire a car) plus your vehicle registration book, and a letter of authorization from the owner if he/she is not with you. There should be a nationality sticker on your car and any trailer. In the Republic, you may not allow an Irish resident to drive your vehicle, except a garage hand who has your written permission.

INSURANCE

It is advisable to have full comprehensive cover. If you intend to cross the border, check that you are covered both sides of it.

FUEL

Fuel stations in villages in the Republic usually stay open until about 8pm, and some open after Mass on Sundays. In the North, 24-hour stations are fairly common, and many stay open on Sundays. Fuel is cheaper in Northern Ireland than in the Republic, where it costs more than in most of Europe. Credit cards are not widely accepted for fuel. Unleaded petrol can be difficult to find – get a list from the local major tourist office.

PARKING

Large towns and cities in the Republic operate a parking disc system instead of, or in addition to, parking meters. The discs carry instructions for use, and are available from local shops and petrol stations. Many town centres in Northern Ireland have Control Zones, indicated by yellow signs, within which cars must not be left unattended. Sometimes these zones are closed off completely. The aim is to prevent car-bombing, and if you leave your car unattended and it is considered a security risk, it is likely to be blown up. There is generally ample and well-signposted parking on the outskirts of the town. Disabled visitors to Northern Ireland can park free of charge in permitted areas if their vehicle displays an Orange Badge.

ROADS

Drive on the left. There are three road classifications in the Republic: National Primary (prefix N, numbers 1–25); National Secondary (prefix N, numbers over 50); and Regional (prefix R). These provide guidelines only on width and surface quality – some primary routes are little more than country lanes. The only motorways are in short stretches north and west of Dublin, and most major roads have two lanes and a wide hard shoulder. The roads in the Republic are on the whole uncongested, but of a variable quality – some minor roads are pitted with pot-holes which can be very hard to spot when there is some surface water. Other potential hazards include loose chippings, livestock and children playing in the road, so it makes sense to keep speeds low on all but the most major roads. On the whole, the standard of driving is not high, and drink-driving and a relaxed attitude to red lights is often in evidence.

Northern Irish roads are classified as motorways, A or B roads, and on the whole are well maintained. Large towns can get congested, and the other potential source of delay is checkpoints. At the wheel of any cars marked with a large red 'R' is a driver who passed the driving test less than 12 months ago, and who should keep to low speeds.

Relying on Irish signposting is a risky business because they can be inconsistent and contradictory. Always make sure that you have a recent local map to hand.

ROAD SIGNS

Road signs are notoriously inadequate in the Republic. They are often missing, or twisted, so a good map and a relaxed attitude to getting lost are essential. Away from the major roads, signposts can be very confusing. To start with, many roads have more than one number, so the sign may not tally with the number on your map. Secondly, many towns and villages have more than one name, in Gaelic and English (wherever possible, Gaelic names are included in the gazetteer of this book). In the Gaelic-speaking Gaeltacht areas, there is sometimes no English translation of place names. Distances can be in either miles or kilometres – the imperial measure features on older, black on white signs, while the new green signs are metric. Quite often a signpost indicates the same place in different directions, usually because one is a more scenic route. So you are bound to get lost sometime amid the spider's web of rural roads, and the best solution is to stop and ask someone. In Northern Ireland, all distances are in miles.

SPEED LIMITS

The limits in the Republic are 30mph (48kph) in built-up areas, and 55mph (88kph) elsewhere unless otherwise indicated. Non-articulated vehicles with a trailer both sides of the border are restricted to 40mph (64kph). The Northern Ireland limits are the same in built-up areas, 60mph (96kph) in country areas, and 70mph (113kph) on dual carriageways and motorways, unless otherwise indicated. Your average speed for a rural journey is likely to be about 30mph (48kph), a point worth bearing in mind when planning your day.

CROSSING THE BORDER

The border between North and South Ireland is a national frontier, and should only be crossed at the 20-odd approved border crossing points, which are marked on all up-to-date maps. Many of the other border roads have been made impassable, but if you do cross on one you could face penalties. The frontier is guarded by soldiers and can appear daunting, but usually traffic is simply waived through. You must stop if requested to, and may be asked for some proof of identification such as a driving licence or passport, or your vehicle registration book, so it makes sense to keep these handy.

FOOD AND DRINK
IN IRELAND

Visitors to Ireland are unlikely to have journeyed over for the cuisine, which is very much potato-based and values quantity over other factors. Still, it is simple and filling, and when it comes to drink the Irish have rather more to offer, not just with Guinness, but with that perfect environment for a drink or two, the Irish pub.

BREAKFAST

Eat a full Irish breakfast and you may feel like skipping lunch altogether, for this is a filling affair including sausage – either chipolatas or black or white pudding – bacon, tomatoes, egg and mushrooms (all fried), with wheaten or soda bread, often preceded by a course of porridge and possibly followed by a soft thick potato cake. If you tire of food from the frying pan, you may come across some fresh and tender scones which are served for both breakfast and tea.

OTHER MEALS

The potato is the mainstay of the Irish diet and a favourite cooking utensil is the frying pan. The potato crops up in many dishes, including soup, colcannon (cooked potatoes fried in butter with onions and cabbage, kale, or leeks, spiced with nutmeg), potato cakes (mixed with dough and fried in butter), and Dublin coddle (a stew made with layers of sausages, bacon, onion and potatoes). Large portions of meat and two veg with lots of gravy are pretty much staple fare, although soups can be very good and there are cafes and restaurants offering the Irish version of more ethnic food, while fast food bars have begun to proliferate in recent years. A filling and cheap 'high tea' comprises fish and chips, followed by bread and jam, and all washed down with tea. Butter usually features high among the ingredients of a meal, and a favourite addition to many recipes is cream: Ireland is not the place to go if you want to slim down.

EATING OUT

Many pubs offer sandwiches, although the quality varies enormously, and tourist menus offering lower-priced set meals are common in cafes and restaurants. Of course, there are some more upmarket establishments which provide food influenced by continental cooking. Many high quality restaurants, serving more adventurous cuisine accompanied by home-grown vegetables, are in out-of-the-way locations, and may open only if there is demand, so phone first to make a reservation. Perhaps surprisingly, some of the best restaurants in Ireland are to be found in County Cork. On the coasts, again particularly in the west, there are some superb seafood restaurants. Galway is famous for its salmon and hosts its own oyster festival in September, when the seafood is served with soda bread and Guinness. Wexford is famous for its succulent mussels, while Kenmare Bay is the source of excellent scallops.

BUYING YOUR OWN FOOD

If you are prepared to do the legwork, you can obtain some superb fresh food ready to be eaten straight away or for cooking. Ireland has a flourishing dairy industry, and every area has its own farmhouse cheeses, and some marvellous, often unpasteurized cheeses like Cashel Blue. These are stocked by some groceries, delicatessens and supermarkets, and you can sometimes buy direct from the maker. They make an excellent lunch with fresh, locally baked bread. Irish bakers specialize in brown soda bread, made from stone-ground

Oysters and Guinness: unbeatable!

wheaten flour.

You can usually buy good fresh vegetables (though nothing very exotic), but in areas where everyone grows their own, even these can be in short supply. On the coast, it is often worth enquiring where you can buy fresh fish, as you may be put in touch with the catcher himself.

GUINNESS

Ireland's best-known drink is Guinness, a smooth, almost black, beer with a creamy off-white head, but its origins are English. In the 18th century, porters in Covent Garden and Billingsgate markets favoured this bittersweet stout, which was known as Porters. It was exported to Ireland, but bad weather held up a shipment, and the Irish began brewing their own. In 1759, Arthur Guinness founded his brewery at St James' Gate in Dublin, and at 60 acres (24.3ha) it was the largest in the world until 1939.

Stout is brewed with softer water than ale, and the drink's distinctive colour and flavour are imparted by the addition of roasted barley. The company makes a range of stouts of varying strengths for different markets, using the same basic ingredients and methods as when it began brewing. Visitors can tour the famous brewery and sample its inimitable brew. Its only stout-brewing competitors are Murphy's and Beamish, both from Cork. The Irish insist that only their pubs treat the drink properly and pour it correctly – a painstakingly slow process.

WHISKEY

Irish whiskey (always spelt with the 'e') was already being enthusiastically consumed in Ireland when Henry II's troops first visited the country in the 12th century. The potion was called *Uisce beatha*, meaning 'The Water of Life', and the natives have displayed their liking for the stuff to this day. It is claimed that whiskey came to Ireland via monks who returned from their missionary travels with a distilled liquid used in the production of perfumes. The Irish put the process to better use, discovering that heating a fermented mixture of water, yeast, unmalted and malted barley allowed alcohol to be extracted as condensation. The resultant liquid acquired a delicious taste if it was then left to rest in wooden barrels.

The pretty village of Bushmills, Antrim, boasts the oldest licensed distillery in the world, licensed in 1608 and undoubtedly operating long before that. Tours of the distillery take in a peek at the huge copper stills where the waters from St Columb's Rill are transformed into the smooth, fiery drink. Some other long-established distilleries survive, and there is a large one at Midleton, Cork, on a site where whiskey has been produced since 1779. In Dublin, the old John Jameson's distillery now houses a museum about the golden liquid.

TEA

Guinness may be the great Irish drink, but the most popular beverage in Ireland is tea, which is used to wash down meals at all times of the day, and for refreshment inbetween times. Most pubs are happy to serve tea and coffee, which is generally accompanied with cream. Incidentally, the famous Irish coffee (made with coffee, sugar, whiskey and cream) was probably invented in America, although some accounts say it originated at Shannon Airport!

PUBS

No visit to Ireland is complete without at least one lengthy stay in an Irish pub. Though some can be a little dingy, most are social centres where the art of conversation is very much alive, and where there is a delightful sense of fellowship with your fellow drinkers. In rural areas many pubs double up as the village store, adding the charm of the unexpected to the atmosphere of the place.

*L*EISURE IN *I*RELAND

Having fun is important to the Irish, and their country offers a number of leisure pursuits which visitors can enjoy in addition to the many places to visit of cultural or historical interest.

Bird watching: Coastal headlands and offshore island for migrating birds, while there are about 60 bird sanctuaries inland.

Boating: You can take a cruise, or hire a boat, to enjoy Ireland's countless waterways.

Canoeing: A year-round sport which is increasing in popularity in a country offering a wide range of water courses.

Climbing: Most Irish mountains can be climbed without special equipment, though a few such as the Mournes will challenge experienced climbers.

Cycling: The quiet Irish roads are perfect for cycling and bikes can be hired.

Fishing: The coast, lakes and rivers provide a massive range of fish, and anglers are faced with a wide choice of venues from which to cast their line. Some require licences – ask at the local tourist office.

Gaelic football: A bewildering but exciting spectacle.

Golf: Ireland's 250 golf courses include some of championship standard and you are sure to find beautiful scenery wherever your clubs take you.

Horseracing: Close to a national obsession, and spread all over Ireland, although the horseracing centre is the Curragh.

Hurling: Popular traditional sport.

Music: The pubs and clubs of Ireland resonate with the sound of music, not all of it traditional.

Pony-trekking: Available at most tourist centres.

Sailing: With Ireland's wealth of water, this is a popular pastime.

Walking: Northern Ireland has many more pathways than the Republic, but when walking in Ireland, make sure you have a good map.

Watersports: These are increasingly popular, and the Irish coast offers some superb surfing. Windsurfing is another popular pursuit, while sub-aqua diving is also on the increase in Ireland.

THE STORY OF
·
IRELAND

The Irish have a very strong sense of their heritage, and a deeper knowledge of their history than many other nations have of theirs. A number of themes have remained over thousands of years: the sense of identity and isolation that comes with being an island; exploitation by a series of invaders; the struggle to survive in a poor economy; and the fundamental importance of the Church in everyday life.

Early settlers The first settlers in Ireland were probably hunters and fishing people who made the short crossing from Scotland in the middle of the Stone Age in about 6000BC. They travelled in skin coracles, and lived near their major source of food: lakes, rivers and the sea. In about 3000BC, they were joined by Neolithic people, some of whose monuments such as graves and religious sites survive.

The arrival of the Celts It was in the late Bronze Age, around 700BC, that the next set of newcomers, the Celts, made their mark. The Celts were a series of groups of people with Indo-European roots who had battled their way across Europe to escape the powerful Romans. They established small farmsteads protected by ditches and a bank of earth (known as ring forts, or raths), which formed the territory ruled by one of the hundred or so Celtic kings of Ireland – each kingdom in turn part of one of the five Celtic provinces of Ulster, Meath, Leinster, Munster and Connacht.

In the west, they were able to use the supply of stone to build more substantial forts (or cashels). As well as warlike tendencies, the Celts had a strong cultural identity evident in the many spirals and curves of Celtic art. The 8th-century Tara Brooch, now in Dublin's National Museum of Ireland, is a good example.

About a thousand years after the first Celts leapt from their boats onto Irish soil, the early Christian missionaries arrived to spread their Gospel in the land. Among those who continued the crusade over the centuries was St Patrick (see page 126), later the patron saint of Ireland. Gradually, a network of sheltered monastic retreats was established, which became centres of not just Christianity, but of art and learning. During the 5th and 6th centuries, Ireland was the missionary base for the spread of Christianity throughout Europe.

Raiders from Scandinavia The rich pickings to be found at these monasteries were partly to blame for the frequency of pirate raids on the country, particularly by the Vikings, or Norsemen. The tall round towers still seen at many monasteries were look-out posts for these Scandinavian 'sea warriors', who sailed their longboats into inlets and up rivers seeking valuables such as gold, metalwork, armour, seed corn, and sometimes land. Where they settled they built walled cities, usually at the mouths of rivers, on the sites now occupied by major coastal towns and cities – ports such as Dublin and Limerick. Battles with the Irish kings continued intermittently during the 9th and 10th centuries, but basically the Norsemen controlled the country. The Vikings did not colonize Ireland: they were warriors and traders, and although they were ruthless in battle, they also brought progress in trading, maritime skills, the use of coins, and the enjoyment of town life.

Scandinavian sea warriors raided much of Europe in their shallow-draughted longships which easily negotiated Ireland's rivers.

The superbly recreated buildings of Ulster Folk Museum offer a fascinating insight into the past.

The Anglo-Normans During this time, the Irish were far from united among themselves, and as many wars were fought between Irish kings as against the invaders. This disunity led to invasion from another source. In 1166, Dermot McMurrough, exiled King of Leinster, appealed for help from England's Henry II. He was able to return with the Anglo-Norman knights of the Welsh border, chief of whom was Richard Strongbow, Earl of Pembroke. Other Norman barons and their armies followed, and Henry II was concerned enough about the power they acquired to assume the Lordship of Ireland himself in 1171.

He and his successors found the Irish a difficult race to quell, and the English were often reduced to simply holding on to conquered territory rather than continue their expansion. Matters were made more complicated by the many Anglo-Normans who were assimilated into Irish life, marrying into Irish families and adopting the customs of the country that they had come over to rule. The land under the English crown was in the end restricted to the 'Pale', an area around Dublin which varied in size according to the fortunes of the invaders. England also had other concerns, such as the Wars of the Roses, and its lack of tenacity in its efforts to subsume Ireland eased the growth of the Fitzgeralds of Kildare, a powerful Anglo-Norman family which ruled much of the southeast and east of the country.

The beginning of the religious divide
When the Tudors came to the throne of England, Ireland remained an irritation. It became a potential threat after the Reformation when Henry VIII rejected the Catholic church. Now Ireland, with its powerful clergy, was a possible ally to aggressive Catholic nations such as Spain. The Irish themselves were split three ways: the Gaelic Catholics opposed Henry VIII; others remained loyal but denied him spiritual primacy; and a third group of Protestants were rewarded for their support with seized church land.

Relations with subsequent Tudor rulers Mary and then Elizabeth I were unsettled, and both queens attempted unsuccessfully to 'plant' Protestant supporters in unsympathetic regions such as Ulster. The chief of Ulster, Hugh O'Neill, eventually turned against Elizabeth when he realized he would not be allowed to rule his territory autonomously. He rebelled but was defeated when his Spanish allies failed to arrive in time, and he signed over his lands to the English with the Treaty of Mellifont in 1603. He and the other chiefs were permitted to remain as landlords only of their land. Many rejected this arrangement and went into European exile in 1607 in an exodus known as the Flight of the Earls.

The Plantation This encouraged the newly-crowned James I to send boatloads of his fellow-Scots over to Ulster to occupy the confiscated lands of the Earls. The Irish, now tenants, rebelled in 1641 but were defeated and later more waves of land-hungry settlers increased the Protestant presence in Ulster. They felled forests, changed farming practices, and built carefully-planned settlements (called 'Plantation' towns) as they imposed their own culture on the land. The 'Plantation' policy changed the character of Ulster and inspired a deep hatred of the newcomers from the dispossessed natives.

The 1641 rebellion had been partly inspired by a belief that the new English king, Charles I, had Catholic sympathies. When he was overthrown by the Protestant Oliver Cromwell, it was inevitable that Ireland would suffer terrible revenge. Cromwell pursued a ruthless policy when he invaded in 1649, and his troops were encouraged into countless massacres and atrocities which remain fresh in the minds of Irish Catholics today. After two years of bloodshed, a quarter of the Catholic population was dead, while others had been deported into slavery, and vast tracts of Catholic-owned land were taken over in the 1652 Act of Settlement.

The magnificent Rock of Cashel was the seat of Munster's kings from about AD370 to 1101.

This painting shows William of Orange at the Battle of the Boyne, when James II was defeated, and Ireland returned to Protestant rule.

The Battle of the Boyne Little changed after the monarchy was restored eight years later, but when James II, who had Catholic sympathies, came to power and clashed with his Protestant parliament, Ireland suffered again. The Protestant William of Orange was invited to take the Irish throne, and his forces defeated those of James II at the Battle of the Boyne in 1690. Now Ireland came fully under Protestant rule and the Catholics were deprived of basic rights, their culture went underground and their act of worship took place behind closed doors.

The settlers and their descendants were good traders, and through their skills the country prospered and many fine buildings that survive to this day were built. The merchant classes grew and, like many invaders of this land before them, became integrated into Irish life. Consequent pressure for more autonomy led to the acceptance by the British of a virtually independent Irish parliament in 1783. But it was short-lived, for in 1798 a rebellion by the Volunteers (a mainly Protestant force originally formed to protect against French invasion) was crushed by the English army. Three years later the Act of Union was passed and Ireland legally became a part of Britain.

The Great Famine The Act was challenged later in the century by a remarkable pacifist campaigner for Catholic rights, Daniel O'Connell, whose popularity was proved when the Protestant voters of Dublin made him their Lord Mayor in 1841. He was outmanoeuvred by the English, however, and his movement lost momentum during the Great Famine as the Irish fought not for rights, but for their lives. The mainstay of the Irish diet on countless tiny farms was the potato, and when blight struck the crop in 1845, 1846 and 1848, the people of south and west Ireland starved. The resulting Great Famine killed a million of them, and an equal number fled the country, mainly for America (see page 36). The Famine had a number of repercussions: there was resentment against absentee landlords who had continued to demand high rents, while other landlords were bankrupted and abandoned their large houses. It was also realized that farms had been broken into unrealistically small sizes, and a trend towards larger farms with pasture began.

Northern regions escaped the worst of the Famine, and indeed at this time were expanding very fast as industrialization brought money and boosted the cities. Belfast in particular grew at a remarkable rate, its population growing twenty-fold in a century. The prosperous Belfast merchants appreciated the importance and protection of Britain in this growth, and strengthened their links over the Irish Sea at the expense of contact with Dublin in the rural south.

Towards Independence It was in Dublin (and mostly, but not solely, among Catholics) that the demand for Home Rule was most active in the late 19th and early 20th centuries. Politicians such as Charles Stuart Parnell championed the cause, while militant Republicans formed their own armed forces. Civil war seemed likely until the onset of World War I diverted their energies. However, there was fighting on the streets of Dublin during the Easter Rising of 1916, when the Republican forces took over several major buildings in the city. The rebel leaders were shot, but sympathy for their cause was strong enough for the Sinn Fein (meaning 'We ourselves') party to win several seats in the 1917 elections. Continuing unrest led to Britain sending its own soldiers, known as the Black and Tans, who dealt ruthlessly with Republican fighters – themselves split into factions – in guerilla warfare throughout the south.

The unrest led Lloyd George to devize the Anglo-Irish Treaty of 1921, which created the independent Irish Free State of 26 counties, retaining six counties in the North as part of Britain. The divided rebels were now fighting a civil war, while alarmed Protestants in the North opted for protection from their own Ulster Special Constabulary. Southern Ireland (Eire) finally became an independent state in 1938, and from 1949 was known as the Republic of Ireland.

Simmering unrest in Northern Ireland, which was deeply divided by religion, came to the boil in 1969 in a series of riots, and eventually British troops were sent in. They are still there, with the unenviable task of keeping the peace in a split community which has suffered terrible violence. In 1985, the signing of the Anglo-Irish Agreement signalled regular consultations between the British and Irish governments, but the Irish question continues to haunt both of them.

THE IRISH AND LITERATURE

Wander into an Irish pub and you are pretty sure to chance across some elegant conversation, for the Irish love words. This respect for language, combined with a dry sense of humour and a wealth of mythology, has helped to create some great writers, most of them closely identified with Dublin.

Jonathan Swift was born in the city in 1667, and went on to become an Anglican cleric as well as a satirical writer whose best-known work is *Gulliver's Travels*. He is buried in St Patrick's Cathedral, where he was honorary canon during his life. The outrageous wit Oscar Wilde was also born in Dublin, but left Ireland before his great theatrical successes. The romantic lyrical poet WB Yeats hailed from Dublin but is most closely identified with Sligo, where he spent many of his holidays. James Joyce, regarded as a mould-breaking novelist, meticulously documented life in Dublin in his stream-of-consciousness writings, especially in *Ulysess*. Sean O'Casey used similar experiences of the city in his hard-hitting plays which dwelt on slum life during the 'troubles' throughout the struggle for independence. The Irish playwright and novelist Samuel Beckett was another writer who took language to its limits in his sparse and challenging plays; he was awarded the Nobel Prize for Literature in 1969.

MUNSTER

Munster is a province of scenic and geological extremes: barren plains, soft green hills, the country's highest peaks, hurtling streams and elegantly idling rivers. The Munster horizon is always close for you are rarely far from one of its many mountains. The result is some of the most beautiful scenery in Ireland, particularly along the coast. Such an environment attracts many visitors, who also flock to visit its numerous historic monuments which reveal so much of Ireland's colourful and fascinating heritage.

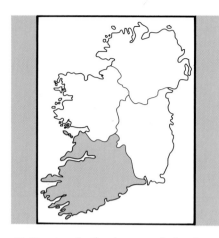

*M*unster is the largest of the four provinces, occupying 9319 sq miles (24,128 km²) and taking in the whole of the south and southwest coasts of Ireland. A characteristic of the region's many ports is that the deep rivers allowed them to be sited far inland, protected from exposure to the wild Atlantic that has battered out the numerous indentations of the west coast. The only comparable long, narrow inlets in the rest of Europe are the fjords of Norway – which perhaps explains why the Scandinavian Norsemen proved so willing to sail up them to make their raids. The Norsemen combined the province's then five regions into two main kingdoms: Desmond in the south, which grew to cover lands controlled by the Fitzgerald family; and Thomond in the north, which was run by the O'Brien family and included most of Clare plus parts of Tipperary and Limerick. The Scandinavians were not the first or last invaders to set eyes on Munster, and by the 16th century the province's coast was dotted with protective fortresses, some of which have survived in their scenic settings. It was this coast that provided numerous emigrants journeying west to America with their last sight of their homeland, as the transatlantic liners eased their way out of Cork Harbour. Today's air travellers see the tower of Bunratty Castle against the clean lines of Shannon Airport: Munster retains its knack for combining extremes to great effect.

Clare County Clare has a strong sense of independence, perhaps because it is separated from its neighbours by the River Shannon and Galway Bay. Indeed, you are rarely far from water here, for the county boasts about 100 lakes. To the west is the Atlantic, which it meets along a wild and dangerous coastline, best enjoyed from Loop Head in the south, or the Cliffs of Moher further north. Inland, Clare is a county of contrasts between green and productive lands and stark and barren rocky plains. In the north is the stark limestone mass of the Burren, which is a favourite spot for botanists and geologists. Further south are gentle pastures and the fertile lands by the Shannon, and on every rolling hill is a flock of sheep.

There is a strong sense of political identity here, and an equally deep love of music. Once a part of Connacht, then a kingdom in its own right (Thomond), Clare was eventually absorbed by Munster. Its name is said to derive from Thomas de Clare, an Anglo-Norman settler granted the area in 1276, though others argue it comes from An Calr, the Gaelic for level surface or plain.

Cork Cork is the largest county in Ireland, and is almost like a miniature of the whole country with its varied scenery and complex history. It is mainly given over to agriculture, although Cork is also home to some of the best restaurants in the country. Its coastline is gentler than that of other western counties, though its extreme southwest has some wild peninsulas. Cork is crossed by a series of ridges and vales running northeast to southwest. Its two main rivers, the Blackwater and the Lee, are separated by the Nagles and Boggerraph mountains in the centre of the county.

The highspot of Cork for visitors must be its county town, self-proclaimed cultural capital of the south, but it also features two of the finest stately homes in Ireland: Fota House near Cobh, and Bantry House in the west. Warmed by the Gulf Stream, the climate is generally mild but moist, in keeping with much of the countryside.

Kerry With its superb coastline, lakes and mountains, County Kerry is a honeypot for tourists. This makes the county one of the most accommodating to the visitor, and if some of its towns have gone overboard in their attempts to attract tourists, there are still remote spots to enjoy, and the scenery is genuinely spectacular. Much of Kerry is made up of three rocky peninsulas, Dingle, Iveragh and Beara, which are deep indentations blasted out by the Atlantic. Their clear air enhances the dark forests and many lakes, and allows you to idly watch a storm approaching across the waves for miles. The most popular peninsula is Iveragh, encircled by a coastal road known as the Ring of Kerry which is crammed with tour coaches during the season.

Away from the coast are countless pretty valleys where tiny stone bridges cross busy streams, and in the middle is the Killarney National Park with its numerous lakes and mountains. Highest of these, indeed the loftiest in Ireland, is 3414ft (1041m) Carrantuohill in the range called Macgillycuddy's Reeks.

Limerick Limerick is blessed with fertile soil which has encouraged a flourishing beef and dairy industry in the county. For the tourist, there is little to shout about, certainly in terms of scenery, but the main attractions are ancient buildings such as the lavish Castle Matrix, and some of the many Fitzgerald strongholds that dot the county. That family (also known as the Geraldines) dominated Limerick for cen-

turies until they clashed with Elizabeth I and were defeated in a brutal war. Also worth seeing is Lough Gur, an ancient lake and hill enclave of great beauty.

Tipperary As with Limerick, the undramatic countryside of Tipperary is fertile and productive, and its richest area is the Golden Vale. This is a massive stretch of superb farming land on a flat limestone plain bounded by mountains, which was planted with Cromwell's soldiers after his conquest of Ireland. The major attraction in the county is the rock of Cashel, an enormous block of rock in the middle of the plain, and one of the greatest historic sites in the country, for it was the seat of the Munster Kings for 700 years until the province ceased being a kingdom in the 12th century.

Other popular spots include the quaint village of Adare, and the Mitchelstown Caves, the largest cave system in Ireland. Of Tipperary's two mountain ranges, the Galties are the prettiest, but are more of a challenge to climb than the Knockmealdowns. Famous from the World War I marching song 'It's a long way to Tipperary', the county was in fact chosen because its name fitted, rather than because of any particular sentiment troops felt for its rich, green land.

Waterford In Waterford, the scenery changes by degrees from its smooth, sculpted coastline with its low cliffs, up luxuriantly wooded valleys towards the grand hills which in turn lead to the starker mountains. Its finest valley follows the course of the majestic River Blackwater. A perennial favourite with invaders, Waterford accommodated Celts, Christians (including the first missionary, St Declan), Vikings, and Anglo-Normans, but proved a tricky problem for the English. More recently it supported the Catholic and nationalist causes, and it still has an influential Gaeltacht district at Rinn.

Today, Waterford is a prosperous county, benefitting from excellent farmland, and extensive commercial activity. Its name is known around the world for the Waterford crystal glass, produced in the county town since 1783. The glass blowers and cutters make every piece individually by hand, and a tour of the Waterford Crystal factory is well worthwhile. If you have time for walking, the best way to enjoy the scenery of Waterford is the Munster Way. This is a 17-mile (27-km) pathway beginning north of Lismore which passes through the Knockmealdown mountains and descends into Tipperary. There are some wonderful coastal walks from which you can enjoy the grandeur of bays such as that at Dungarvan in Waterford.

Bantry House in Cork was built for local landowner Richard White, who was made Baron Bantry by the English in recognition of his loyalty to them.

Places *of* Interest

There are many of these picturesque cottages in Adare, which attracts tourists by the busload.

ABBEYFEALE (Limerick) Ref: G2

Mainistir na Féile, Abbey of the River Feale. Named after a Cistercian abbey founded by Brian O'Brien in 1188, this is a small market town crouching among the foothills of the Mullaghareik Mountains on the banks of the River Feale. Little of the original foundations remain, but the abbey church has been incorporated into the structure of the Roman Catholic church. About 1½ miles (2.4km) northwest, still on the Feale, are the ruins of the 14th-century Geraldine castle of Portrinard.

ADARE (Limerick) Ref: G2

Áth Dara, Ford of the Oak. Thatched cottages and tree-lined streets give Adare an unusual appearance for an Irish village, but its history is typically turbulent, mainly concerning attempts to conquer the O'Donnell's castle (dismantled by Cromwell's troops in 1657). Part of it survives near the river, displaying interesting 13th-century windows. A Franciscan friary was founded here in 1464, and its remains include a nave, choir, and a south transept of late Irish-Gothic origin. There is also a graceful tapering tower and a fine sedilia.

In the village, close by the 14-arch bridge, are the remains of an Augustinian friary founded in about 1316. Adare Manor has been the family home of the Earls of Dunraven since the 17th century, although the present neo-Gothic building dates from the last century. There is much of interest inside, but access has been limited by its transformation into a hotel.

What to see Adare Castle Great Hall (13c); Adare Manor (19c); Augustinian friary (14c); Franciscan friary (15c); Garraunboy Castle (15c); Trinitarian Abbey (13c).

Begun in 1832, Adare Manor is built in a grand neo-Gothic style and stands in wooded grounds.

AHERLOW Tipperary
Ref: G3

Eatharlach. This is a beautiful and secluded glen between the Galtee Mountains and the wooded ridge of Slievenamuck. The Galtees form the highest inland range in Ireland and are particularly popular with walkers and botanists. The glen formed an important pass between the Golden Vale of Tipperaray and Limerick, and it has witnessed numerous battles between the Thomond O'Brien kings and the Fitzpatricks. The O'Briens held the glen for 300 years, and early in the 13th century founded Moor Abbey near Galbally village at the head of the valley. However, the ruined church that survives with its narrow 70ft (21.5m) tower probably dates from after a fire of 1472. A 16ft (4.8m) statue of Christ the King can be found on the lower slopes of Slievenamuck.

ANASCAUL (Kerry)
Ref: H1

Abhainn an Scáil, the River of the Hero. The village of Anascaul lies inland from Dingle Bay and is dominated by the 2000ft (610m) peaks towering behind it. The surrounding countryside is of interest to plant-lovers, especially in May and early June when the banks of streams and ditches are golden brown with royal fern. Other local plants of note are the green-gold Irish spurge, large flowered butterwort, and a variety of orchids. The South Pole village inn was named in memory of Tom Crean, a one-time owner and the man who discovered the bodies of some of Scott's polar expedition team. About 1½ miles (2.4km) northwest is Knockane hamlet and the remains of a multiple-cist cairn, with a boulder displaying a Chi-Rho cross close by. Three miles (4.8km) southwest along the coast is Minard Castle, a stronghold of the Knights of Kerry which was virtually destroyed by Cromwell's troops in 1650.

ARDFINNAN (Tipperary)
Ref: G3

Ard Fhíonáin, St Fíonán Height. A 14-arch stone bridge spans the River Suir at this picturesquely sited village, and a (private) 12th-century Anglo Norman castle stands on the river bank. The oldest surviving part of the structure is a fragment of the late 13th-century keep. However, two of the later square towers on the curtain wall are intact, in spite of a cannon assault from a neighbouring hill by General Ireton in the 17th century. His taking of the castle dispelled local

belief that it was impregnable. There was also a monastery in the village in the 7th century, founded by St Fionan the Leper, but no trace remains. The ruins of a Carmelite lady's abbey can be seen 1½ miles (2.4km) southwest. The Suir has carved a deep gorge, so dividing the area's low hills.

ARDNACRUSHA (Clare)
Ref: G3

Ard na Croise, the Height of the Cross. At Ardnacrusha there is a showpiece hydro-electric station which was built between 1925 and 1929. Here, a dam holds the waters of the Shannon and, further upstream, Lough Derg, forming a huge reservoir. The work also involved digging out 252 million cu ft (7.1 million m³) of earth to form two canals, totalling almost 9 miles (14.5km), to make a head race and tail race carrying water to the station and back to the Shannon above Limerick. A 92ft (28m) waterfall drives the turbines.

  Also of interest to the visitor are the massive plant at the station itself; the barge navigation locks; the wier and intake at O'Briensbridge; fish ladders for migrating salmon at the east end of the weir; and the huge embankments which bound parts of the race and contain the river between Killahoe and the weir.

ASKEATON (Limerick)
Ref: G2

Eas Géitine, the Waterfall of Géitine. Askeaton stands on the River Deel, and its castle stands on an island near the bridge. It dates from the 12th century, but the finest surviving building is the 15th-century Great Banqueting Hall, which measures 90 by 30ft (27.5 by 9m). Its vaulting reveals evidence that basketwork was used during construction. The castle also has a 15th-century tower on a limestone outcrop. In the Franciscan friary on the east bank of the river, there are exquisite windows to be seen and the friary has spectacular cloisters, enclosed by 12 arches fashioned from black marble and supported on columns. Parts of a 13th-century church are preserved in the walled-off south transept of the Church of Ireland parish church.

  What to see Askeaton Castle (12c); Franciscan friary (14–15c); parish church.

BALLYBUNION (Kerry)
Ref: G2

Baile an Bhuinneánaigh, Bunyan's Homestead. Ballybunion is a popular Atlantic-coast resort offering excellent surfing, bathing, golf and many caves to explore. The extensive beach is divided by a promontory featuring a ruined

The 18-hole golf course at Ballybunion is regarded as one of the country's finest, and offers superb coastal views.

wall of the Fitzmaurice family castle. There are some fine caves to the south end of the strand, and to the north are precipitous, cave-riddled cliffs. Further south, the Cashen river has many teal, mallard and widgeon, while grouse and woodcock can be found inland on Knockanore Hill, which offers superb views across the River Shannon to the spires of Limerick.

  What to see beach; Cashen river; Knockanore Hill.

BALLYDUFF (Kerry)
Ref: H3

An Baile Dubh, The Black Homestead. A lane at the end of this village leads to Rattoo Church and the Round Tower, built on the site of an old monastery. In its graveyard, the 15th-century church was constructed using materials from an earlier building. The 92ft (28m) tower includes an interesting round-headed doorway surrounded by an architrave in raised relief. The circumference of the base of the tower is 48ft (14.5m). East of the tower are the remains of a 15th-century abbey, with a three-light east window.

29

BALLYLONGFORD (Kerry) Ref: G2

Béal Átha Longfoirt, the Ford-mouth of the Fortress. Situated on the Shannon estuary, this village marks the starting point of an occasionally submerged path taking you 2 miles (3.2km) along the river bank to a beautiful inlet and the ruins of 15th- and 16th-century Carrigafoyle Castle. The original fortifications included a square barn with rounded turrets on the landward side, with more towers guarding the sea entrance. A spiral staircase allows access to the battlements. Just north of the village are the remains of the Franciscan Lislaughtin Abbey, founded by John O'Conor in 1477. There is a four-light east window executed in the pointed style, a

beautifully-carved sedilia on the south side of the altar, and three fine windows on the south side of the choir.

BANTRY (Cork) Ref: H2

Beanntraí. A characterful coastal market town, Bantry is set between hills and a deep harbour providing shelter for many small vessels. The 21-mile (34-km) long bay was twice used for attempted invasions by French fleets; in 1689 in support of James II, and under General Hoche in 1796. Bantry House stands with its Italian gardens on a wooded hill at the head of Bantry Bay, and is open for tours. It houses numerous art treasures including mosaics from Pompeii, Russian icons, and one of Waterford's finest crystal

chandeliers. Additionally, it offers luxurious bed and breakfast accommodation. Across the bay and north of Adrigole is the spectacular Tim Healy Pass (named after the first governor-general of the Irish Free State), which rises to 1084ft (330m) and offers magnificent views.

What to see Bantry House; harbour; Tim Healy Pass.

BUNMAHON (Waterford) Ref: H3

Bun Machan, Mouth of the River Mahon. A pleasant coastal resort with a sheltered, sandy beach backed by 200ft (61m) cliffs. During the summer the stone walls of the village are covered with colourful blankets of thrift, or sea pink.

Bunratty Castle was built in 1460, and has a fine keep.

BUNRATTY (Clare) Ref: G3

Bun Raite, Mount of the River Raite. A castle has stood on this site since 1251, but the present structure dates from the mid-15th century when it was built by Sioda MacConmara. It became a stronghold of the O'Briens, kings and later earls of Thomond. Bunratty Castle is noted for the towering arched recess of its main doorway, and its impressive collection of medieval furniture and artworks, utensils and weapons. It frequently hosts medieval candlelit banquets. An adjoining folk park features Irish farmhouses and cottages.

BURREN (Clare) Ref: F2

Boirinn, Stony Place. The Burren is a great upland limestone wilderness covering some 50 sq miles (130km²). Surface streams vanish into pot and swallow holes as they cross from the shale to the limestone. An excellent example of this can be seen near Slieve Elva, where many streams disappear into underground caverns. Corkscrew Hill, on the Ballyvaughan to Lisdoonvarna road, is characteristic of the whole region. Many rare plants are to be found in the fissures and cracks in the rocks of The Burren, and the area holds many stone forts and dolmens.

BUTTEVANT (Cork) Ref: H2

Cill na Mallach. A rock overhanging the River Awbeg here carries the ruins of a castle built by the de Barry family, and the town's strong monastic tradition is supported by the remains of a 13th-century Franciscan friary. Only the church remains of the original monastic complex, and an interesting feature is the way the crypt was built below the choir to support it on the site's steep incline towards the river. The windows show the respective preferences of 13th- and 15th-century stone masons for sandstone and limestone. Two early de Barry tomb recesses can be seen in the walls of the nave. The town's name probably derives from a war cry, meaning 'push forward'.

The coastline near Caherdaniel has some breathtaking scenery as well as some pretty islands within Derrynane Bay.

THE EVOLUTION OF CASTLES

Bunratty Castle was built during a boom in castle-building by the major native Irish families in the mid-15th century; Bunratty was for the MacConmaras, the MacCarthys were building at Blarney, and the MacNamaras at Knappogue. Guns had been used to attack masonry since 1326, so thick walls were obligatory. Early Norman castles had generally been simpler affairs of a motte-and-bailey fort, the timber building topping an earth mound inside a moat, and the bailey being merely an adjoining cattle pen. Sometimes prehistoric burial mounds provided an easy to develop site.

But by the 12th century, these vulnerable structures were being rapidly replaced with stone castles, and during the peak Norman building years of 1190 to 1215, some fine city type castles were built, including those at Dublin, Kilkenny and Limerick. They were designed to resist attack even if the walled city had fallen. They comprised four ranges of buildings surrounding a courtyard, with massive circular towers in each corner. There were smaller variations, in reality no more than a fortified house with corner towers, examples being Enniscorthy (Wexford) and Malahide (Dublin). It was only in open areas that the conventional high towered building on rising ground was deemed suitable.

The notion of a castle as a stately home came in by the end of the 17th century, and during the early 19th century crenellations were added to purely residential structures to add to their status.

CAHERDANIEL (Kerry) Ref: H1

Cathair Dónall, Dónall's Stone Fort. The stone fort from which this charming Derrynane Bay village derives its name still stands by the road. About 2 miles (3.2km) east are the remains of St Crohane's Hermitage, a curious little structure hewn from solid rock. To the southwest can be found the ruined Derrynane Abbey in the grounds of Derrynane House, home of patriot Daniel O'Connell (1775–1847). He believed in social reform, tolerance of Catholics, and the union of all Irishmen into a single nation, earning himself the nickname 'the Liberator'.

CAHIR (Tipperary) Ref: G3

An Chathair, The Stone Fort. A spacious little town that straddles the River Suir at the east end of the Galtee Mountains, Cahir is a well-known fishing centre. The *Book of Lecan* notes the destruction of a fort here in the 3rd century, and the well-restored present castle dates from the 15th century. It includes a massive keep and high wall with seven towers. The keep has a portcullis, chambers, and a round tower with a trap door leading to the castle prison. The Earl of Essex took the castle after a ten-day siege in 1599. On the banks of the river are the remnants of Cahir Abbey, founded in the reign of King John. Four miles (6.5km) north is the Mote of Knockgraffon, which may have been the site of coronations of Munster kings before this event switched to Cashel.

What to see Cahir Abbey; castle (15c); Mote of Knockgraffon.

CAHIRCIVEEN (Kerry) Ref: H1

Cathair Saidhbhín, Little Sadhbh's Stone Fort. Cahirciveen is a long, narrow street of a town in the shadow of the 1245ft (380m) high Bentee, which also overlooks the waters of Valentia Harbour. Cahirciveen's main building is a Roman Catholic church built in memory of Daniel O'Connell in 1888. The cornerstone and arch keystone were gifts from the Pope. The ruins of Ballycarbery Castle lie to the west, and north is the stone fort of Cahergall, while west of

this is the carefully-restored stone fort of Leacanabuaile, whose site has been occupied since the 6th century. There are two other impressive ringforts in the area.

What to see Ballycarbery Castle: Cahergall (stone fort); Leacanabuaile (stone fort).

CAMP (Kerry) Ref: G1

An Com, The Hollow. This small cluster of houses at the seaward end of Glen Fas is a good starting point from which to explore one of the highest peaks of the Slieve Mish range, the 2713ft (827m) high Caherconree. The Curaoi

stone fort built 2050ft (625m) up on a promontory has a 350ft (107m) long, 14ft (4.2m) thick wall. Local legend relates that Blunaid, wife of the 1st-century King of Munster, fell in love with a man called Cuchullain. As a signal for him to attack the castle, she poured milk into a nearby stream (still known as White Stream), whereupon the hero killed Curaoi the king and carried off his queen.

CAPPOQUIN (Waterford) Ref: H3

Ceapach Choinn, Conn's Plot.

Kerry's famous scenery is dotted with religious sites. This one is near Cahirciveen.

Glanshalane River joins the Blackwater near the foot of the Knockmealdown Mountains, a range accessible from this market town. Cappoquin is also a good base from which to explore Blackwater Valley, and the woodland and flanking hills create some of the finest scenery in the country. Mount Melleray Cistercian Abbey, a heavy Gothic building founded in 1833, is 4 miles (6.4km) to the north.

CARRANTUOHILL (Kerry)
Ref: H2
Corrán Tuathail, Tuathal's
Curved Mountain. Carrantuohill is
a 3414ft (1040m) mountain (the
highest in Ireland) dominating the
MacGillycuddy's Reeks range.
Views from its roomy summit are
breathtaking, embracing other
mountains, lakes and Atlantic
inlets. The best ascent is probably
from Gortbue school at the
mouth of Hag's Glen to the north,
and up Devil's Ladder, while the
road approach is by Beaufort
Bridge. Lough Acoose lies at the
west end of the range and is the
starting point for the finest ridge
walk in Ireland: a circuit of Caher,
Carrantuohill, Beenkeragh and
Skregmore.

CARRICK-ON-SUIR
(Tipperary) Ref: G4
Carraig na Siúire, Rock of the
River Suir. The River Suir is at its
prettiest here, and the town of
Carrick-on-Suir offers good
angling and golf. It has interesting
monuments, too, especially the
Elizabethan Manor House, built by
the 10th Earl of Ormonde ('Black
Tom') for a visit by the Queen,
later cancelled. The bridge has
medieval origins. Lough
Coumsshingaun nearby is a rock-
climbing centre, and north is
Crotty's Lake, named after an
18th-century highwayman who
hid here.
   What to see Crotty's Lake; Lough
Coumsshingaun; the Manor
House (16c).

CARRIGALINE (Cork)
Ref: H3
Carraig Uí Leighin, Lyon's Rock.
A picturesque village of some
charm, Carrigaline was once
famous for its pottery. It is
overlooked by a castle built on a
rocky cliff in 1177 by Milo de
Cogan. The Perpendicular church
has a remarkable leaden effigy of
Lady Newenham, who died in
1754. Two miles (3.2km)
northwest is Balla Castle, built as a
McCarthy fort and thought to be
one of the oldest inhabited castles
in the country. Drake's Pool in the
Owenboy estuary celebrates an
event in 1587 when Sir Francis
sheltered his outnumbered ships
from the Spanish fleet.

CASHEL (Tipperary)
Ref: G3
Caiseal, Stone Fort. Cashel sits in
the shadow of the Rock of Cashel,
and it is one of Ireland's greatest
historical sites, holding a number
of buildings of huge importance.
This ancient royal site covers
about 200 acres, and is worth re-
visiting at night when it is
superbly floodlit. The Rock's

ROUND TOWERS

Cashel is one of about 70
places in Ireland where
distinctive tall, slim and round
towers have survived. They
usually date from the 9th
century, and should not be
confused with the short and
squat Martello towers built as
coastal watchtowers for the
Napoleonic invasion. These,
much older, towers are
generally near monastic and
other ecclesiastic sites, and
while serving as watchtowers,
were also used for storage and
to house bells. Viking attackers
soon learnt to head for the

round tower for its strategic
importance and for the valuable
goods stored there.
   The towers reach to between
50 and 120ft (15 and 36.5m),
the top tapering towards a
stone-capped peak, although
not all of these have lasted.
Near the top are usually four
windows, one for each point of
the compass. Doors are set
high up, usually at about 12ft
(3.5m), thus requiring a ladder
to gain entry, with obvious
benefits in times of seige. These
are clearly the features of a
defensive watchtower, and

structures solely designed for
this purpose had one long
ladder inside. Most, however,
had a number of floors, linked
by trapdoors.
   In addition to Cashel, towers
can still be seen at: Ardmore
(Waterford), Cloyne (Cork),
Glandalough (Wicklow),
Kildare, Kilkenny,
Monasterboice (Louth), and
Scattery Island opposite Cappa
(Clare). Towers have also been
incorporated into the streets of
Clondalkin in the southwest
suburbs of Dublin and Roscrea
(Tipperary).

buildings include a cathedral, the
Hall of Vicars Choral, the 11th-
century St Patrick's Cross,
Cormac's Chapel of 1127, and an
85ft (26m), 10th-century round
tower. Quirke's Castle is a 15th-
century structure converted into
a hotel – as is the Queen Anne
style deanery of 1730. Principal
stronghold of the kings of
Munster from the 4th to the 12th
centuries, Cashel has seen St
Patrick preaching, the crowning
of Brian Boru, Henry II
conquering, and Gerald, Earl of
Kildare, burning the cathedral in
1495.
   What to see Dominican Friary
Church; Hore Abbey; Longfield
House; Quirke's Castle; Rock of
Cashel (site of numerous
historical buildings).

CASTLEISLAND (Kerry)
Ref: G2
Oileán Ciarraí, the Island of
Kerry. The colour of the red
marble for which this market
town is noted comes from the
iron oxide content of the local
rock. It is named after a castle
built by Geoffrey de Marisco in
1226, the ruins of which can be
seen. To the north is Knight's
Mountain, which rises to 1079ft
(329m), and near this is
Desmond's Grave – resting place
of the 15th and last Earl of
Desmond, Gerald, executed here
in 1583. There are interesting
marine caves 2 miles (3.2km) east
of the town at Ballyplymouth.
   What to see Castle (13c);
Desmond's Grave; Knight's
Mountain; marine caves.

CASTLETOWNBERE (Cork)
Ref: H1
Baile Chaisleáin Bhéarra, the
Town of the Castle of the Bear.
The natural harbour of this little
town and angling resort is
sheltered by Bear Island, which
can be seen almost directly
opposite in Bantry Bay. It became
important as the chief route out
for copper, once mined to the
west at Allihies, and is now a
fishing port. To the southwest are
the few remains of Dunboy Castle.
This ancient fortress of the
O'Sullivan Bere family resisted Sir
George Carew's force of 4000
men in 1602, after the battle of
Kinsale, until the walls were
shattered and its occupants killed.
   What to see Dunboy Castle
(ancient fortress).

CLONMEL (Tipperary) Ref: G3

Cluain Meala, Pasture of Honey. A handsome and prosperous town which is a centre for greyhound racing and other sports. Portions of the 14th-century walls remain, including those at the old St Mary's Church, but the West Gate is an imaginative re-build from 1831. The central landmark is the Main Guard, begun by the Duke of Ormonde in 1662. Nearby is the 19th-century Franciscan church with older tower and choir, while the mid-19th-century Catholic St Mary's has a fine stucco ceiling. In 1815, an Italian called Charles Bianconi set up a countrywide road passenger service while based at Hearn's Hotel in Parnell Street.

What to see Church of SS Peter and Paul; the courthouse; Franciscan Church (19c); Main Guard (17c); St Mary's Church (one Catholic [19c], one Church of Ireland [19c with earlier sections]); town walls (14c); West Gate (19c).

COBH (Cork) Ref: H3

An Cóbh, The Cove. Erosion of limestone troughs by river water formed the deep harbour at Cobh which was once a port of call for transatlantic liners (including the doomed *Titanic*). The town itself boasts a fine 19th-century Roman Catholic cathedral which has a 47-bell carillon and is built of blue Dalkey granite. The town has a maritime museum in a converted church, including a display on the *Lusitania* disaster of 1915, many of whose victims are buried in the churchyard at Clonmel, and who are commemorated by a memorial on the Quay.

What to see Cathedral (19c); Maritime Museum.

CONNOR PASS (Kerry) Ref: H2

An Chonair, The Path. This mountain pass is one of the highest roads in the country. It crosses the Dingle Peninsula from Dingle to the bays of Brandon and Tralee. A rapid climb between the peaks of Ballysitteragh (2050ft [625m]) and Slievanea (2026ft [617m]) culminates in a 1354ft (41m) summit with marvellous views. Several small loughs can be seen far below to the north, while even further north is the bulk of Brandon Mountain. Tiny, rock-encircled Lough Doon occupies a corrie above the pass on the east side of the road. The road passes the winding base of great cliffs in its northward descent, curving over a deep gorge.

CORK (Cork) Ref: H3

Corcaigh, Marsh. Cork is the Republic's second largest city, and although it offers no spectacular sights, it has a splendidly relaxed atmosphere and there is much to enjoy. The River Lee flows through the city in two channels, spanned by numerous bridges. The principal artery, Patrick Street, was, until the late 1780s, a deep water dock for ocean-going vessels (on Grand Parade you can see capstans to which ships were moored). The surviving shipyard shows that the sea remains an important source of work, but Cork is also a centre for other industries and for business, as well as boasting a lively cultural life, including international choral and film festivals. It is very well situated to be a touring base.

Near the centre of Cork is a remnant of a 1300 Augustinian friary, the Red Abbey Tower, which was used as a vantage point by John Churchill, later the Duke of Marlborough, during the 1690 siege. On South Main Street is Christ Church, built on a Norse foundation of about 1050, and thought to be the scene of Edmund Spenser's marriage to Elizabeth Boyle in 1594.

Up on the hilly north side of Cork is St Ann's Church, Shandon, known as the Lion of Cork and

Once a base for transatlantic steamers, Cobh harbour protects a large fishing fleet, and hosts a regatta every August.

Cork's Grand Parade is lined with elegant shops.

the Pain brothers has been preserved. The city museum in Fitzgerald's Park, Mardyke is the former home of the Beamish brewing family, while the city's other famous brewers, Murphy's, are based on the site of an old hospital at Lady's Well whose waters are believed to have curative powers.

Six miles northwest of Cork, the famous Blarney Stone sits atop the 15th-century castle of the MacCarthys. Kissing the stone (no easy task, as you have to hang upside down over an abyss) is supposed to impart the gift of words. Some claim that this story was invented by a tour operator last century, but there is still often a queue of visitors prepared to give it a try.

What to see The Blarney Stone; Christ Church; Elizabeth Fort; Fitzgerald's Park; MacCarthy Castle (15c); Patrick Street; Red Abbey Tower (14c); River Lee; St Ann's Church; St Finbarr's Cathedral; University College, Cork.

CROOKHAVEN (Cork)
Ref: J1
An Cruachán, The Little Round Hill. Offering a safe anchorage away from the fury of the Atlantic, this remote village is a popular meeting place for yachtsmen. The local coastline and peninsula divides into three forks, Brow Head, Mizen Head (whose massive 700ft [213m] cliffs form the southwest tip of Ireland) and Three Castles Head. Between them are the beautiful sandy beach of Barley Cove, and the cliff-girdled Dunlough Bay.

built during the 18th century on the site of medieval St Mary's Church (destroyed during the seige of 1690). Its tower has graduated turrets and has two sides faced in red sandstone, the other two with limestone. It houses eight bells, cast in Gloucester in 1750, which visitors are allowed to play.

On the city's south side can be found the French Gothic St Finbarr's Cathedral, which took 15 years to complete and was finished in 1880. Designed by William Burgess of London, it features three spires, and a striking west front with a trio of recessed doors, elaborate carvings and a beautiful rose window.

Nearby is the ivy-clad wall of Elizabeth Fort, where Cork's citizens gathered in 1603 to defy James I. About half a mile (1km) west of the cathedral is the University College Cork, founded in 1845. Although the expansion of the college has taken over the site of the former County Gaol, the 19th-century classical gate by

A TURBULENT HISTORY

Cork has a turbulent history which begins with the foundation of a monastery by St Finbarr in the 6th or early 7th century, when it was a small island surrounded by marshes. This ecclesiastical complex grew rapidly, attracting scholars and the not so welcome Norsemen. Although they came as sea-bandits, they took to trading in the area, laying the strong foundations of the commerce on which the city still flourishes.

In 1172, Henry II took control of Cork from the Desmond chieftain Dermot MacCarthy. The city was then a

target in struggles for possession for several centuries – which is why nothing of the medieval city remains. In Tudor and Stuart times, Cork had an unhappy knack for backing losers: it supported the pretender to the throne Perkin Warbeck, sided with Charles I against Cromwell, and had to surrender after standing by James II in 1690. On that occasion, the attacking Williamite forces beseiged and took the city, destroying the stone fortifications which had survived since Norman times. Cork suffered once again in this century's wars.

CROOKSTOWN (Cork)
Ref: H2
An Baile Gallda, The English Town. This village lies off the southern road from Cork to Macroom, near the head of the striking Bride Valley. To the southwest, a monument on the Dunmanway road, at Bealnablath, commemorates the death of General Michael Collins in an ambush in 1922. Southeast, near Templemartin are the remains of a large fort called Garranes, which incorporates triple ramparts and is also known as Rath Raithleann. It is said to have been the 6th-century birthplace of St Finbarr, whose father was a metal worker for the ruling chief.

CROOM (Limerick) Ref: G2
Cromadh, Crooked Ford. Because of its nearness to the old Thomond border, Croom has a long history of battles and bloodshed which have left only shattered fragments of its 13th-century castle. About 1 mile (1.6km) west at Carrigeen are the rectangular church and incomplete round tower of the ancient monastic foundation of Dysert. The 65ft (20m) tower has five storeys, and the walls are 4½ft (1.4m) thick. Six miles (9.6km) east is the lovely octagonal tower of 15th-century Glenogra Castle, and 4 miles (6.4km) northeast is Ballycahane House.

DINGLE (Kerry) Ref: H1
An Daingean, The Fortress. Described as the 'last parish before America', or 'the most westerly town in Europe', Dingle's steep streets and old world air nestle among the hills of the beautiful Dingle Peninsula. Throughout the Middle Ages, Dingle was a prosperous port trading with Spain. The site of a fort before the Norman invasion, it suffered greatly during the Desmond troubles, and as consolation, Elizabeth I donated £300 for the repair of defences. The 1804 parish church occupies the site of an older structure. A Geraldine tablet to a Knight of Kerry, dated 1741, can be seen in the transept, and the graveyard features a carved Desmond tomb from 1540 and several interesting carved stones from the town halls – remnants of which can be seen in Green Street. This is a Gaelic-speaking area, popular with language students.
What to see Parish church.

DONERAILE (Cork)
Ref: H3
Dún ar Aill, Fort on a Cliff. Poet and novelist Canon Sheehan was parish priest here from 1895 to

AMERICAN LINKS

Ireland is the closest European country to America, and emigration to that land was a feature of Irish life long before the Great Potato Famine of 1845–47. For example, Wilsons still live in Dergalt, Tyrone, which Woodrow Wilson's grandfather left for America in 1807, and President John F Kennedy's great grandfather emigrated in 1820. However, a trickle became a flood during the Famine, when about 1½ million Irish fled across the Atlantic. The trend has continued, and today it is hard to find families without relatives in the USA. The beacon that pulled those early emigrants through the gruelling journey to America was that land's rapid expansion during the 19th century, though many of them stayed on the east coast, particularly in New York. It took determination to succeed, and a yearning for the homeland is often expressed in popular songs of the 19th century in America.

Michael Regan, great grandfather of Ronald Reagan, was born in Ballyporeen, Tipperary, and the Kennedy ancestral home is in Dungastown, Wexford. Theodore Roosevelt's mother was descended from people of Larne, Antrim. The ancestors of the first man on the moon, Neil Armstrong, came from Fermanagh, while motor magnate Henry Ford's father, William, emigrated from Ballinascarthy, Cork in 1847. Hollywood actresses Maureen O'Hara and Maureen O'Sullivan were both actually born in Ireland.

Canada, Australia and New Zealand have also attracted emigrants and are home to Irish settlements, but none are on the scale of the exodus to America.

There are some beautiful natural harbours all around the Dingle Peninsula.

1913, carrying out much of his research on the relationship between Irish clerical life and the problem of rural population. There is a statue to him in front of his church. Doneraile Court was built in about 1730, but altered in the last century. The fine entrance arch was by the Pain brothers.

Three miles (5km) to the north of Doneraile, on the edge of a small lake, are the ruins of Kilcolman, the house where Edmund Spenser lived and worked between 1587 and 1598. His outrageous views on the Irish people made him very unpopular and he barely escaped with his life when the castle was attacked and burned.

DROMBEG STONE CIRCLE (Cork) Ref: H2

Situated about 2 miles (3.2km) east of Glandore, Drombeg Stone Circle is a fine Druidic altar thought to date from about 150BC. It is made up of 17 stones, set in a 30ft (9m) diameter circle, with two 6½ft (2m) portal stones set on one side. Its interior was covered with a layer of gravel, and two pits

have been discovered, one containing an urn of cremated remains.

A little to the west is a group of hut circles and a cooking place. The larger hut has 4ft (1.2m) thick walls and is 15ft (4.5m) across, and is linked to the other hut which has a roasting oven. These huts have been dated at roughly AD200, but it seems that the site was of some importance for a considerable length of time before and after this, being occupied periodically, perhaps at the winter solstice.

DROMOLAND CASTLE (Clare) Ref: G2

This huge mansion was built in 1830 by the brothers Pain, and is now a hotel. It is the birthplace of William Smith O'Brien, a leader of the Young Ireland party. The grounds contain an old tower and an ancient stone fort known as Mooghaun, enclosing 27 acres (11h) within its three great walls. Late Bronze Age objects, known as the 'Great Clare Find', were discovered not far from here in the mid-19th century.

DUNGARVAN (Waterford) Ref: G4

Dún Garbhán, Garbhán's Fort. This was an important town even before the Anglo-Normans came to Ireland. Part of the castle keep has survived from the stronghold built here in 1185 by King John, and some of the town walls also remain. The parish church graveyard has a curious stone gable with five circular openings. There are also remnants of a 1295 church which were incorporated into St Augustine's Catholic Church of 1828 in Abbeyside on the east bank of the Colligan River, not far from the strange Shell Cottage. The single-arched, 75ft (23m) bridge across the river was built by the Duke of Devonshire in 1815 for the then massive cost of £50,000. The Master McGrath Memorial 2½ miles (4km) northwest of Dungarvan recalls a famous greyhound.

What to see St Augustine's Church; Castle and town walls; holed gable in parish churchyard; Master McGrath Memorial; Shell Cottage.

DUNMORE EAST (Waterford) Ref: H4

Dún Mór, Big Fort. An angling and seaside resort that has cashed in on its undoubted higgledy-piggledy prettiness, Dunmore East derives its name from the great dun which partially survives. Black Knob Cliff with its promontory fort known as the Shanooan can be seen on the south side of the village. Access to Merlin's Cave beneath the Cliff is via a footpath. About 2½ miles (4km) north is the Harristown passage grave, with a 22ft (6.5m) long passage widening to 4½ft (1.3m) at the west end. The grave was originally roofed with stone slabs, and the orthostatic kerb within which it lies is 30ft (9m) in diameter. The 430ft (130m) viewpoint of Knockadirragh lies 2½ miles (4km) northwest.

What to see Harristown passage grave; Knockarragh; Merlin's Cave; Shanooan.

Drombeg Stone Circle seems to have been used for ceremonies for 2000 years, but excavations have not revealed all its secrets.

ENNIS (Clare) Ref: G2

Inis, Holm. Ennis is a busy market and county town on the River Fergus, with narrow and tortuous streets. It makes an excellent base for exploring County Clare, and offers plenty of brown trout fishing. A statue on the site of the old courthouse commemorates Daniel O'Connell, MP for the area from 1828 to 1831. Nearby at Newbridge Road is Steele's Rock, which is carved with a lion and recalls O'Connell's friend Honest Tom Steele. He sat for hours on this rock from where he could see the home of the woman who had spurned him. Ruins of a Franciscan friary founded in 1242

can be seen at the end of Church Street. Some splendid carvings and tombs, some of them 15th century, can be seen in the town's church.

What to see Church; Franciscan friary; Steele's Rock.

ENNISTYMON (Clare) Ref: F2

Inis Díomáin, Dioman's Holm. A holiday (especially for fishing) and small market town, Ennistymon grew up around a castle built by Turlough O'Brien in 1588. Situated on the River Collenagh, it is noted for its fishing. At this point in its course the river hurtles over a rocky bed before

joining the sea at Liscannor Bay. Poet Brian Merriman was born here in about 1747. A hill above the town is surmounted by a ruined church dating from 1778, and Ennistymon's notable Roman Catholic church was built in 1953.

What to see Cascades Walk; River Collenagh; Roman Catholic church.

FERMOY (Cork) Ref: H3

Mainistir Fhear Maí, the Monastery of the Men of the Plain. The Scottish-born John Anderson built this community straddling a wide and beautiful stretch of the River Blackwater towards the end of the 18th century. Today,

Fermoy is renowned for its fishing – salmon on the river, trout in the tributaries. Knocknaskagh rises 1046ft (319m) from the Nagles Mountains in the west, and 2 miles (3.2km) northwest is Labbacallee, or the Hag's Bed: probably the finest wedge-shaped gallery grave in Ireland (see separate entry). The ruins of an old Roche Castle and a 1227 Dominican Abbey can be found near the Funcheon River, which has a quaint and narrow bridge with 13 arches. Further along the River Blackwater are the castles of Carrigabrick, Cragg, Hyde and Licklash.

What to see Dominican Abbey (13c); Labbacallee (wedge-shaped gallery grave); Roche Castle; River Blackwater; River Funcheon.

FETHARD (Tipperary) Ref: G3

Fiodh Ard, High Wood. The walls, gates and other defensive structures seen here reveal that, as long ago as the 14th century, Fethard was a fortified town. Everard's Mansion, which was incorporated into the British military barracks, carries the town's armorial bearings. A castle stands east of the parish church, incorporating the west tower and nave of a medieval structure. Interesting remains of an Augustinian friary founded in 1300 include a carving built into a wall at the east end.

Five miles (8km) south is the ruined church of Donaghmore with a finely-carved Irish-Romanesque doorway. Knockelly Castle with its 16th-century tower is 3 miles (4.8km) northeast, and the same distance southeast is tri-towered Kiltinane Castle. Dating from the 13th century, it was captured by Cromwell in 1649, and is still inhabited.

What to see Augustinian friary (14c); Donaghmore; Everard's Mansion; Kiltinane Castle (13c); Knockelly Castle.

FOTA ISLAND (Cork) Ref: H3

Fóite. This island, 9 miles (14.5km) east of Cork, has an 800-acre (323ha) wildlife park with a wide variety of species on view. It is open from mid-March to the end of October. The animals roam about the landscaped 18th-century grounds of Fota House. Its estate is also home to one of the best arboretums in Europe. The train from Cork crosses an estuary teeming with birdlife.

The old streets of Ennis meet in O'Connell Square, where there is a statue to the Catholic campaigner Daniel O'Connell.

FOYNES (Limerick)
Ref: G2

Faing. Flying boats used to head across the Atlantic from Foynes and it remains a busy seaport with a fine pier. A 25ft (7.6m) limestone cross on a nearby hill commemorates Stephen Edmund Spring Rice, brother of the first Baron Monteagle. To the south is the 572ft (174m) Knockpatrick Hill which offers lovely views over the Shannon Valley. At its top are early church ruins from a foundation said to have been created by St Patrick, and a holy well is nearby.

GALLARUS ORATORY
(Kerry) Ref: H1

Gallaras. This stone oratory is without doubt the most important piece of early Christian architecture of its type remaining in Ireland. Thought to date from the 8th century, the little church has a high ridged roof looking like an upturned boat. The walls are 3½ft (1m) thick, and the internal dimensions are 10 by 15ft (3 × 4.5m). No mortar was used in building the oratory, but the stones are so well-fitted that the structure is waterproof. There is a

small round headed window at the east end. At the top of each gable is a socketed stone, each of which would once have been the base of a cross. St Brendan is said to have laid the ancient trackway of Saint's Road close by, which goes to the summit of Brandon Mountain.

GALTEE MOUNTAINS
(Tipperary) Ref: G3

Na Gaibhlte. Ireland's finest inland mountain range extends from Tipperary across the Limerick border to merge with the Ballyhoura Hills. The highest point is 3018ft (920m) up on the border at Galtymore, directly north of the Mitchelstown Caves (see separate entry). From the summit ridge there are fine views north towards the Glen of Aherlow and the Golden Vale, while 2712ft (827m) Lyracappul rises to the west. There are easy routes to the summit peaks from the Mitchelstown to Cahir road

The Gallarus Oratory may be the first church in Ireland built in stone instead of wood, and has survived for over 1000 years.

(N8) on its south side. Several small lakes lie on the north slopes, including Lough Curra beneath Galtymore and Lough Muskry under 2636ft (800m) Greenane, near a rock known as O'Loughnan's Castle. Pigeon Rock Glen offers a good viewpoint on the south side of the range.

ANCIENT GAMES

Galway, Kilkenny, Limerick, Tipperary, Waterford and Wexford are the counties rated strongest in the Irish national game of hurling. This sport is said to date from pre-Christian days and is mentioned in the legends of the Red Branch Knight and the Fianna. Two teams of 15 are required, each with a goalkeeper, six backs, two midfields and six forwards. The game is similar to, but less

regulated than, field hockey, and the 3½ft (1m) long sticks have curved striking blades. A goal (worth three points) is scored when the leather ball is hit under the crossbar, with a point scored for each hit over the bar and between the high posts. Players can catch the ball in their hands, but cannot throw it, and it must be picked off the ground with a stick.

Gaelic football has elements

of soccer and rugby, and players may handle the ball, but otherwise team structure and scoring is as in hurling. There are hundreds of hurling, Gaelic football and handball (another traditional game) teams around the country. Women have their own version of hurling called carnogie, played with shorter sticks by teams of twelve. This game is popular in cities, unlike hurling.

The gardens on Garinish Island were created from bare rock – all the topsoil was imported. The picture shows part of the Italian Garden.

GLENBEIGH (Kerry) Ref: H1

Gleann Beithe, Valley of the Birches. A small fishing and bathing resort sitting under the 1621ft (494m) Seefin Mountain near the River Beigh, Glenbeigh offers magnificent scenery. One of Kerry's finest walks follows a great amphitheatre of mountains, known as the Glenbeigh Horseshoe, from Seefin to Drung Hill. Here can be seen excellent views of a series of glacial corries and loughs, the largest of which is Coomasaharn. Follow the road southwest to Kells to enjoy the splendid sight of Dingle Bay and the mountains of the Dingle Peninsula.

GLENGARRIFF (Cork) Ref: H2

An Gleann Garbh, The Rough Valley. The huge masses of rock which gave this secluded deep valley and harbour its name are now covered by the most luxuriant foliage of holly, arbutus, fuchsia, yew, pines, oaks and many other trees and shrubs. Natural shelter of the surrounding lofty hills has endowed the valley with the most genial climate in Ireland, and this is a lovely spot for boating, fishing and swimming. Almost in the middle of the harbour is Garinish island, which can be reached by boats leaving from a shaded glen near the village street. This barren rock was transformed into a tropical garden paradise by Mr and Mrs John Annan Bryce and Harold Peto. It is an island of surprises: Italian and Japanese gardens, a simulated Grecian temple, and plants with tropical, antipodean and even Antarctic origins.

GLIN (Limerick) Ref: G2

An Gleann, The Valley. The River Shannon on which Glin is situated is 3 miles (4.8km) wide here. Once a salmon depot, it is now more concerned with the dairy industry. Parties of ten or more can tour, by arrangement, the Georgian castle, which is noted for its paintings, furnishings and plasterwork. The site has been home to the Fitzgerald family for 700 years, although the present castle dates from the 1780s, with the castellations added 40 years on. Nearer the Shannon Estuary is the ruined keep of the older castle, destroyed in 1600. The 19th-century Hamilton's Tower overlooks the pier.

GLANDORE (Cork) Ref: J2

Cuan Dor. Glandore is an attractive fishing village overlooking the coastal inlet of Glandore Harbour, and it is surrounded by lovely scenery. Glandore Castle is now part of a private house, and nearby are the ruins of a medieval church. Kilfinnan Castle on the southeast side of the village has massive defensive walls and was a seat of the Townshend family. It now forms part of a hotel. On the opposite side of the inlet is the village of Unionhall, where Dean Swift lived in 1723, at Rook Cottage.

GLANWORTH (Cork) Ref: H3

Gleannúir. A pleasant village known for its woollen manufacture, Glanworth has a 13-arch bridge spanning the River Funshion. It also has a ruined 13th-century castle (destroyed in 1649), and a 13th-century early-English church of the Dominican friary. The Elizabethan mansion of Ballyclough House lies to the east, and a mile (1.6km) south at Moneen are the remains of a multiple cist cairn erected on a neolithic ritual enclosure.

GOUGANE BARRA (Cork) Ref: H2

Guagán Barra, St Finbarr's Cleft. A broodingly romantic mountain lake which forms the source of the River Lee, reached by a road just northwest of Keimaneigh Pass. A feature of the surrounding mountains are the numerous streams which become foaming cataracts after heavy rain. The tiny half-acre island, reached by a causeway, was St Finbarr's hermitage, founded in the 7th century. Just off the causeway is St Finbarr's Well and an ancient cemetery held in great veneration. The island holds a cluster of buildings, a tiny chapel, and a large court, set with stations of the cross, which survives from an 18th-century building. Keimaneigh Pass means 'Deer's Pass', from a story that deer once jumped across it to escape their pursuers. Its lush greenery and craggy cliffs make it one of the country's most romantic beauty spots.

What to see St Finbarr's hermitage (on the island).

HOLY CROSS ABBEY (Tipperary) Ref: G3

Mainistir na Croiche, the Monastery of the Cross. Located a few miles from Thurles, this is one of the most picturesque Christian monuments in Ireland, charmingly set beside the banks of the River Suir. Roofless since the 17th century, it has recently been fully restored to become an active parish church as well as a tourist attraction. The name derives from a portion of the True Cross thought to have been presented by Pope Pascal II to Donogh O'Brien in 1110. The abbey was founded in 1169, and its relic attracted many pilgrims whose offerings greatly enriched the building. The Cistercian Abbey Church incorporates late 12th- and 15th-century architecture and has well preserved stone carvings and traceries. A 15th-century hunting scene is preserved in the north transept. On the wall of the River Suir bridge outside the abbey is an inscription relating to the rebuilding of the bridge in 1626. Two miles (3.2km) southeast is the keep of Killough Castle, and 3 miles (4.8km) southwest is a quartet of castles – Clogher, Clonyharp, Graigue and Milltown.

What to see Abbot's House; Cistercian Abbey Church (12c); Killough Castle; River Suir bridge.

There are nature trails in the Gougane Barra Forest Park, but you can simply wander if you wish.

HOSPITAL (Limerick) Ref: G3

An tOspidéal, The Hospital. This little town derives its name from a hospital for the Knight's Hospitallers which was founded in 1215. The original church survives and features three magnificent effigy tombs, one of them thought to be that of the founder, Geoffrey de Marisco. The 537ft (164m) hill of Knockainy to the west is said to be the otherworld seat of the goddess Anu, and was the scene of rituals related to her as late as the 19th century.

INCHIGEELAGH (Cork) Ref: H2

Inse Geimhleach. Inchigeelagh is a resort of anglers and artists situated on the River Lee near the eastern extremity of Lough Allua.

This lake and the expansions of the Lee present a charming picture with their water lillies. To the southwest is Sheehy Mountain (1797ft [548m]) with its lower slopes cloaked in fir trees, and best climbed via Pipe Hill. A McCarthy stronghold, Carrynacurra Castle, can be found 1 mile (1.6km) northeast of the village.

What to see Carrynacurra Castle; Sheehy Mountain.

INISHANNON (Cork) Ref: H2

Inis Eonáin, Eonán's Holm. Picturesquely placed on the River Bandon, this was a walled town of some importance in the 15th century. The ruins of several castles can be seen nearby, including Dundanier Castle, which dates from 1476 and stands

at the junction of the Rivers Brinning and Bandon.

INISHCEALTRA (Clare) Ref: G3

Inis Cealtrach, Island of Churches. Also known as Holy Island, this is a tiny islet in Scarriff Bay, the prettiest arm of Lough Derg, about 1 mile (1.6km) from Mountshannon. It is a 17th-century monastic site made conspicuous by its tall round tower. The monastery was ravaged by the Danes of Limerick in 834, and was rebuilt and extended by King Brian Boru in 1027. In addition to the tower, there are the remains of five churches, graves with inscriptions in early Irish dating from the 8th to 11th centuries, a cell known as 'The Confessional', and a drystone structure called 'The Cottage'.

MUNSTER

KANTURK (Cork) Ref: H2
Ceann Toirc, the Head of the Boar. Kanturk is a market town and meeting point for six small roads and the River Blackwater tributaries Dulua and Allow. Just to the south is Old Court Castle, a MacCarthy stronghold during the Elizabethan period. Dermot MacOwen MacDonagh MacCarthy built the castle in the Anglo-Norman style in 1601. It includes a large 120 by 80ft (36.5 by 24m) quadrangle with a large, square, four-storey tower in each corner. The builder was told to cease work on the structure when its obvious defensive strength aroused the suspicions of the government. It became known as MacDonagh's Folly.

KENMARE (Kerry) Ref: H2
Neidín, Little Nest. Set among the Kerry Hills, Kenmare is a good base from which to explore the Iveragh and Beara peninsulas, and has a fascinating history. It was founded in 1670 by a handful of English soldiers. These colonists withstood almost continuous assault while building up a fishery and iron works. In 1688, the town was besieged by 3000 men, and the defenders escaped packed into two vessels, reaching safety in Bristol two weeks later.

Kenmare was re-colonized by William II, and is today an industrial (including lace and woollens) and tourist centre. South of the old abbey is a Druid's Circle comprising 15 stones around a tomb of a capstone on three uprights. The 13th-century Dunkerron Castle stands on a rock 2 miles (3.2km) west of the town.

KILKEE (Clare) Ref: G2
Cill Chaoi, St Caoi's Church. Kilkee is a pleasant resort sheltered from the Atlantic by the Duggerna rocks. Between Doonberg to the northeast and Loop Head to the southwest is a spectacular 16-mile (26-km) stretch of coast which has been eroded into a series of caves and chasms. One just west of the town forms a natural amphitheatre which is used for concerts. The cliff walk southwest affords views of precipitous Bishop's Island, where ancient monastic remains can be found, the ruined tower of Doonlickas Castle, and a magnificent stack known as Green Rock. Loop Head has a fine lighthouse.
   What to see Carrigaholt village; Loop Head; Moneen Church (with its portable 'Little Ark' for services in times of suppression).

KILLALOE (Clare) Ref: G3
Cill Dalua, St Dalua's Church. Delightfully situated on the banks of the River Shannon, this town stands close to the falls of Killaloe, about 1 mile (1.6km) from Lough Derg. Two noteworthy features are the central square and the multi-arched bridge. St Flannan's Cathedral is a cruciform building dating from the 12th century and restored in 1887. Its Romanesque doorway came from an earlier church and was built into the nave's south wall. Nearby is the 12th-century St Flannan's Oratory with its steep-pitched stone roof and 11th-century west doorway. Close to the Roman Catholic parish church is the equally old St Molua's Church which was moved from its original site on Friar's island in 1929 when the isle was to be flooded for a hydro-electric scheme. A number of earthern forts are in this area, including Beal Boru 1½ miles (2.4km) west of Killaloe bridge from which King Brian Boru took his title. His Kincora Palace is thought to have stood near this fort in the 10th or 11th century.
   What to see Beal Boru; St Flannan's Cathedral (12c); St Flannan's Oratory (11–12c); St Molua's Church (pre-12c); Shannon hydro-electric scheme.

KILLARNEY (Kerry) Ref: H2
Cill Airne, Church of the Sloes. Killarney is one of the finest beauty spots of Ireland, standing near the country's Lake District. It is a major tourist centre. The most distinguished building is St Mary's Cathedral, designed by Alexander Pugin and completed in 1855. This is a cruciform building which carries a massive square tower capped by a spire. At the east end of the town on Fair Hill is the Franciscan Church with its outstanding stained-glass window by Harry Clarke and decorative woodwork. Two miles (3.2km) south is Muckross House and Gardens. These latter are particularly splendid when the azaleas and rhododendrons are blooming in May and June. Ruined Muckross Abbey, founded in the 15th century for Franciscan monks by Donal MacCarthy Mor, is beautifully situated near the wooded shore of the Lower Lake. The town is a noted angling centre and has two golf courses. Southwest of Killarney is Ross

This is 'Ladies View' near Killarney, one of many magnificent vistas on the Ring of Kerry, the road which runs around the Iveragh peninsula.

Castle and its massive 15th-century keep. Said to have been home of the O'Donoghues, the stronghold has been well preserved and is one of the finest castles in the country.

What to see Dunloe Castle (13c); Franciscan Church; Hill of Aghadoe; Innisfallen Abbey; Muckross Abbey 15c); Muckross House; Ross Castle (14c); St Mary's Cathedral (19c); Seven Sisters (stone circle two miles [3.2km] east at Lissyvigeen).

KILLORGLIN (Kerry) Ref: H1

Cill Orglan, Orgla's Church. Killorglin is a little town on a hill south of the Castlemain Harbour headwaters, on the River Laune which is noted for its salmon fishing. The ruined 13th-century Castle Conway (the town's original name) is one attraction, but Killorglin is famous for its three-day Puck Fair held every August. Possibly originating in pagan times, this occasion centres

Killarney exploits its picture-book charm to the full.

around a goat (puck) with monstrous beribboned horns set up on a platform at the head of the town. Everything else stops for the fair, which draws thousands of visitors. To the south are the high mountains of MacGillycuddy's Reeks.

What to see Castle Conway (13c); MacGillycuddy's Reeks; Puck Fair (held during August).

KILMACTHOMAS (Waterford) Ref: H4

Coill Mhic Thomáisín, Mac Thomas' Wood. Known for its Irish tweeds, this town on a steep hill astride the Mahon River is a popular touring centre. Six miles (9.6km) northwest and accessible on foot is Lake Coumshingaun, which is almost completely surrounded by precipitous cliffs rising 1288ft (393km) to form a fine glacial cirque. The sole outlet is a stream running to the Clodaigh River. About 4 miles (6.4km) northwest are the forest-clad slopes of 2478ft (755m) Knockanaffrin.

KILMALLOCK (Limerick) Ref: G3

Cill Mocheallóg, St Mocheallóg's Church. Once a major town, Kilmallock has declined in importance, but has some magnificent remnants of its past. The collegiate Church of SS Peter and Paul is 15th century with a 13th-century transept with a fine south door. The modern church of the same name dates from 1879. Remains of the 13th-century Dominican friary stand on a picturesque river site, and include a 90ft (27m) square tower rising from the junction of choir and nave. The conventual buildings lie north of the church and include a well-preserved day room and kitchen. King's Castle is a tall, 15th-century gate tower on the Limerick Road.

What to see Blossom's Gate; Church of SS Peter and Paul (15c and 19c); Friary (13c); King's Castle (15c); Museum; Spitalfield ($\frac{1}{2}$ mile [0.8km] north).

KILRUSH (Clare) Ref: G2

Cill Rois, Church of the Wood. A port and market town on the estuary of the Shannon, Kilrush has the remains of a small pre-Romanesque church with a flat-headed doorway and round-headed window. A mile (1.6km) south is the steamer pier from where visitors reach Scattery Island, which has an outstanding collection of stone monuments dating from the 11th or 12th centuries. St Senan founded a settlement on the island in the 6th century. It suffered greatly from Norse attacks in the 9th and 10th centuries, and the oldest building on the site is a 122ft (37m) tower (reputedly Ireland's tallest and oldest) that served as a refuge. East of the tower is a much-altered pre-Romanesque cathedral, and north is a 12th-century Romanesque church with a fine chancel arch.

What to see Church; Scattery Island.

*I*RELAND'S *L*AKE *D*ISTRICT

Most of this area's famous Lake District forms the extensive Bourn-Vincent Forest Park. There are three major lakes at Killarney, and there is also Lough Guitane, 5 miles (8km) southeast, and numerous mountain tarns. Luxuriant woodland clothes the banks of all the lakes, and erosion has formed some striking caves.

The best way to enjoy the lakes at Killarney is by boat. Starting from the landing stage near Lord Brandon's Cottage at the west end of Upper Lake the water-borne traveller will assume the lake is landlocked, but a 10yd (9m) wide passage opens at a narrow promontory called Colman's Eye and leads into the Long Range. Later, the river divides to enter Lower Lake to the left, or Middle Lake to the right. The limestone on which Middle Lake lies has been eroded into fantastic

shapes along the shoreline, and has dissolved to form the Colleen Bawn Caves on the north side. After passing a whirlpool known as O'Sullivan's Punch Bowl, the traveller enters Lower Lake. This is the largest lake at some 5000 acres (2024ha) and it contains about

30 islands. After about 2 miles (3.2km) is O'Sullivan's Cascade – three separate falls which plummet from a total height of 70ft (21m). A charming view of the cascade can be enjoyed from a little grotto beneath a projecting rock in the lowest basin.

Sorting out the nets in Kinsale.

KILSHEELAN (Tipperary) Ref: G3

Cill Síoláin, Síolán's Church. The Comeragh Mountains rise south of the charmingly placed village on the banks of the River Suir. The countryside to the north is dominated by Slievenamon, the 'Mountain of Women' of legend. Local ruins of an early-Irish church include a Romanesque style chancel, arch and doorway added in the 12th or 13th century. About half a mile (0.8km) west is the beautifully set mansion of Gurteen le Poer, a house in a fine estate with an interesting dolmen in the grounds. Northwest are the castles of Newtownanner and Anner, while towards Clonmel are the ruined Derrinlaur Castle and 17th-century Tickincor Castle. A mile (1.6km) east is Poulkerry Castle, scene of a massacre by Cromwell in 1650.

KINSALE (Cork) Ref: H3

Cionn tSáile, Head of the Sea. Kinsale is a yachting and sea fishing centre of great character which has played an important part in Irish history. The 16th-century Dutch-gabled courthouse has an interesting museum; and Desmond Castle (or French Prison) is a distinguished 16th-century townhouse which was used to hold French prisoners during the Napoleonic wars. St Multose's Church is one of the few medieval parish churches in use today, and features a curious tower and spire, and an ornamented doorway. Kinsale was occupied by the Spanish in 1601, but a siege by 12,000 men recovered the town. The battle marked the last stand of medieval Gaelic Ireland against the power of the English Renaissance state. James II was based here for his doomed attempt to recover the English crown.

What to see Charles Fort (17c, in Summercove, has a romantic ghost story); Courthouse (16c); Desmond Castle (16c, French Prison); Gift House (17c); Holeopen Bay (12c castle ruins); St Multose's Church (12c).

KNAPPOGUE CASTLE (Clare) Ref: G3

An Chnapóg, The Hummock. Knappogue was built in 1467 and was in the MacNamara family until 1815. Its dominant feature is a massive central tower. The castle has been fully restored and hosts many medieval-style banquets. It is a major tourist attraction. Inscribed pillars on the back gate give distances in English and the rarely-used Irish mile, which measures 2240yd (2048m).

LABBACALLEE GALLERY GRAVE (Cork) Ref: H3

Leaba Caillighe, Hag's Bed. This is the largest and most complex wedge grave in Ireland, and lies 1½ miles (2.4km) southeast of Glanworth. It narrows from 20ft (6m) to 11ft (3.3m) from end to end, and a slab divides it into two chambers. This slab seems to have had a corner deliberately broken off, perhaps to enable the free passage of the soul. Three large capstones form the roof of the gallery, and the whole structure was once covered by a large cairn. The headless and partially dismembered skeleton of a woman was found on the floor of the smaller chamber when it was excavated, together with burnt animal bones and a bone pin, which may have been the closing pin for a leather bag. Other human remains were found in the large chamber. From this it is assumed that the primary burial was of an important woman, perhaps a matriach, with her family cremated and buried in the secondary chamber.

LAHINCH (Clare) Ref: F2

An Leacht, Grave Mound. A popular resort on Liscannor Bay, Lahinch has an excellent sandy beach and a championship golf course. The famous Cliffs of Moher rise to the northwest, affording magnificent views. Two natural curiosities in the neighbourhood are the Puffing Holes (water spouts) on the coast at Freagh, and the Dropping Well. Interesting ruins can also be found at O'Brien's Bridge 4 miles (6.4km) southeast where the Dealagh River meets the sea. One is of Dough Castle, the other the nave and chancel of 15th-century Kilmacreehy Church. The chancel has a deeply-splayed east window and a decorated recess in the north wall. Nearby Liscannor has the ruined O'Connor Castle, and is the birthplace of submarine inventor John P Holland.

What to see Dough Castle; Freagh (puffing holes); Kilmacreehy Church; O'Connor Castle.

LIMERICK (Limerick) Ref: G3

Luimneach, Barren Patch of Land. The Republic's third city is a sum of three parts which were added as it developed: Englishtown (the oldest part, on an island bounded by the Shannon, also once known as High Town); Irishtown (which began life as a second walled town, and is across Mathew and Ball's Bridges, and dominated by St John's Cathedral), and Newtown Pery (mainly Georgian terraces, named after developer Edward Sexton Pery).

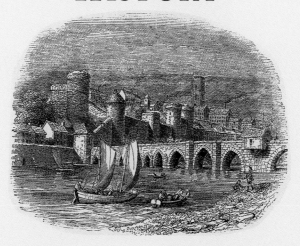

*L*IMERICK'S *H*ISTORY

The first settlement at Limerick was a base for Viking marauders in the 10th century, who were finally driven out by King Brian Boru early in the next century. Limerick was then repeatedly burned to the ground in an unstable period until the arrival of the Normans at the end of the 12th century, who built King John Castle and a bridge to replace the ford over the Shannon. The city was resolutely Jacobite in the 17th century and won a notable victory when under seige by 26,000 of William III's troops in 1690. A surprise attack on the Williamites' supply train stopped munitions reaching the beseigers, but a year on the city had to give way, and the Jacobites were allowed to sail to France.

The English later reneged on other parts of the peace treaty, a betrayal that still rankles with some Limerick people. After fortifications were removed in 1760 the city expanded beyond the castle walls in a welter of fine business streets crossing the area now known as Newtown Pery.

The main sites of the city can be enjoyed from a circular walk, starting in the chief thoroughfare, O'Connell Street. Turn down Sarsfield Street and cross the river, turning right along Clancy's Strand. At the west end of Thomond Bridge is the Treaty Stone, where the 1691 treaty of surrender was signed. On the far bank of the river is King John's Castle. The southeast bastion was built on the site of a former tower, and all the corner towers were lowered to accommodate heavy artillery. Massive drum towers stand at the north and southwest angles, and the ancient gateway penetrates the 10ft (3m) thick north curtain wall.

Leave the castle along Castle Street and turn right along the Parade, continuing along Nicholas Street to reach St Mary's Cathedral. This was begun in the 12th century and features a mixture of styles from subsequent expansions. There is a squat, battlemented west tower, and a fine Romanesque doorway. There are interesting monuments and a modern five-light window. Exit along Bridge Street and facing the river you will find City Court, which dates from 1764. Beyond Rutland Street in Patrick Street is the town hall of 1805, and the custom house of 1769 stands near the opposite side of Mathew Bridge. Do not cross Abbey River here: go along George's Quay to take Ball's Bridge. Continue up Broad Street and John Street to reach St John's Church. It was here that the fighting at the end of the 17th century between the city and William III was fiercest.

Take a detour about 200yds (180m) east, to see part of the ancient wall. Massive defensive gateways can be seen inside the entrance to St John's Hospital. Nearby St John's Cathedral is a handsome Gothic building with a graceful 280ft (85m) spire. From the exquisite, stone Georgian St John Square walk down Griffin Street and turn right on Upper William Street towards the city centre. There is a library, gallery and museum in People's Park.

What to see St Alphonsus Redemptionist Church (19c); City Court (18c); Fanning's Castle (16c); Hunt Museum; King John's Castle; Museum; St John's Cathedral; St Mary's Cathedral; Tait's Clock (Victorian, erected to Sir Peter Tait); Town hall (19c); Treaty Stone.

Most of the medieval structure of Limerick's King John Castle remains. A drawbridge once stood where the steps lead to the main road.

LISDOONVARNA (Clare)
Ref: F2

Lios Dúin Bhearna, the Enclosure of the Gap Fort. Lisdoonvarna is an inland resort and is Ireland's premier spa town, with a number of springs known as Gowlane, Twin Wells and Rathbaun. Summer is a convivial time in the town and a number of 'matchmaking' festivals have been run. Lisdoonvarna sits on the edge of the strange, contorted landscape known as The Burren, and there is much to see in the surrounding area. About 3 miles (4.8km) north at Pollnagollum is a 6¾ mile-(11km-) long cave. Eight miles (12.8km) east is a type of ancient Irish church called Teampull Cronan, which is delightfully situated in a little dell, surrounded by ash trees. Grotesque heads set into the exterior walls probably date from the 12th century. St Cronan's Well rises nearby. Five miles (8km) southwest is the round tower known as Doonagore, and the 15th-century castle of Ballynalackan stands on a clifftop site 2½ miles (4km) northwest.

    What to see Ballynalackan (15c); Doolin (fishing and bathing village 5 miles [8km] away); Doonagore; Lisdoonvarna springs; Pollnagollum cave; Spectacle Bridge (strange structure with an open circle over its arch, on the River Aille); Teampull Cronan.

LISMORE (Waterford)
Ref: H3

Lios Mór, Big Ringfort. This is a charming small town unspoilt by tourism, despite the interesting sights it offers. A monastery was founded here by St Cartach in the 7th century, and it soon gained fame as a university – King Alfred was said to be one of its students. Repeatedly sacked by Vikings, Lismore nevertheless became a centre for culture and Christianity by the time its first castle was erected in 1185. Much of it still remains. St Carthach's Cathedral was restored in 1633, but includes older sections. A mile (1.6km) east is a flat-topped conical mound, probably the site of a 12th-century castle. Several miles west at Ballysaggarthore are the Gothic gates and bridge of a project for which the money ran out before the house could be built.

    What to see Ballysaggarthore; Lismore Castle; St Carthach's Cathedral.

Lough Gur's beauty attracts many visitors, and people have chosen to settle here since the Stone Age – the area is rich in archeological finds.

LISTOWEL (Kerry)
Ref: G2

Lios Tuathail, Tuathal's Ringfort. Two ivy-clad towers are all the remains at Listowel of a 13th-century Fitzmaurice castle, the last Desmond stronghold to fall in the 16th-century wars. Gunsborough, 4 miles (6.4km) northwest, was the birthplace of Earl Kitchener (of Khartoum) in 1850.

LOUGH GUR (Limerick)
Ref: G3

Loch Goir. There is a wide variety of bird life to be enjoyed at Lough Gur, a small lake where, according to legend, the last of the Earls of Desmond sleep. Many antiquities came to light when the lake was drained late last century, providing information on Neolithic and Bronze Age man. Stone circles, an Early Bronze Age tomb, two Viking forts, and the well-preserved 15th-century Bourchier's Castle are among the interesting sights.

Lismore Castle stands magnificently above the town, and is surrounded by gardens.

MACROOM (Cork)
Ref: H2
Maigh Chromtha, Sloping Plain. This beautifully sited market town and its massive square castle was granted to Admiral Sir William Penn by Cromwell. The USA State of Pennsylvania is named after his son William who founded it as a refuge for oppressed Quakers on land granted by Charles II. The first Macroom Castle was probably built in the reign of King John, but the structure has burnt down many times. The present ruins include a quadrangular keep from the 15th century. Three miles (4.8km) east off the N22 is an old MacCarthy fortress, called Carrigaphouca Castle which stands on a high ridge of rock with a ruined dolmen nearby.
What to see Ballingeary (clapper-bridge made of stone slabs); Carrigaphouca Castle; Macroom Castle.

The Mitchelstown Caves are a massive pre-glacial underworld.

MALLOW (Cork) Ref: H2
Mala, the Plain of the Rock. A prosperous town in good farming country where sugar is processed, Mallow sits in the beautifully wooded valley of the River Blackwater. It was once a fashionable spa, and is now known for its angling and its racecourse. Mallow also has a strong literary tradition. At the southeast end of the town are the ruins of a fortress built in about 1600 by Sir Thomas Norreys.
What to see Buttavant (ruined 13c friary and modernized castle); Elizabethan Clock House; Liscarroll Castle (13c); Spa well.

MIDLETON (Cork)
Ref: H3
Mainistir na Corann, Monastery of the Weir. This small market town at the head of the Owenacurra estuary was founded by the Brodrick family (later the Earls of Midleton) in about 1670, although the local abbey was founded at the end of the 12th century. There is an attractive 18th-century market house in the main street, a church designed by the Pain brothers, and Midleton College. This was founded as a free grammar school in 1696, and was attended by the Irish statesman and orator John Philpot Curran. Midleton is famous for its distillery, begun in 1826, where the world's largest pot still (31,648galls [142,500l]) was used until 1975. Limestone caves can be seen just northeast at Fox's Quarry, and the remains of 15th-century Cahermone Castle lie 1 mile (1.6km) to the east.
What to see Cahermone Castle (15c); distillery; Fox's Quarry (limestone caves).

MITCHELSTOWN (Cork)
Ref: H3
Baile Mhistéalai, Mitchel's Homestead. Largely rebuilt in the 18th and 19th centuries, Mitchelstown is home to The Kingston College for Decayed Gentlefolk, founded in 1780 to accommodate Protestants in distress. It has a charming group of buildings which form three sides of College Square. The castle has interesting landscaped gardens. The town is famous for its cheese. Ten miles (16km) away (actually in Tipperary) are the Mitchelstown Caves. The Old (or Desmond) caves are difficult to reach and were the hiding place of the Sugan Earl of Desmond in 1601, who was betrayed by someone seeking the £1000 reward for finding him. The New Cave was discovered in 1833 and comprises 1½ miles (2.4km) of passages with many galleries full of stalactites and stalagmites. A ladder is needed for part of the descent and it is essential to go with a guide.
What to see Castle and gardens; Mitchelstown caves.

GAELTACHTS

In 1921, the Republic government decided to encourage the use of Gaelic and provided special treatment for Gaelic-speaking districts, or Gaeltachts, which are mainly in the west and north of Ireland. The language originated in the 7th century, but 900 years on, English began to overtake it in usage. Certain districts now enjoy grants for their own radio stations, and have colleges for students wishing to improve their Gaelic. Some poor regions such as the Dingle Peninsula, Connemara and the Aran Islands (in Galway) have also benefitted from the tourism Gaeltacht status encourages.

Other Gaeltachts include: a region west of Macroom, Cork; Donegal's northern area around Gortahork, Falcarragh and Derrybeg; Gibbstown, near Donaghpatrick in Meath; and south of Dungarvan in Waterford. Naturally, the language is spoken in various dialects which adds a further complication for outsiders learning Gaelic.

Use of the language goes hand in hand with folklore and traditional music, especially in the southwest. Some areas have adopted Gaelic dress such as Aran sweaters, and homespun white coats (bainins, or bauneens). However, the modernizing of Ireland remains a powerful influence resulting in the use of the international English language, and although teaching of the Irish tongue is compulsory at school, only about a third of the population is competent in the language.

Atlantic waves batter the Cliffs of Moher in Clare.

MOHER CLIFFS (Clare)
Ref: G2

Aillte an Mhothair, Cliffs of the Ruin. These magnificent cliffs form a 5 mile (8km) range overlooking the Atlantic from up to 668ft (204m), starting at Hag's Head in the southwest and finishing at O'Brien's Tower at the northeast end. This tower was erected in 1835 by Cornelius O'Brien for visitors to enjoy the view without being alarmed by the drop, but its spiral staircase is now destroyed. Under it is a huge ridge called Goat Island. The cliffs are topped by black shale over dark sandstone, sandwiching a stratified layer containing unusual fossils. A 200ft (60m) stack can be seen offshore from the tower.

MOURNE ABBEY (Cork)
Ref: H2

Mainistir na Móna, Monastery of the Bog. Situated on the east side of the Mallow to Cork road, this area was a walled town with a Preceptory of the Knights Templar in the reign of Edward III. After the Knights Templar were suppressed it was given to the Knights of St John of Jerusalem. The remains of the church itself are unremarkable, but a Templar tombstone can be seen 1½ miles (2.4km) from Rathcormack at Kilshannig graveyard. Near the abbey site is the tower of Castle Barrett.

NENAGH (Tipperary)
Ref: G3

An tAonach, The Fair. Nenagh was an important Anglo-Norman settlement, and then a Franciscan centre until the friary was destroyed by Cromwell's troops. Nenagh Castle was built around 1217 by Theobald Walter Butler, the first of the great Butlers of Ormonde, and its remains dominate the town. It has a cylindrical keep (or donjon) of five storeys with walls up to 20ft (6m) thick. Some of the holes in the fortress were inflicted during the castle's many battles, and one by a farmer trying to get rid of a sparrow's nest. An interesting fort can be seen 4 miles (6.4km) away at Rathurles, and the ruins of a 15th-century church stand within its ramparts. The area around Nenagh is rich in prehistoric sites, ruined castles, monastic remains, and other antiquities.

What to see Ballynaclough castle and church (13c, 3 miles [4.8km] southeast); Courthouse (19c) Church of St Mary; Nenagh Castle (13c); Nenagh Friary (13c); Tyrone Priory (1 mile [1.6km] southeast).

NEWMARKET-ON-FERGUS (Clare) Ref: G2

Cora Chaitlín, Kathleen's Weir. This village is set in a flat area between the estuaries of the Shannon and the Fergus, and is a horse-racing centre (hence the name, taken from the English Newmarket). Opposite Dromoland Castle (see separate entry) is a belvedere from which Sir Edward O'Brien used to watch local horse racing, and members of the O'Brien family are buried in the parish church at Kilnasoolagh nearly 1 mile (1.6km) to the west. There is an interesting monument by sculptor William Kidwell of Dublin. Four miles (6.4km) east at Finlough are the remains of Tomfinlough church, on the site of an early monastic foundation. Two miles (3.2km) south is Urlanmore Castle, once a stronghold of the McMahons. This has a three-storey tower at one end, plus the remains of a fine hall. Some walls feature outline paintings of animals.

Parknasilla is something of a subtropical paradise, its climate warmed by the mild Gulf Stream.

What to see Dromoland Castle; Kilnasoolagh church; Tominlough church (14c); Urlanmore Castle.

PALLAS GREEN, NEW (Limerick) Ref: G3

Pailís Ghréine, Grian's Palisade. At Old Pallas Green, nearly 2 miles (3.2km) southwest of Pallas Green, are a motte and the remains of a manorial church. About 3 miles (4.8km) north is the former O'Grady stronghold of Castle Garde, a five-storey tower linked to a more recent wing, and thought to be the oldest inhabited house in Limerick.

PARKNASILLA (Kerry) Ref: H2

Pairc na Saileach, Willow Field. Parknasilla is a well-known beauty spot where the estuary of the Sneem meets Kenmare River. There are many pleasant walks along winding paths through woods and over rustic bridges, and boat trips to the numerous islands out to sea. Do not confuse Garinish Island with its namesake near Glengarriff. Parknasilla offers good sea fishing and a nine-hole golf course, while the absence of a sandy beach forces bathers onto the pier and into the many coves. Just to the east is Blackwater Bridge, famous for its pretty setting.

QUIN (Clare) Ref: G2

Cuinche. This little village is surrounded by beautiful scenery and rich archeological remains, and is famous for its well-preserved Franciscan friary. Founded in 1433 on the remains of an Anglo-Norman castle, this has a virtually complete church with high altar, cloisters, and a graceful tower. From the top of the friary tower can be seen a number of castles. One of the most interesting is Danganbrack, a tall tower of 16th-century origin with very high chimneys. It lies nearly a mile (1.6km) to the east. On the opposite side of the river is 13th-century St Finghin's Church, a long rectangular building with triple-lancet east windows.

RATHCORMACK (Cork) Ref: H3

Ráth Chormaic, Cormac's Ringfort. Rathcormack can be found in the lovely countryside of the River Bride, whose banks support numerous fine houses. Beyond the river to the west is the hilltop site of Georgian Kilshannig House, a mansion built by Davis Ducart in the 18th century. Lisnagar is a similarly dated and splendid mansion lying southwest of the village. Two

ST BRENDAN'S JOURNEY ACROSS THE ATLANTIC

Four miles (6.4km) south of Quin is the Craggaunowen Project, which is devoted to re-creating some of Ireland's ancient history. One of its most interesting exhibits is the Brendan, a leather-hulled boat made by scholar and sailor Tim Severin in which he crossed the Atlantic in 1977. The journey repeated that in the legend of St Brendan, who in the 15th century sailed from Kerry and is thought to have reached Newfoundland via the Faroes and Iceland. He described his boat as 'ribbed with wood and with a wooden frame . . . they covered it with ox-hides tanned with the bark of oak and smeared all the joints of the hide on the outside with fat.' Brendan and his fellow monks endured an incident-packed voyage in which his boat was followed by whales, was hit by burning rocks from a volcano, and passed bird-covered islands and ice floes.

Tim Severin set out to prove that Irish monks could have reached America in a light boat with a wooden frame covered with leather, and used the hides of 49 oxen in making his replica boat. He and his four crew had some remarkably similar encounters with whales, islands of birds, and ice floes during their journey. Like St Brendan, they eventually reached Newfoundland.

miles (3.2km) east, on a tributary of the Bride, is Castlelyons village with its friary, castle and ruined church. A ruined cairn and a holy well are features of 727ft (221m) Corrin Hill, off the Fermoy road, northwest of the town.

RATHKEALE (Limerick) Ref: G2

Ráth Caola, Caola's Ringfort. Rathkeale is a market town with remains of 13th-century St Mary's Abbey. The Protestant church contains the Southwell monument of 1676. Half a mile (0.8km) away is Castle Matrix, a 15th-century tower house that has been very well restored. It includes a tiny top floor chapel and a medieval bedroom, and houses a collection of objets d'art.

RATH LUIRC (Cork) Ref: H2

An Ráth, The Ringfort. The name of this market centre near the Limerick border was changed for a time to Charleville in honour of Charles II (1630–85). In 1690, the Lord President of Munster entertained the Duke of Berwick in his fine mansion. The Lord President's hospitality towards his guest was rudely repaid by the burning of the house to the ground. A short distance away in the old church of Ballysallagh is the grave of Clarach Mac Domhnaill, the 17th-century Gaelic poet. Five miles (8km) north is Bruree, where there is a pretty six-arch bridge across the Maigue and the remnants of a de Lacy fortress.

THE ARRIVAL OF CHRISTIANITY

The gradual conversion of Celtic Ireland to Christianity probably began in around AD430 when missionaries began to arrive, mainly from Britain. One by one, monasteries were established. But, sadly, little survives of these early Christian foundations, as the buildings were mainly made of wood.

However, some of the later, simple stone structures seen in Co. Kerry give an idea of the ascetic life of the first monks. Skellig Michael has good examples of hermits' stone cells, often called beehive huts because their shape resembles

old-fashioned beehives. Existing in such a place, marooned in the Atlantic, was physically tough, but the idea of living in this environment was to enable the monks to concern themselves with artistic and literary pursuits.

As Christianity began to grow, the monasteries became wealthy and powerful centres, providing an impetus for a 'Golden Age' of learning and art. Illuminated manuscripts and exquisite metalwork were produced at this time, as were intricately carved crosses, known today as Celtic or high crosses.

ROSCREA (Tipperary)
Ref: F3
Ros Cré, Cré's Wood. Roscrea is home to a rich collection of antiquarian remains. A 60ft (18m) round tower on Church Street has a doorway 15ft (4.5m) up for protection, and carries the faint image of a ship on the inner face of a window. The tower was originally 20ft (6m) higher, but was damaged when a cannon backfired in 1798. Further along Church Street is the 1812 parish church, with its entrance formed by a 12th-century monastery façade. The modern (Catholic) St Cronan's Church, in Abbey Street, has a pillar with an animal carving, possibly dating from the 8th century, and in the churchyard entrance is a square, castellated tower of a 1490 friary.

What to see St Cronan's churches (Church of Ireland, 19c; Catholic, 15c origins); Damer House (18c); Mona Incha Abbey (2 miles [3.2km] southeast); Rosemary Square (ornate Victorian fountain).

SKELLIG ISLANDS (Kerry)
Ref: H1
Na Scealaga, The Rock-splinters. The Skellig Islands lie 8 miles (12.8km) off the coast of Kerry, and can be reached by boat from Reenard, Knightstown and Portmagee on Valentia Island. The massive jagged rock arch of Little Skellig can only be viewed from the sea, and is a sanctuary for

Four miles (6.4km) southwest of Thurles is Holy Cross Abbey, which was founded in 1169 and has been recently restored.

thousands of birds. Great Skellig (also known as Skellig Michael) is the largest island, and is an important early-Christian site. Visitors who climb the forbidding cliffs from the landing stage via crude stone steps will find the ruins of St Finian's Abbey, founded in AD560. Here there are six beehive cells (drystone huts with a distinctive 'beehive' shape) and a number of other interesting monuments from the many centuries that the island has been inhabited by monks.

SKIBBEREEN (Cork)
Ref: J2
An Sciobairín. Skibbereen is a market town and fishing port standing on the Ilen River about 1 mile (1.6km) away from where the river forms a winding estuary joined to Baltimore Bay. The rather desolate surrounding district saw appalling suffering during the 19th-century potato famine. The fine Grecian cathedral was built in 1816, and there are pleasant Georgian houses around the green. South of the town is

Abisdealy Lough, and beyond it are the bay and headland of Toe Head. A mile (1.6km) west are the remains of the Cistercian abbey of Abbeystrowry. Southwest, the old castle of the O'Driscoll family perches on a rock, while the ruins of the family's stronghold, Dunamore Castle, can be seen on Clear Island, west of Sherkin Island.

What to see Abbeystrowry abbey; Abisdealy Lough; Cathedral (19c); Dunamore Castle; O'Driscoll Castle.

The façade of Thurles Cathedral was modelled on Pisa Cathedral.

SNEEM (Kerry) Ref: H1

An tSnaidhm, The Knot. This is a pretty village which has become something of a tourist centre. The Catholic church dates from 1865 and contains the grave of Father Michael Walsh, a 19th-century parish priest immortalized in the song 'Father O'Flynn'. The east window is a memorial to poet Aubrey de Vere who died in 1902. The much-altered Protestant church probably dates from Elizabethan times, and advertises the good local fishing with its salmon weather-cock.

TALLOW (Waterford) Ref: H3

Tulach an Iarainn, the Hill of the Iron. Once a town of some importance, Tallow went into decline in the 19th century, and its name derives from the iron ore once exploited here. It sits in the valley of the River Bride, a tributary of the Blackwater, and was part of the territory granted to Sir Walter Raleigh in 1586. He assigned the town to Sir Richard Boyle (later Earl of Cork) who 'planted' it with English Protestants. There are a number of almshouses, and a horse fair is held in early September. Nearby stands Lisfinny Castle, and 3 miles (4.8km) west are the ruins of Mogeely Castle. Not far away is Conna Castle, and east of this is Tallow Hill which offers excellent views.

What to see Conna Castle; horse fair (held in September); Lisfinny Castle; Mogeely Castle; Tallow Hill.

TEMPLEMORE (Tipperary) Ref: G3

An Teampall Mór, The Big Church. A town famous for its cattle fairs in the last century, Templemore grew up as an establishment of the Knights Templar, who had a strong castle and monastery here. The parish church of c.1790 has a fine spire, and there are castle and abbey remains in the town park. A few miles away stands the 1557ft (475m) Devil's Bit Mountain which offers pleasant views. There is a 45ft (14m) high cross to commemorate the Marian Year 1954 on the summit. Just over 3 miles (4.8km) south is Loughmoe Castle. Its rectangular tower dates from the 15th century and is vaulted on both the ground and first floors. The rest of the building (now ruined) is 17th century.

Sneem is spectacularly set among domineering mountains.

What to see Carden's Folly; Court and market house (19c); Devil's Bit Mountain; Loughmoe Castle (15 and 17c).

THURLES (Tipperary) Ref: G3

Durlas, Strong Fort. This market town was of great strategic importance in the Middle Ages and there are many castle ruins in the surrounding area. The Roman Catholic cathedral is a fine building with a façade modelled on that of Pisa Cathedral. The bell tower is 125ft (38m) high. St Mary's Church features a 16th-century Archer tomb. Two miles (3.2km) north is Brittas Castle, a replica of Warwick Castle which was never completed because the owner was hit by falling masonry. A modern residence has since been built within its confines. To the southwest of Thurles is Holy Cross Abbey (see separate entry).

TIPPERARY (Tipperary) Ref: G3

Tiobraid Árann, Well of the River Ara. Like many towns bearing the name of a county, Tipperary is less important than one might assume. Sited on the River Ra in the Golden Vale, south of the Galtee Mountains, it had far greater significance in medieval times. It was also a centre of Land League protest in the 19th century. There is an interesting museum by the swimming pool with exhibits from the warring years of 1919–23. The famous 1914 song 'It's a long way to Tipperary' was written by Englishman Jack Judge, who had never been to the town.

TRALEE (Kerry) Ref: G2

Trá Lí, Strand of Lí. Tralee is a tourist and climbing centre at the gateway to the Dingle Peninsula. The town is closely identified with the Desmonds, and the last episode in the drama of their downfall took place at Glenageenty, 8 miles (12.8km) to the east. The last earl was captured by English forces and executed, with his head sent to England for display on London Bridge. Only a fragment of wall survives of the great castle of the Desmonds, once the family seat. The Dominican church of Holy Cross features fine stained glass by Michael Healy.

What to see Annagh church (southwest of town, has a 13c carving of an armed horseman); Thomas Ashe Memorial hall; Ballyseedy House (18c, 3 miles [4.8km] east); Courthouse; Denny Street 1798 memorial; Holy Cross church; Ratass Church (early Irish, 1 mile [1.6km] east).

Reginald's Tower of 1003 now houses Waterford's city museum.

TRAMORE (Waterford)
Ref: H4
Trâ Mhór, Big Strand. A 3-mile (4.8km) sandy beach and a pier tell their own story of the popularity of Tramore as a holiday resort. The bay is much exposed to southern gales, and in 1816 a troop ship returning from the Peninsular War (1808–14) fought against the French was wrecked here with the loss of 363 lives. West of the bay are the Doneraile cliffs, crowned by three towers on the summit of Great Newtown Head, acting as markers for ships. One huge iron figure is called 'Metal Man', and girls who hop around its base three times will be married within a year, according to legend. Five miles (8km) west is the ruined 17th-century Dunhill Castle. Five miles (8km) in the other direction at Kilmacleague is a ruined church with an ancient font, built on the site of a monastery.

VALENTIA ISLAND (Kerry)
Ref: H1
Dairbhre, Place of Oaks. A 7 by 2 mile (11.2 by 3.2km) island of mainly rocky surface, Valentia Island is separated from the mainland by a narrow strait which is spanned by a bridge at Portmagee. Geokaun Mountain (880ft [268m]) and Bray Head (792ft [241m]) are splendid vantage points. The island is home to the most westerly harbour in Europe, and the first transatlantic telegraph cable was laid from here in 1857. Permanent contact was established in 1866, and it was joked that communication was better with New York than Dublin. The cable station closed 100 years later. A delightful excursion can be made from Knightstown harbour to the tiny Church Island, east of Beginish Island, where there are the remains of an ancient oratory and some beehive huts.
   What to see Bray Head (792ft [241m], western end of island); Church Island (boat excursion); Geokaun Mountain slate quarries; Glanleam gardens.

WATERFORD (Waterford)
Ref: H4
Port Láirge, Bank of the Haunch. Waterford has some splendid Georgian architecture and interesting structures from its past, and while never spectacular it is a lively and enterprising city providing the visitor with excellent entertainment.
   Most of the Georgian splendours are around the Mall, and nearby

A KNACK FOR
SELF-PRESERVATION

Waterford has shown a knack for self-preservation and for money making throughout its long history. It was established by the Vikings in the 9th century, and became their key settlement, known as Vatnfjordhur. Its strategic importance for control of the southwest made it a target for the Anglo-Normans in 1170 when it was violently taken. An already formidably fortified town was further strengthened (much of this work remains) and Waterford stayed loyal to the English crown throughout subsequent struggles, receiving many favours in return.
   Well equipped with its long

quay, Waterford prospered as a European port from the 16th century onwards, trading with France, Spain, Portugal and Newfoundland. The only city to withstand the attacks of Cromwell, the city negotiated terms with General Ireton and continued to grow. In the late 18th century, Waterford established itself as the best glass manufacturer in Europe, and although the industry went into decline, it has since been revitalized and is again world famous.

**WATERVILLE (Kerry)
Ref: H1**

An Coireán, The Little Whirlpool. A famous salmon fishing resort which also has a sandy beach and a nine-hole golf course, Waterville sits on a narrow neck of land between Ballinskelligs Bay and Lough Currane. The scenery at the upper end of this lake is particularly beautiful. At the north end of Lough Currane is Church Island which has the ruins of a 12th-century church and a beehive cell thought to date from the 6th century. A little north, at the foot of Bentee mountain, is Cahirciveen (see separate entry). About 9 miles (14.4km) off Valentia Island are the three Skellig Islands (see separate entries).

What to see Ballinskelligs (Gaelic speaking village); Cahirciveen; Church Island; Leacanabuaile Fort; Skellig Islands; Valentia Island.

YOUGHAL (Cork) Ref: H3

Eochaill, Yew Wood. There is much to see both within and outside Youghal's 15th-century town walls. The old town lies at the foot of a long steep hill. Here, Main Street is spanned by a wide arch carrying a four-storey structure topped by a clock tower, known as Clock Gate. Nearby is the much altered 15th-century tower house called Tynte's Castle, and opposite is a fine house from c.1706; the Red House. At the north end of Main Street is the Dominican North Abbey. Ireland's largest medieval parish church can be found in William Street: The Collegiate Church of St Mary was built in the reign of King John (1199–1216) and has been restored several times. There is an Early English west doorway and a separate belfry tower with 8ft (2.4m) thick walls. Other features are the 14th-century baptismal font, the oak roof and arches of the nave and the massive pulpit with canopy carved in bog oak. Many of the memorials in the church date from the 16th and 17th centuries. North of the church is Myrtle Grove, an Elizabethan gabled house, once home to Sir Walter Raleigh, but not open to the public. Two miles (3.2km) away is Rincrew Hill, crowned by the ruins of Rincrew Abbey.

What to see Clock Gate (1771); Collegiate Church of St Mary; Dominican Priory (13c); Myrtle Grove; St John's House (a cell of a Benedictine priory); the Red House; Rincrew Abbey (12c); Stancally Castle (7 miles [11.2km] north on a rock over the Blackwater); Tynte's Castle.

the spired Christ Church Cathedral dates from 1770, although it was altered in 1891. It replaced an ancient Norse cathedral founded in 1050, but John Roberts' design followed the shape of the original. Two noteworthy monuments inside are the Fitzgerald, of white Carrara marble, and the Rice. This dates from 1469 and represents a decomposing body with a frog nestling on the intestines. The Catholic Holy Trinity Cathedral of 1796 is further along the Quay, and is also by John Roberts. Also of interest are the museum and art gallery in O'Connell Street, the 19th-century courthouse, and the similarly-aged clock tower. A tower and belfry remain from the

Dominican friary, dated 1226.

Off the Parade are remains of the Grey Friars or French Church, originally a Franciscan friary in 1240 and given to Huguenot refugees in 1695. Only the nave, chapel and 15th-century tower have survived. There is a triple-light east window in the chancel. Some of the Viking origins of St Olaf's Church remain, but most of it was built in 1734.

The best view of the city, and one which reinforces the importance of its harbour, is from the swing bridge across the Suir, which replaced an 18th-century wooden toll bridge by celebrated American bridge builder Lemuel Cox. There are numerous portal dolmens around the city, dating

Waterville, a seaside resort in Victorian and Edwardian times, has retained its charm.

from around 2000BC. The most remarkable is 4 miles (6.4km) southwest at Knockeen. Some 4 miles (6.4km) roughly west of the city, above the River Suir, stands the mid-Georgian house of Mount Congreve, with notable gardens which can be seen by appointment. Northwest of here are the ruins of Kilmeadon Castle.

What to see Christ Church Cathedral (18c); Clock Tower and Quay (19c); Courthouse (19c); Cromwell's Rock; French Church; Holy Trinity Cathedral (18c); St Olaf's Church; Waterford Glass Factory.

LEINSTER

The flat and well watered province of Leinster offers some of Ireland's greenest, lushest countryside, and its most golden beaches, though it is also the most densely populated and industrialized area of the country. Rolling farmland, bogs and woods dominate Leinster, contrasting with the hills of Wicklow to the east. All roads lead to Dublin, capital of the Republic, and generally regarded as one of Europe's most attractive cities.

*T*he gentle coast of Leinster offers no resistance to attackers, and consequently the province bears the mark of foreign influence, much of which has centred on Dublin, once a Viking settlement, and later the focus of English involvement in Ireland. Today, the golden beaches of this coast attract many visitors, who can also be tempted inland by the deep green countryside and some marvellous ancient historical sites.

Carlow This is a tiny county northwest of Wexford, its low plains mostly occupied with farming land producing sugar beet and crops for the food processing industry. The busy farms are often hidden by undulating hills and the greenery of woods and hedgerows. The finest panorama of the county is probably seen from the ancient stone fort of Rathgall. Other places of historic interest in Carlow are the ancient remains at St Mullin's near the River Barrow, Ballymoone Castle, and the dolmens at Tobinstown and Brown's Mill.

Dublin The county of Dublin covers the city and its environs (the only other major settlement is Dun Laoghaire). Any visitor to Ireland should plan to spend some time in this magnificent city which, while not without problems (there are some areas of acute poverty) is characterized by a glorious vitality. Of the sites within easy range, Powerscourt House and gardens (see Enniskerry entry) is at the top of the list. County Dublin also has a varied and beautiful coastline which has more in common with the rough sea border of south Wexford than the accommodating east coast, and the county itself has been described as one of the most attractive in Ireland.

Kildare It could be argued that County Kildare is plagued by main roads that whisk the visitors through the least attractive areas and leave the best untouched. The best way to enjoy Kildare is from the waters of the Grand Canal, once a commercial thoroughfare, now a cruising channel with a walkable towpath. The surrounding countryside is relatively flat, so the views are extensive, and include many buildings of historical interest, plus the big stone estate walls that indicate

Kildare's central location in the Pale. Any description of Kildare must include St Brigid, and horses. St Brigid had a nunnery in the middle of Kildare city 1500 years ago, and her name echoes down the centuries in churches, wells and place-names. Just as prolific is the love of horses, for the wide plain of the Curragh is the home of Irish racing, and the whole county seems to follow the sport avidly.

Kilkenny The county of Kilkenny has some of the most beautiful countryside in the southeast of Ireland: a compact, green landscape dissected by wandering lanes. This provides a marvellous setting for some magnificent sites: ruined Jerpoint Abbey near Thomastown in the heart of the county, with Kells Priory a few miles northwest; Graiguenamangh Abbey overlooking the eastern border with Carlow; the ancient friary and castle of Inistioge; and Kilkenny, the finest medieval city in Ireland.

Laois There are few major sites in County Laois (pronounced Leash), and it is missed from the itineraries of many visitors, but it

does have its own quiet charm. It is mainly flat, low country where forests alternate with bogs and rich pasture. The River Barrow marks most of its eastern border, and the northern frontier with Offaly is formed by the Slieve Bloom mountains. The main tourist attraction is the Rock of Dunamase, a fortress standing 200ft (61m) above its surrounding hills.

Longford This is another county that has stayed pretty much off the beaten track. It has pockets of great beauty at many of its lakes, but the overall impression is of a plain and placid area. In Annaly, it has one of the most famous regions of Irish history, long dominated by the O'Farrell family. They were Lords of Annaly for centuries and they retained their independence long after other chieftains had submitted to the English. Exiled in 1691, the family later reached the Argentine and became very powerful there.

Louth This is the smallest of Ireland's 32 counties, covering a short stretch of coast that is punctuated by quaint seaside resorts. It also has the interesting town of

Previous page: *The upper lake at Glendalough is famed for its tranquillity.*

province, and was home to Tara, seat of the High Kings of Ireland. Even more ancient is the Brugh na Boine complex of megalithic graves, the most famous of which is Newgrange. Through the county runs the River Boyne, whose banks saw the great battle of 1690 when William III defeated James II. These famous royal sites are dotted about on the most fertile soil in Ireland, where rolling green pastures blend into rich plantations and prosperous farmsteads.

Offaly The bogs of County Offaly are a major source of fuel and moss peats, which makes the area economically important, but not particularly attractive to the vistor. In the northwest is the flood plain of the Shannon, and in the southeast rise the mountains of Slieve Bloom. In between, there are few sights of interest, apart from Clonmacnoise, a key monastery in early Celtic Ireland.

Westmeath Although it is an inland county, water is a major feature of Westmeath, for in its north it boasts some truly magnificent lakes. One of the best is tree-shrouded Lough Derryvarragh, with its strange hidden quality as if it has chosen to escape the crowds. Between Loughs Lene and Baneare stands the fascinating group of monastic remains at Fore.

Wexford You could be forgiven for disbelieving that Ireland has a sunny and dry corner, but not after visiting Wexford, on the southeastern tip of the country, which has a very mild climate. That said, there is little to detain you here – there are frustratingly few traces of the county's eventful history (the Danes founded the county town in the 9th century). The south and east coasts offer some of the finest sea angling in Europe, and south of Rosslare are some lovely bays and promontories. The farmers of Wexford have to work hard to get much reward out of their poor soil, but through their veins runs the hardy Norse and Norman blood of past invaders, a mix which gives the region's people a separate identity from the rest of Ireland.

Wicklow Such is the diversity of County Wicklow's scenery that it is known as 'The Garden of Ireland'. Its breathtaking views are all the more welcome for being within easy reach of Dublin. Back from its coastline of sandy beaches are the massive Wicklow Mountains, which form a 40-mile chain extending from Dublin City to the foothills of Wexford. Standing out among the peat-covered domes is the quartzite cone of Great Sugarloaf, rising above the Glen of the Downs, one of Wicklow's beautiful valleys and gorges. Such a landscape produces fantastic waterfalls, and one of the best is near Enniskerry at Powerscourt, the famous house whose grounds are worth a trip in themselves. The other major attraction of the county is 532 acre (215ha) Avondale Forest Park.

Spectacular views against silhoutted mountains at Wicklow Head.

Drogheda, and the historic monasteries of Mellifont and Monasterboice. The highlight, however, is probably the Cooley Peninsula, between Dundalk Bay and Carlingford Lough. Visiting this remote district is rather like stepping back in time, a feeling which is intensified by the knowledge that it plays a central role in the major legends of Ireland. There is a story of Queen Maeve of Connacht starting a war to win a bull she coveted, and immobolizing her enemies with a magical sickness. Only the warrior Cuchulainn is able to fight, and he holds her army off single-handed. There are countless tales associated with these real people, who lived in the 1st century AD. Visit Louth to sample the atmosphere of such stories.

Meath Meath is one of the great historical counties of Ireland. Once, combined with Westmeath, it formed the country's fifth

Carvings in St Michan's Church, Dublin.

PLACES of INTEREST

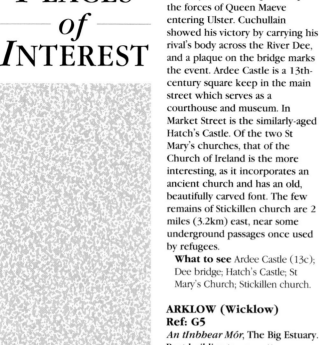

ABBEYLEIX (Laois) Ref: G4

Mainistir Laoise, the Monastery of Laois. The Cistercian abbey after which this pleasant town is named has long since disappeared, but what is evident is the work carried out by an 'improving' landlord in the 18th century. Viscount de Vesci re-built the whole community around a planned network of tree-lined streets, some of them with elegant Georgian houses. The Protestant church and market house are of some interest – although many visitors are here for the angling on the River Nore. Just southwest is the Viscount's old home, set in attractive parkland, sometimes open to the public, where remains of an ancient oak wood, and a 12th- or 13th-century monk's bridge survive.

ARDEE (Louth) Ref: E4

Baile Áth Fhirdhia, the Town of Ferdia's Ford. Irish legend has it that in this ancient town, Cuchullain, leader of the Red Branch Knights, fought Ferdia for four days in an attempt to stop the forces of Queen Maeve entering Ulster. Cuchullain showed his victory by carrying his rival's body across the River Dee, and a plaque on the bridge marks the event. Ardee Castle is a 13th-century square keep in the main street which serves as a courthouse and museum. In Market Street is the similarly-aged Hatch's Castle. Of the two St Mary's churches, that of the Church of Ireland is the more interesting, as it incorporates an ancient church and has an old, beautifully carved font. The few remains of Stickillen church are 2 miles (3.2km) east, near some underground passages once used by refugees.

What to see Ardee Castle (13c); Dee bridge; Hatch's Castle; St Mary's Church; Stickillen church.

ARKLOW (Wicklow) Ref: G5

An tInbhear Mór, The Big Estuary. Boat-building town, pottery centre, and coastal bird-spotting base, Arklow is one of the major resorts on the east coast. The

Athlone's Norman castle has guarded a key crossing over the Shannon for centuries.

ruins of a great Ormond fortress demolished in 1649 stand on a bluff overlooking the river mouth. Remains of a 13th-century Dominican friary can be seen in a field near the parish priest's house. The mock-Tudor Shelton Abbey is 2 miles (3.2km) along the Avoca river to the northwest, and is noted for its fine grounds. It is now a state forestry education centre. Famous beauty spots within easy reach of Arklow include Glendalough, Glenmalure, the Vale of Clara and the Meeting of the Waters at the Vale of Avoca.

What to see Dominican friary; Glendalough; Glenmalure; Ormond fortress; Shelton Abbey; Vale of Avoca; Vale of Clara.

ASHFORD (Wicklow) Ref: F5

Áth na Fuinseoige, the Ford of the Ash. A number of attractions can be found near this pretty village. One mile (1.6km) northwest is the deep, shrub covered chasm of Devil's Glen, where the River Bartry falls almost 100ft (30m) into the Devil's Punchbowl basin. Mount Usher Gardens are closer to the village, and have rare shrubs and trees in a 20-acre (8-ha) 'wild' garden made after the ideas of William Robinson in the late 19th century.

Unusual rock formations including the mitre-shaped Bishop's Rock can be seen at Dunran Glen, to the north. The lovely old-world Hunter's Hotel is 1 mile (1.6km) east at Newrathbridge.

What to see Carriage museum; Devil's Glen; Dunran Glen; Hunter's Hotel; Mount Usher Gardens.

ATHBOY (Meath) Ref: E4

Baile Átha Buí, Town of the Yellow Ford. The west tower of a 15th-century Carmelite priory is incorporated into the church of Athboy, which also features a 15th-century effigy of a knight and his lady. Nearby are parts of medieval town walls dating from a time when Athboy was a stronghold of the Pale. A mile (1.6km) east is the Hill of the Ward, a hilltop fort with a central enclosure surrounded by four pairs of banks and ditches. This was once Tlachtga, one of the principal assembly places in the ancient kingdom of Meath, and scene of many mass human sacrifices.

ATHLONE (Westmeath) Ref: F3

Baile Átha Luain, the Town of the Ford of Luan. Athlone is

renowned more for its historical associations than for what has been preserved. It stands where the Dublin to Galway road crosses the country's biggest river, the Shannon, and thus occupies a strategic position. This has made it the site of countless battles throughout history. A celebrated tussle took place at the bridge in the town centre in 1691 between Jacobites and Williamites, when the defenders destroyed it in the face of heavy artillery fire to keep the Williamites out. Adamson Castle has its origins in a 1210 castle house built, in turn, on the site of a primitive fortress and now houses a museum.

What to see Abbey ruins; Athlone Castle; Church of SS Peter and Paul; Franciscan friary remains; John McCormack's Birthplace (on The Bawn); St Mary's Church; Town wall remains.

ATHY (Kildare) Ref: F4
Áth Í, the Ford of Ae. Another town in a strategic position on a ford, a dubious privilege which inevitably means battles in times of war. There are therefore a number of local castles close by. Castle Woodstock is a 13th-century structure badly damaged in 1649, while White Castle dates from 1575. It has a massive rectangular wall with turrets at each corner, and overlooks the 1796 Crom-a-boo Bridge (the name derives from a Desmond warcry). The political theorist Edmund Burke attended the school at the Quaker settlement Ballitore, 8 miles (12.8km) to the east. The ruins of Castle Inch are 3 miles (4.8km) east, while those of Ballyadams are 4 miles (6.4km) southwest. Belan House, by 18th-century architect Richard Cassels, is 6 miles (9.6km) southeast.

AUGHRIM (Wicklow) Ref: G5
Eachroim, Horse Ridge. The River Aughrim is formed nearby by the convergence of the tiny Ow and Derry rivers. The village forms a good base from which to climb 3039ft (926m) Lugnaquilla Mountain, approached via Aghavannagh Valley. Northwest by 3 miles (4.8km) at Ballymanus is a splendid Georgian farmhouse, birthplace of Billy Byrne, who led Irish insurgents against the king's army in 1798.

Abbeyleix House was designed by James 'the Destroyer' Wyatt. His nickname derives from a penchant for rebuilding rather than restoring.

AVOCA (Wicklow) Ref: G5

Abhóca. Late spring or autumn are the best times to enjoy the Vale of Avoca, scene of the Meeting of the Waters – the confluence of the Avonmore and the Avonbeg – and the best view is from Lion Bridge. This was once the entrance to Castle Howard, now called Croneblane. The scene is immortalized in the Tom Moore song 'The Meeting of the Waters'. Avoca is also known for its copper, lead and zinc deposits. Up on the 618ft (188m) high Cronebane Ridge is the Mottha Stone, a 14ft (4.2m) long boulder said to be the hurling stone of Irish hero Fin MacCool.

BALLINAKILL (Laois) Ref: G4

Baile na Coille, the Homestead of the Wood. Only a few ruins remain of the castle which once guarded this Kilkenny-border community. The stronghold survived attack by Cromwellian troops in 1641, but was abandoned in 1680. A mile (1.6km) north is Haywood House, first built in 1773 but destroyed in a fire, and rebuilt in 1950. It now serves as a Salesian missionary college, and its grounds include sunken gardens designed by Sir Edward Lutyens. A mile southwest at Rusconnell are the remains of a 13th-century church.

BALLINDERRY (Westmeath) Ref: F3

Baile an Doire, the Homestead of the Oak Grove. This is the site of the remains of two crannogs among the bogs, 1½ miles (2.4km) northeast of the village of Moate. The first dates back to the 10th century, and was occupied off and on for 700 years. As the foundations sank into the bog, another dwelling was built on top of them. One find on the site was a carved 10th-century wooden gaming board, now in Dublin's National Museum. Just over a mile (1.6km) southeast is the second crannog, which was originally occupied in the Bronze Age.

BALLYMAHON (Longford) Ref: F3

Baile Uí Mhathaín, Ó'Mathaín's Homestead. A five-arch bridge spans the River Inny in this angling resort in the heart of Goldsmith Country. Oliver Goldsmith was born 3 miles (4.8km) east at Pallas in 1728, though two years later the family moved to Lissoy, 5 miles (8km) southwest.

BALLYRAGGET (Kilkenny) Ref: G4

Béal Átha Ragad, the Ford-mouth of Ragget. This little River Nore town boasts the 15th- and 16th-century remains of a former

ANCIENT LAKE DWELLINGS

Crannogs are artificial islands upon which people built homes to create lake dwellings, a practice that seems to have begun in the Neolithic period (4000–2400BC). Those at Ballinderry are thought to have been used as late as the 17th century. To build a crannog, a mound was created above the water, using layers of logs, stones, peat, brush, animal bones and any other material to hand. Then a wood and stone structure was built on top. It is likely that many crannogs were built on marshland which over the years turned into lakes. The remnants of wooden palisades at some suggest that they had a defensive as well as domestic function. Some of the structures were quite sophisticated, for example one at Lough-na-cranagh, Fair Head, has drystone facing which rises 7ft (2.1m) above water level.

The damp foundations provide excellent conditions for preserving objects from the past, and have allowed archeologists to piece together the history of certain sites. At Ballinderry, for example, layers of wicker floor, gravel and clay have been used to reinforce the surface over the years. Other crannogs can be seen at Drumcliff (Sligo) and Lough Gur (Limerick).

Ormonde castle. Surviving parts include four round towers linked by crenellated curtain walls to form a rectangle round the strong keep. Closer to the river is an 80ft (24m) high motte with a deep fosse, which when complete would have housed an archer's tower.

BALTINGLASS (Wicklow) Ref: G4

Bealach Conglais, the Road of Cúglais. A little town dwarfed by 1285ft (391m) Baltinglass Hill, which offers a fine viewpoint and is crowned with the remains of a passage grave with Bronze Age burial chambers, and an Iron Age hillfort called Rathcoran. A Cistercian abbey known as Vallis Salutis stands by the River Slaney. It was founded in 1148 by Dermot

Baltinglass Abbey occupies a fine site by the River Slaney.

MacMurrough, king of Leinster, whose invitation led to the Norman invasion of Ireland. The remains are considerable and include twin rows of Gothic arches and some sculptures in the south nave. Four miles (6.4km) north is Grange Con park, which boasts a herd of white fallow deer brought over from Welbeck Abbey in Nottinghamshire.

What to see Baltinglass Hill; burial chambers; Grange Con park; Rathcoran; Vallis Salutis.

BIRR (Offaly) Ref: F3

Biorra, Watery Place. The Camcor and Little Brosna rivers join here to provide an attractive setting for an unusually well laid-out town. Birr is dominated by its castle, which is a veteran of many sieges since the 16th century, and has also been extended many times. In 1620, it passed into the hands of Lawrence Parsons, and has

stayed in the family every since (Birr itself was known as Parsonstown for a while). The 3rd Earl of Ross was a famous astronomer who built what was then the world's largest telescope, and its remains can still be seen, although the reflector is at the Science Museum, London. In the castle grounds are limes, chestnuts, Wellingtonias, Greek and other firs, a Cedar of Goa, Himalayan juniper, Monterey cypress and possibly the world's tallest box hedges – 35ft (10.6m) high.

BRUGH NA BOINNE (Meath) Ref: E5

This is an area on a great bend of the River Boyne with a remarkable concentration of prehistoric monuments whose origins and rationale are still the object of much speculation. For a complete description, see the

entry for its most impressive monument at Newgrange.

CALLAN (Kilkenny) Ref: G4

Callainn. The Church of Ireland parish church of this busy town is the adapted chancel of a church built in 1460, although there is also a tower remaining from a 13th-century structure. There are fine sculptured details on the doorways, and a good collection of 16th- and 17th-century gravestones in the nave. The town also has the remains of a 15th-century Augustinian friary, including an ornamental sedilia and a decorative doorway and window. There is also a Catholic church in Callan dating from 1836 which has an unusual west tower topped by an obelisk-like spire. A well-preserved Norman motte with traces of the bailey can be seen in the town.

CARLINGFORD (Louth) Ref: E5

Cairlinn, Hag's Bay. Carlingford is a Cooley peninsula village with a long history – there was a castle here from at least 1210, and so many structures were fortified that even the church of the 1305 priory has a battlement. Worth seeing are Taaffe's Castle (with a good spiral staircase) and a fortified house called the Mint, both 16th century. Nearby is Carlingford Lough, a lovely lake set against the Cooley and Mourne Mountains. Vikings beached their ships when they arrived at the Lough's mouth at Cranfield, and carried out raids from a settlement here for many years. Cloughmore stone was said to be thrown to its spot in the Forestry Division drive by Finn MacCool (although glacier movement seems a better explanation for how 40 tons [40,640kg] of granite got there).

What to see Blockhouse Island (has a colony of terns); Carlingford Lough; Cloughmore stone; Kilbroney Park; Mint (16c); Narrow Water Castle (16c, 3 miles [4.8km] west); Taaffe's Castle (16c); Warrenpoint (pleasant resort).

CARLOW (Carlow) Ref: G4

Ceatharlach. More than 600 rebels were slaughtered here during the 1798 insurrection, and you could be forgiven for assuming that the keep of the 13th-century castle was destroyed in one of the many battle's strategically-important Carlow has witnessed. In fact, a Dr Philip Middleton, hoping to reduce the thickness of its walls in readiness for a new role as a mental hospital, blew them up by mistake. Carlow has a fine classical-style polygonal courthouse dating from 1830, and an interesting 151ft (46m) octagonal tower on its neo-Gothic cathedral of the same period. Two miles (3.2km) east at Browne's Hill is Ireland's biggest dolmen, featuring a 100-ton (101,600kg) capstone supported on five granite blocks.

CASTLEDERMOT (Kildare) Ref: G4

Díseart Diarmada, Dermot's Hermitage. A monastery was founded here in the 9th century, and granite crosses from around that time have survived. Later, the town was walled in and came under the protection of the Fitzgerald family. Hugh de Lacy built a castle here in the 12th century, but the crenellations on its 60ft (18m) round tower are more recent. Abbey Street is home to the remains of a 13th-century Franciscan friary, and at the north end of the town is the only remnant of the Hospital of the Crutched Friars from the same period, St John's Tower, or the Pigeon Tower. Three miles (4.8km) northwest is Kilkea

Narrow Water Castle is a 16th-century tower house in a superb setting some 3 miles (4.8km) west of Carlingford Lough.

Castle, once the seat of the Marquess of Kildare. The present building is a 19th-century restoration of the medieval castle, now a hotel.

What to see Castledermot castle; Franciscan friary; Kilkea castle; St John's Tower.

CASTLEPOLLARD (Westmeath) Ref: E4

Baile na gCros, the Town of the Crosses. This makes a good touring and angling centre for the Westmeath Lakelands, lying in a region of small hills. Northwest by 1½ miles (2.4km) is 17th-century Tullynally Castle, residence of the Earls of Longford, standing in 1500 acres (607ha) of parkland. It was classicized in 1775, and later transformed into a flambuoyant Gothic edifice.

THE BOOK OF KELLS

The colour, detail and ornamental tracery of the *Book of Kells* have earned it the description 'the world's most beautiful book.' Certainly it is the most sumptuous of the illuminated manuscripts to remain from the Middle Ages. It survived Viking raids and was stolen in 1007, being recovered – minus its gold – ten weeks later under a sod. The *Book of Kells* was a holy work of art, not a book for reading, and was the work of a team of craftsmen. It unites all four gospels in the story of Christ's life. All but two of its 680 pages are coloured, and the initial letters are beautifully worked in a harmony of detail and design. Key events such as the Nativity and the Crucifixion are given full page illustrations, and other pages are enlivened by witty renderings of birds and animals filling the empty spaces. In the 17th century, Bishop Henry Jones of Meath donated it to Trinity College, Dublin, although a replica can be viewed in the church at Ceanannas Mór. It is thought that Giraldus Cambrensis was referring to the *Book of Kells* when he wrote in 1185: 'Here you may see the face of Majesty divinely drawn . . . look more closely and you will penetrate the very shrine of art. You will make out intricacies, so delicate and subtle, so exact and compact, so full of knots and links . . . that you might say that all this is the work of an angel, not of a man.' Viewing the original in Dublin is recommended.

CEANANNAS MÓR, or KELLS (Meath) Ref: D5

Ceanannas Mór. Better known by its anglicized name, Kells, this town is famous as the source of *The Book of Kells*, an illuminated Latin manuscript of the Four Gospels, produced before AD800 (see box). Ceanannas Mór is set near the wooded banks of the River Blackwater, and was a royal residence for centuries before St Columba founded a monastery here in 550. Note the five windows on the 100ft (30m) round tower, probably to keep an eye on the five roads that approach the town. The nearest high cross to the tower is one of five in the town, but this is the largest and oldest, carved, like the others, with scenes from the Bible. The carvings on the south face show Adam and Eve, Cain and Abel, the three children in the fiery furnace, and Daniel in the lion's den. The cross in the market place served as a gallows in 1798. Some 12th-century walls remain, south of the churchyard, and also of interest is St Columcille's (Columba's) House. This has a 38ft (11.5m) high roof which is a continuation of the 4ft (1.2m) thick side walls.

St Columba's Oratory, the tiny building in which the Book of Kells *(Ceanannas Mór) may have been produced.*

CLONARD (Meath) Ref: F4

Cluain Ioraird, Iorard's Pasture. This was once the centre of a large monastic complex with a college attracting thousands of students from throughout Europe – including St Columba, St Brendan, and St Ciaran. Nothing of this extraordinary heritage remains, although the modern church houses a 15th-century font made of grey marble and displaying biblical scenes on the external panels, and may be a relic of the abbey. A nearby mound may have served a sepulchral function, while to the northwest are the remains of what may have been a motte and bailey.

CLONDALKIN (Dublin) Ref: F4

Cluain Dolcáin, Dolcán's Pasture. A tiny old-world village, Clondalkin lies in the centre of an industrial complex. Preserved here is a round tower from the ancient monastery founded by St Cronan, and rising to 84ft (25m). The conical cap, plinth and outside stair are probably original. Opposite is a graveyard housing two granite crosses, a baptismal font, and the remains of a medieval church largely destroyed by a gunpowder explosion in a nearby mill in 1787. At the end of the town is the 16th-century tower Tully's Castle.

CLONMACNOISE (Offaly) Ref: F3

Cluain Mhic Nóis, the Pasture of the Descendants of Noas. This is one of the most important and interesting of Ireland's monastic sites, and can be reached by boat from Athlone, or by turning off the N62 at Togher. A monastery was founded here by St Ciaran in 548, and its success and wealth led to it being burnt 26 times between 844 and 1012 by the Vikings. Ireland's last high king, Rory O'Connor, was buried here in 1198. The 15th-century cathedral (restored 1689) has a fine doorway displaying the figures of saints Francis, Patrick and Dominic. By the west door is King Flann's Cross, or the Cross of the Scriptures. This early 10th-century cross is richly decorated with scenes from the Last Judgement and the Crucifixion, plus animal and human figures. The Crucifixion is also depicted on the 11th-century South Cross, while only the shaft remains of the 9th-century North Cross. An 11th-century stone-lined causeway starting at the east of the cathedral eventually leads (via a road) to Nun's Church of 1167. It still has its decorative west door and chancel arch, which is Irish Romanesque in three orders.

What to see Cathedral; King Flann's Cross; Norman Castle (13c, north of the car park); Nun's Church (12c); South Cross.

COURTOWN HARBOUR (Wexford) Ref: G5

A seaside resort which grew in the last century following the building of the harbour from 1820 to 1830. This harbour silts up repeatedly, limiting the local fishing industry and making the town dependant on tourism and golf. An ancient 7ft (2.1m) cross stands in the grounds of Courtown House north of the village. Beyond this is another fine beach at Ballymoney, north of which is Tara Hill, 831ft (253m) taller than the more famous Tara in Meath.

Sandwiched between lovely beaches, Courtown Harbour is one of Ireland's most pleasant seaside resorts.

DELVIN (Westmeath) Ref: E4

Dealbhna. Delvin is a picturesque village set among woods near the Stoneyford River. At the top of the main street is Delvin Castle, a 13th-century stronghold built by the Nugent family who later abandoned it for Clonyn Castle. The ruins of this in turn lie west of the village in the grounds of a 19th-century castle. The area is best known as the birthplace, and sometime setting, for the works of Brinsley McNamara. He emphasized the disillusionment that set in after the drive for national independence and saw some of his books publicly burnt before his death in 1963.

DOWTH (Meath) Ref: E5

Dubhadh. This is a prehistoric burial chamber with some intriguingly-decorated stones. It is part of the Brugh na Boinne site described as a separate entry under Newgrange.

DROGHEDA (Louth) Ref: E5

Droichead Átha, Bridge of the Ford. A bustling industrial town with a port, Drogheda began as a ford between the Bullring and Shop Street, at St Mary's Bridge. Vikings settled here in 911, and two towns grew up on either side of the river. They were warring rivals until 1412. Of the ten town gates built in the 13th century, only St Laurence's Gate survives, with its two four-storey drum towers. A 15th-century two-storey belltower (Magdalene Tower on the site of the 1224 Dominican priory) still bears the scars of Cromwellian artillery.

Millmount House Museum tells the story of the town from a site that was once a Viking ceremonial meeting place and of a 12th-century castle. The Millmount itself is a massive grass mound surrounded by a low wall, probably a prehistoric grave. Good rococo decoration can be seen in the Church of St Peter in William Street, site of a castle burnt down by Cromwell with one hundred defenders still inside. The other St Peter's Church in West Street holds the head of St Oliver Plunket, executed in 1681, and kept separate from his body in Downside Abbey. In the northwest of the town is the Butter Gate, an octagonal tower with a round-arched passage.

What to see Butter Gate; Cornmarket; St Laurence's Gate; St Mary's Abbey; Magdalene Tower; Millmount House; St Peter's Churches; Townley Hall (18c, 4 miles [6.4km] west).

DUBLIN (Dublin) Ref: F5

Baile-Átha Cliath, the Town of the Ford of the Hurdles. Dublin is the greatest port in the republic, and with its airport and converging roads, railways and canals, the communications and distributional heart of Ireland. The city is divided by the River Liffey, and its north and south sides have quite distinctive personalities.

The oldest parts of Dublin are in the area around St Patrick's Cathedral, begun in 1191, and since twice restored. Inside are the tombs of Jonathan Swift and his 'Stella', Hester Johnson.

A little to the north is Christ Church Cathedral, which has its origins in 1172, when it replaced a wooden church erected in 1038. The structure is one of the best Irish examples of early Gothic architecture, and has a particularly beautiful nave with magnificent stonework. Nearby is Fishamble Street, scene of the first performance of Handel's Messiah in 1742.

The early Gothic Christ Church Cathedral was superbly restored in 1871, financed by a distiller.

LEINSTER

There is little to suggest a castle about Dublin Castle to the east. It was begun in 1204 but largely rebuilt in the 18th century, although one of the original sections is the record tower. The richly appointed State Apartments are open to the public and include ceilings painted by Vincenzo Valdre, a picture gallery, and the Throne Room with its heavy throne believed to have been presented by William of Orange. The State drawing room has been restored to its 18th-century style; and in the square Apollo room next door is a 1746 plaster ceiling depicting the sun god.

A little to the east of Dublin Castle is Powerscourt House, built for the Powerscourt family in 1771 to a design by Robert Mack. After more than a century as a clothing and textile base, this is now the Powerscourt Townhouse Centre of select shops and restaurants. Moving further east, the seat of Parliament, Leinster

House, was the huge and lavish town house of the Duke of Leinster after it was completed by Richard Cassels in 1748. To save expense, he worked to a similar plan for the Rotunda Hospital, the oldest maternity hospital in the world, which is in Parnell Square on the north side of the city.

Still south of the Liffey, St Stephen's Green is one of the biggest squares in Europe, and includes a beautiful park complete with artificial lake, laid out in 1880. Among its notable buildings is University Church, designed in a neo-Byzantine style which gave rise to some controversy after its completion in 1856. Its interior is decorated with some beautiful Irish marble. The University itself has now relocated to the suburbs of Dublin, but this area was once very much the centre of Irish learning, for nearby is the home of Trinity College on College Green.

College Green was a meeting place and burial ground in the

city's Viking days, and is home to two major landmarks: Trinity College and the Bank of Ireland. The College was founded in 1591, and its oldest surviving part is a row of Queen Anne red brick buildings called the Rubrics, begun in 1700 and now used for student accommodation. In its library is the world-famous *Book of Kells* (see Ceanannas Mór entry). The Bank of Ireland with its curving, windowless Hall, has all the grandeur of a Parliament – which is what it was built as from 1729 to 1739, only being sold when the British succeeded in dampening the ardour for independence.

The oldest example of Dublin's numerous elegant Georgian squares is Henrietta Square, begun in 1720, but the best-preserved are in the Fitzwilliam and Merrion Squares area (the latter has a long list of famous past inhabitants, including the Wildes, WB Yeats and Daniel O'Connell, and is the centre for art galleries).

Unfortunately, many of the other Georgian squares are badly decayed or have been destroyed.

Across the river on Dublin's north side, one of the designers of the port below Custom House was Captain Bligh, of *Mutiny on the Bounty* fame. The house itself is one of Ireland's finest buildings, and is best viewed from the other side of the Liffey, from where its fine proportions are apparent. Beneath its dividing freize are 13 heads of riverine gods, representing 13 Irish rivers. The fourteenth head is a female representation of the Atlantic Ocean. The building is topped by a graceful copper dome with four pedimented clocks, above which rise the 16ft (14.8m) figure of Hope, resting on her anchor. A little to the north is St Mary's Pro Cathedral, whose façade with it six-pillared Doric portico is a copy of the Temple of Theseus in Athens. The Roman Catholic church was completed in 1825, and was originally supposed to be built in O'Connell Street where the General Post Office is, the change of plan being for fear of official opposition. Facing it is Tyrone House, designed by Richard Cassels and built mainly in 1740. Its sombre aspect is in part relieved by the six square pillars in its portico. It forms part of the Department of Education. Nearby Waterford Street was formerly known as Tyrone Street, and was changed because of its associations with the surrounding 'red light' area.

To the west are some of the outstanding public buildings in Dublin. This includes the massive General Post Office (always known by its initials) which dates from 1818. It was from here that the reading of the Proclamation of the Irish Republic signalled the start of the 1916 Easter Rising. Four Courts, completed in 1802 by Gandon and Thomas Cooley, has a 440ft (134m) river frontage and a 64ft (19.5m) central dome. Its site was earlier occupied by the Abbey of St Saviour, founded in 1224, and stones from this survive in a length of city wall at Cook Street.

A trio of churches in the vicinity are all of interest. St Michan's Church in Church Street houses an organ played by Handel in 1742. This building has a vault renowned for its qualities of preservation: corpses have mummified naturally here and remained in remarkably good condition for centuries. A few streets away is St Mary's Abbey, which dates from 1156 and includes a preserved 1180 chapter house – the 6ft drop to its floor

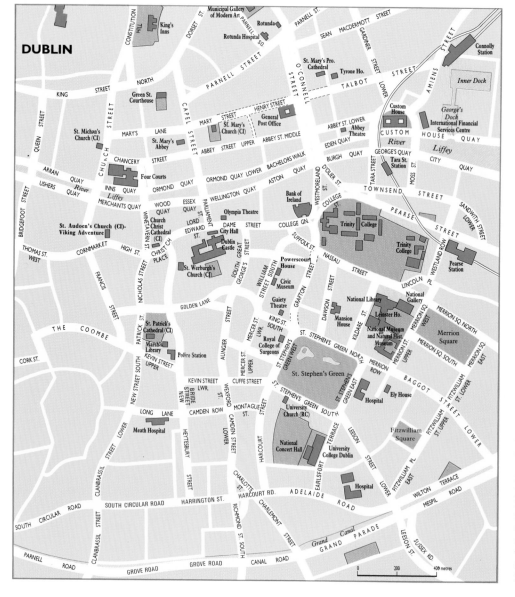

66

indicates how levels have risen over the centuries. This was once a huge foundation with the largest pre-Reformation building on the north side of the Liffey. Nearer the river is St Mary's Church, which became a parish church in 1697 and was the scene of the baptisms of many famous people. It has a fine galleried interior with box pews and early 18th-century figures carved on the organ case.

In the north of the city, Francis Johnston's St George's Church of 1814 in Temple Street North is notable among other things for its great breadth, and its celebrated chime of bells. To the northeast is one of the world's most perfect Palladian buildings, the Casino by William Chambers in the grounds of the now-demolished Marion House in Malahide Road.

Dublin offers a full theatrical, cultural, sporting and social life, and its most famous theatre is the Abbey Theatre, founded in 1904 as part of a Celtic literary revival. This revival in the centre of British influence is typical of the contradictions of Dublin, where luxury and poverty are common neighbours. The city is also home to one of the world's largest breweries, which makes one of the most famous drinks on earth: Guinness.

What to see Abbey Theatre (Abbey Street); Bank of Ireland

A CITY OF CRAFTSMEN

Dublin's many and varied trades were traditionally based in their own streets. For example, the pastry cooks were all in Sackville Street, outside the old city walls, to minimise the risk of fire in the city (after all, the Fire of London started at a baker's). Sackville Street, now called O'Connell Street, is still a centre for pastry makers whose goods are to be found throughout Dublin in shops which your senses will forbid you from passing.

Parallel to O'Connell Street is Capel Street, where men's clothing shops compete to sell

the fineries made by the city's master tailors. James Joyce, innovative writer and snappy dresser, said it was the best street in the city that he loved.

Candle-making is a real Dublin speciality. The oldest established firm is Rathbornes, which has been hand-casting beeswax candles in the city since 1488. Of course, churches were major customers, but Rathbornes also made affordable candles for the poor. The family began trading from workshops close by the Church of St Werburgh, but are now based in East Wall Road.

Countless other trades have flourished in the city's history: the city's breweries and distilleries provided business for the coopers; bookbinding was a speciality; and Lever Brothers began making soap here. Visitors can see crafts old and new at two venues. A former sugar refinery, distillery and iron foundry is now the Tower Design Craft Centre in Pearse Street – a street where you can still find gold, silver and pewter workers. At Marley Park, Rathfarnham, a 200-year-old courtyard has been converted into craft workshops.

(18c, College Green); Christ Church Cathedral (Christ Church Place); Civic Museum (William Street South); Customs House (Custom House Quay); Dublin Castle (13c and 18c, Cork Hill); General Post Office (O'Connell Street); Iveagh House (St Stephen's Green); Municipal Gallery of Modern Art (Parnell Square); National Gallery (Kildare Place); History Museum (Kildare Street); Newman House

(University College, St Stephen's Green South); Powerscourt House (18c, William Street South); Rotunda (Parnell Street); St Andrews Church (Westland Row); St Ann's Church (Dawson Street); St Audoen's Church (Church of Ireland, High Street); St Audoen's Church (Roman Catholic, High Street); St George's Church (Temple Street North); St Mary's Abbey; St Mary's Pro-Cathedral (Roman Catholic); St Mary's

Church (Church of Ireland, Mary Street); St Michan's Church (Church Street); St Patrick's Cathedral (13c, Patrick Street); Trinity College (College Street/ Westland Row); Tyrone House (Marlborough Street); University Church (St Stephen's Green South).

No visit to Dublin is complete without a leisurely stop-off in one of its 800 or so pubs.

OUT OF THE SHADOW

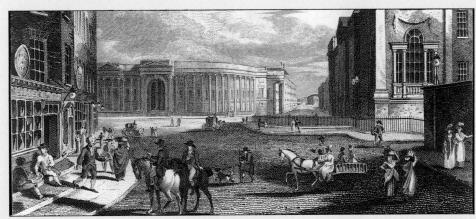

The Vikings destroyed a Celtic township on the Liffey but kept its old name when they established Dubh Linn (Dark Pool) in 840, which soon merged with the town on the opposite bank, Baile Atha Cliath. After the Anglo-Normans invaded Ireland, Henry II set up a court at Dublin in 1172 to restrict the power of Strongbow (Earl of Pembroke) and his men, and the city became the focus of British influence for the next seven centuries. Many of the city's finest buildings date from the prosperous Georgian period when Dublin was a focus of economic and political development. Gradually, independent Irish movements diluted the British influence, and won tolerance for Catholics – for example campaigner Daniel O'Connell became the first Catholic Lord Mayor of Dublin in 1829.

A struggle for trade unionism led to the Great Lock-Out of 1913 when many workers and their families died of cold and hunger, and three years later the main battles of the Easter Rising were fought in the city. Similarly, when independence was won in 1921, and Dublin became the capital of Eire, it was the scene of much of the fighting during the subsequent Civil War. Dublin has since grown from the ashes of this conflict, and out of the shadow of the British Empire, to become one of the cultural centres of Europe.

Left: *Trinity College has been central to the development of the Anglo-Irish tradition.*

DULEEK (Meath) Ref: E4
Damhliag, Stone Church. This small village's name derives from an early stone church, said to have been the first of its kind in ancient Ireland. A number of other churches have since occupied its site, and the monastic relics include three early gravestones, the remains of St Cianan's Church, and two 10th-century high crosses. The north cross is stumpy and features figures and abstract designs. The south cross is shaftless and can be found in the ruined 15th-century St Mary's Augustinian Priory. Three miles (4.8km) southwest is the White Cross, a memorial to the de Bathe family. This in turn is not far from Athcarne Castle, a fortified Elizabethan mansion from 1578.

What to see Annesbrook memorial cross (1¾ miles [2.8km] south); Athcarne Castle; Athcarne bridge (16c); High crosses; St Mary's Priory; White Cross.

Parts of the Georgian splendour of Dublin have survived well (Fitzwilliam and Merrion Squares are examples), while in others it has decayed badly.

DUNDALK (Louth) Ref: E5
Dún Dealgan, Dealgan's Fort. A very busy town south of the Moyry Pass (the 'Gap of the North'). Seatown Tower is the belltower of a 1240 Franciscan friary, and two features of Seatown Place are a seven story windmill and Kincora House, birthplace of 19th-century Arctic explorer Sir Francis McClintock. The elegant church of St Patrick's was completed in 1850 and was inspired by King's College, Cambridge. The Church of Ireland Church of St Nicholas has a 14th-century tower, and its graveyard holds two interesting memorials dating from the 16th century. One of the most pleasing buildings in the town is the courthouse, which was completed in 1818 and borrows the portico design and dimensions of the Temple of Theseus in Athens.
  What to see Castletown Hill; Courthouse (19c); Kincora House; St Mary's College; St Nicholas' Church (both); St Patrick's Church; Seatown Tower (13c); Windmill.

DUN LAOGHAIRE (Dublin) Ref: F5
Dún Laoghaire, Laoghaire's Fort. A holiday resort 9 miles (14.4km) from Dublin with a magnificent granite harbour and two huge piers. The 51-acre (20.6-ha)

harbour was completed in 1859 after 43 years' work, and was the biggest artificial haven of its time. The piers have a combined length of 8450ft (2575m), and the East Pier is the most popular promenade. Look out for the famous 'Forty-foot gentlemen only' sign for bathers. Pronounced 'Dun Leary', this town is a major ferry port and yachting centre, and the venue for the Dublin Bay Week Regatta. James Joyce once lived in the Martello tower which now houses a museum about him, and includes unusual items like his guitar.
  What to see Joyce Museum; Monkstown Castle (15c); Monkstown Church; National Maritime Museum (in what was Mariner's Church).

DUNLEER (Lough) Ref: E4
Dún Léire, Léire's Fort. This once important town has now decreased in size to become a village. Transitional features are displayed by the west tower of the 19th-century Protestant Church, and its hall contains three gravestones, relics of an early monastic site called Lann Leire. About 3 miles (4.8km) southeast is Rokeby Hall, a mansion designed for Primate Robinsons of Armagh by Francis Johnston in 1794.

EDENDERRY (Offaly) Ref: F4
Éadan Doire, Hill-brow of the Oak Grove. Many of this town's buildings were constructed by the Marquess of Devonshire after he had acquired Blundell's Castle by marriage. This hilltop castle lies south of the town, and a mile (1.6km) further south is the Grand Canal. Monasteroris Friary (2 miles [3.2km] west) was founded in the 14th century, and beside its ruins is a small parish church with a dovecote on a mound. Near the town, 290ft (88m) above sea level, is the source of the River Boyne, and the 240,000 acre (97,000ha) Bog of Allen extends to the West.

EDGEWORTHSTOWN See Mostrim

ENNISCORTHY (Wexford) Ref: G4
Inis Corthaidh. Well situated on the steep west bank of the Slaney, Enniscorthy is charming, hilly and historic. It has a very well-restored castle with a comprehensive county museum inside. The castle was built in the 13th century by the Prendergast family, and features a keep flanked by three drum towers and a turret. One tenant was poet Edmund Spenser, in 1581. Beside the striking six-arch bridge is The

With its twin piers, octagonal Victorian bandstand and 19th-century buildings, Dun Laoghaire has retained the atmosphere of a resort town from times past.

Cotton Tree, where in 1798 English cavalry officers are said to have tethered their horses while on their way from the Battle of Vinegar Hill. A windmill stump on the summit of the 390ft (119m) hill was the rebel's final headquarters, and offers a good view of the town.

ENNISKERRY (Wicklow) Ref: F5
Áth na Sceire, the Ford of the Reef. Enniskerry is a delightful little picture-book village on the Cookstown River. Its main attraction is half a mile (0.8km) to the south: the 34,000-acre (14,000-ha) Powerscourt estate, one of the great gardens of Europe. An avenue of trees including giant beeches more than 200 years old line the entrance. The mansion was designed in 1740 by Richard Cassels and was badly burned in 1974, but the gardens and their famous waterfall are well worth a visit. They were created between 1745 and 1767, and re-styled in the 19th century. They include English, Japanese and Italian

gardens leading up to a superb vantage point with views of the Great Sugar Loaf Mountain. There are some rare plants and a pet cemetary.

FORE (Westmeath)
Ref: F4

Baile Fhobhain, Town of the Spring. Set in the exceptionally beautifully Fore Valley, this town is on the site of a monastery founded in the 7th century, of which a few remnants can be seen. There is a 9th- or 10th-century church with a fine doorway featuring a huge cross-inscribed lintel with Syrian affinities. There are also some abbey remains. Fore is famous for its six so-called Wonders, which are: the water that will not boil; wood that cannot be burnt; the monastery built on quaking sod; a mill without a race; the Cylcopean stone above the doorway of St Fechin's Church; and a stream that flows uphill.

FRESHFORD (Kilkenny)
Ref: G4

Achadh Ur, Fresh Field. St Lactin, of royal descent and a disciple of St Comgall of Bangor, created a religious foundation here in the 7th century. Its church was replaced in the 12th century, and again in the 18th with the current parish church. This incorporates the west gable and beautiful Romanesque porch of a 12th-century structure, and has an Irish inscription asking for a prayer for the builders. Freshford has some fine Georgian houses and a pleasant green. Just over 2 miles (3.2km) south is Rathealy, with the remains of a ringfort with houses and a souterrain.

GLASSAN (Westmeath)
Ref: F3

Glasán, Streamlet. Locally known as the 'Village of the Roses' because of the profusion of roses that once grew here, Glassan is a small community near Lough Ree. An octagonal dovecote can be seen in the nearby ruins of Waterstown House. A hill 1½ miles (2.4km) east of the village on an unclassified road to Kilkenny West is said to be the geographical centre of Ireland, and is surmounted by a circular structure known as The Pinnacle,

A detail from a gate at Powerscourt, one of the great gardens of Europe.

built in 1769. One of the few habitable medieval castles in the country, Portlick Castle stands the shore of Lough Ree.

A WEALTH OF GARDENS

Ireland's mild climate and Gulf Stream currents are a boon to horticulture and have helped to produce some beautiful gardens. Two styles are readily discernible. Powerscourt's statues, ornamental water and terraces are very much in the Victorian formal mode, rather like Mount Stewart with its compartmentalized garden with different colour schemes in its separate 'rooms'. However, in other Irish gardens the focus is more on planting to complement the natural beauty of the landscape. This is partly due to William Robinson's *The Wild Garden* of 1870, which recommended a combination of landscape and plants instead of more artificial Victorian schemes. Exotic plants flourish by a dramatic lough, while rhododendrons and azaleas make a spectacular display at Glenveagh in Co. Donegal. The steep banks of the river at Annesgrove, Co. Cork, feature a marvellous collection of plants gathered in this century by Richard Grove-Annesley. Another great plantsman, Hugh Armytage Moore, has created a superb garden with waves of azaleas and rhododendrons at Rowallane, Co. Down. Birr, in Co. Offaly, is a garden which, like Rowallane, uses rocky outcrops for rock gardens.

GLENDALOUGH (Wicklow) Ref: F5

Gleann dá Loch, Valley of the Two Lakes. Set in one of the most picturesque glens in Ireland near two lakes more than 2000ft (610m) up are the remains of a 6th-century monastic settlement. St Kevin first built a church on the south side of Upper Lake, but as his followers became more numerous, the monastery moved to the lower part of the glen. The 103ft (31m) round tower was recapped in the original mica slate in 1876, when the ruins of St Kieran's Church were also discovered in a mound of earth. Other remains include the early barrel-vaulted oratory and high-pitched roof of St Kevin's Church, and the late 11th-century (since restored) St Saviour's Church. There is a Bronze or Early Iron Age stone fort on the eastern edge of Upper Lake, and there is also a 7th-century Cathedral with an east window probably imported from England. St Kevin began his hermit's life in a 7 by 4ft (2 by 1.2m) excavation in a cliff 30ft (9m) above the water, known as 'St Kevin's Bed'.

What to see Cathedral (7c); St Kevin's Bed; St Kevin's Church; St Kieran's Church; St Savour's Church (12c); Stone fort.

GOREY (Wexford) Ref: G5

Guaire. Gorey is a pleasingly laid out market town, and was the storm centre of the 1798 Insurrection – a granite Celtic memorial cross stands near the spot where the rebels camped on 418ft (127m) Gorey Hill. There is some superb stained glass by Harry Clarke in the Protestant Church. To the south is the Augustinian abbey of Ferns. Built in 1160, this has a strange square tower with a conical roof. To the west, Bunclody is an excellent starting point for exploring the Blackstairs Mountains. Not far away is Huntington Castle (used in the film *Barry Lyndon*) at the end of the tree-lined street of Clonegal.

What to see Bunclody; Clonegal; Ferns Abbey; Huntington Castle; St Mark's Church (19c).

GOWRAN (Kilkenny) Ref: G4

Gabhrán. Gowran is a village which was of great political and strategic importance in medieval times. James, 3rd Earl of Ormonde, lived in a strong castle here before he moved to Kilkenny in 1391. No trace of the castle remains, but the ruins of Ballyshawnmore Castle are south of the village. The present Gowran Castle dates from 1815. The early English Collegiate Church of Gowran, *c.*1275, is one of the finest parish churches in Ireland. The tower was added in the 14th or 15th centuries, and is now incorporated in a 19th-century church on the site of the old chancel. Features of the church include a finely pointed black marble arch, elegant windows delicately ornamented in quatrefoil, and a stone featuring the ancient Celtic alphabetical writing system known as ogham.

GRAIGUENAMANAGH (Kilkenny) Ref: G4

Gráig na Manach, the Hamlet of the Monks. Situated on the River Barrow near the Carlow border, this small market town is best known for its Cistercian monastery called Duiske – once the name of Graiguenamanagh. It was founded by the Earl of Pembroke in 1207, apparently modelled on the abbey of Strata Florida in Wales, and was the largest Cistercian church in Ireland. It was restored – not very well – last century. Interesting monuments in the churchyard include two granite high crosses with biblical decorations, brought from Ballyogan and Aghailta. An effigy of a cross-legged knight in 14th-century armour has been moved from the churchyard to the interior.

HOWTH (Dublin) Ref: F5

Beann Éadair, Eadar's Peak. A popular resort and fishing fleet centre, Howth forms the northern horn of the crescent of Dublin Bay. Howth Castle is a long, battlemented building on the west side of the town dating from 1564, although it was restyled in 1910. The hall contains an interesting collection of relics, including the great sword of the 1st Lord of Howth. Its grounds have a noted rhododendron display, worth seeing in May or June, and a large dolmen known as Aideen's Grave, made of ten enormous masses of quartzite, with a capstone said to weigh 70 tons (71,00kg). Tradition has it that Aideen, wife of Oscar, slain near Tara at the end of the 3rd century, lies buried here. The Collegiate Church of St Mary (or Howth Abbey) stands on a bank above the harbour, and is thought to have been founded in 1235, although it has been very much altered and extended. The oldest parts, probably 11th century, are

St Kevin's Church is the most famous building in Glendalough.

the west end of the nave, and the porch. Howth has attractive cliff walks, especially to the north to the 1814 Bailey Lighthouse.

What to see Aideen's Grave; Bailey Lighthouse; Church of St Mary; Howth Castle; Ireland's Eye (small island a mile offshore, good for picnics).

JERPOINT ABBEY (Kilkenny) Ref: G4

Mainistir Sheireapúin. A handsome ruin in the Nore Valley which was once surrounded by a town. The abbey was founded in 1158 by Cistercians, and its oldest parts – the chancel and transepts of the church – are Irish Romanesque. The barrel vault and stone roof of the chancel are original, but the east window was added in the 14th century. In the next century, the square central tower with its stepped battlements was added. The strange effigy of Bishop O'Dullany (who died in 1202) holding a crozier being chewed by a serpent, is one of a number of outstanding monuments with carved effigies. Just northwest, at Newtown Jerpoint, is the parish church of St Nicholas, noted for

its groin-vaulted rood gallery. Southeast by 1½ miles (2.4km) at Ballylowra are two megalithic tombs and the re-erected Liaghan ogham (ancient Celtic alphabet) stone.

KILBEGGAN (Westmeath) Ref: F4

Cill Bheagáin, Beagán's Church. A branch of the Grand Canal which used to flow through Kilbeggan brought prosperity to this town on the River Brosna, and many of its buildings reflect its elegant past. There is a neat limestone market and courthouse, and the old distillery building dates from 1749. South by half a mile (0.8km) is a green mound known as the Church of the Relic, said to mark the site of an abbey. Three miles (4.8km) northeast is Newfrost, a Georgian mansion dating from 1749.

KILDARE (Kildare) Ref: F4

Cill Dara, Church of the Oak. Once an important ecclesiastical centre, this county town by the Curragh plain is now famous for its horse breeding and training, and it retains a slightly old-world

atmosphere. There are extensive barracks because the plain to the east is an important military centre. At the eastern end of the town is Donnelly's Hollow, where Irish boxer Dan Donnelly beat English champion George Cooper in 1815 – the victor's footprints as he left the scene of this celebrated match have been preserved. There are two golf courses in the area.

Kildare has a 105ft (32m) round tower. Although it has a superb Romanesque doorway 14ft (4.2m) above the ground, the addition of a battlemented top was not a success. Nearby, St Brigid's Cathedral incorporates parts of a 13th-century church and holds several antiquities. St Brigid established a nunnery here in the 5th or 6th century. A fine viewpoint known as the Chair of Kildare can be visited in the low Red Hills to the northwest.

What to see Chair of Kildare; Donnelly's Hollow; round tower; St Brigid's Cathedral (part 13c); Tully Church; Tully House (1 mile [1.6km] southeast).

The Japanese Gardens at Tully House near Kildare.

A LOVE OF HORSES

The county of Kildare is closely identified with horses, and facilities for racing, hunting, breeding and training can be found all over, especially in the northern regions. In the centre of the county, near Kildare itself, is The Curragh, a great, mainly unenclosed plain measuring about 6 by 2 miles (9.6 by 3.2km) which is the headquarters of Irish racing. On most mornings visitors can see some of the finest Irish bloodstock being exercised on the carefully maintained gallops. The Irish Sweeps Derby, St Leger and Guineas are run here. The National Stud with its Japanese gardens is at Tully, 2 miles (3.2km) from Kildare, and may be visited. The Irish horse breeding industry is better known for its jumpers than for flat-racers, and the leading stud farms are to be found in the counties of Kildare, Meath and Tipperary.

Punchestown, just outside Naas, comes alive for three days of racing in April, and the sight of superb horses against a vast landscape and a foreground of grassy hillocks splashed with the white and gold of spring blackthorn and furze is unforgettable. The point-to-point meetings that take place at this venue are considered very fashionable. Summer evening meetings are held at the Phoenix Park course near Dublin City, and Galway race-week is run during the holiday season. The Irish Grand National is run at Fairyhouse, near Ratoath, Meath.

Above: *Imposing Kilkenny Castle was much restored last century, but some of its medieval origins remain.*

Left: *Kilkenny sports its share of Irish bars, some of which offer live music as well as a good pint.*

KILKENNY (Kilkenny)
Ref: G4

Cill Chainnigh, St Canice's Church. Situated high on the banks of the River Nore, Kilkenny's winding passages and lanes and rare Elizabethan architecture have made it one of the most attractive towns in Ireland. Its castle was built at the end of the 12th century by William Earl Marshall, Strongbow's son-in-law. Heavy bombardment by Cromwell in 1650 destroyed one tower and the south range of the castle, but the rest of this Gothic-Classical structure with conical tops to its three drumtowers still stands, looking rather like a French château. It now houses an art gallery. Below is Kilkenny College, founded in 1666, and whose 18th-century buildings are best enjoyed from the Canal Walk.

Back across John's Bridge is St Mary's Church, which dates from the 13th century but has been modernized, and contains interesting medieval and later monuments, including heraldic shields of Kilkenny families. Nearby, St Mary's Steps lead to the Shee Almshouses, begun in 1582. Grace's Castle was surrendered in 1566 by James Grace, who became constable of the gaol into which it was converted – it now makes a fine courthouse. St Canice's Cathedral stands on a hilltop and is a spectacular, battlemented building with a round tower, begun in 1251. Other 13th-century ruins include Balack Abbey, St John's Priory, and St Francis Abbey (now part of Smithwick's Brewery).

What to see Courthouse; John's Bridge; Kilkenny College; The Mall; Rothe House; St Canice's Cathedral; St Mary's Cathedral (RC); St Mary's Church (CI, 13c); Shee Almshouses; Tholsel (18c town hall with wooden tower).

*H*IGH *C*ROSSES

The south of Co. Kilkenny is particularly rich in high crosses dating from the 8th century. There are good examples at Kilkieran and 2 miles (3.2km) away in Co. Tipperary at Ahenny. Carved stone crosses are among the earliest Christian monuments in Ireland, and the ringed high cross was probably inspired by portable wooden crosses depicted in some early carvings. Carvings often represented the Crucifixion, but over the centuries other scriptural scenes, and then vine-scrolls, spirals and other ornamentation became popular. It is thought the ring was used to brace the angles of the cross.

At the beginning of the 10th century, sandstone came into use again, and a series of splendid monuments from this time survives across Ireland's central plain. Then, towards the end of the next century, a new type of cross was carved. The ring was now frequently omitted, and the whole length of the shaft was taken up with a single figure, such as the crucified Christ in full relief.

KILMAINHAM (Dublin) Ref: F5

Cill Mhaigneann, Maighne's Church. Kilmainham is an area of Dublin named after a little 7th-century church which may have stood where the high cross can now be seen. In Kilmainham is the Royal Hospital which was built in around 1680 for old soldiers, and is the oldest surviving secular building in Ireland. A museum in the old Kilmainham Gaol has displays about the patriots and political prisoners once incarcerated here. A stark carving over the door depicts a servant in chains. Nearby is the War Memorial Park commemorating those who died in the First World War.

KILTERNAN (Dublin) Ref: F5

Cill Tiarnáin, St Tiarnán's Church. An ancient church and a fine portal dolmen can be found at this place in a lane off the main road near the border of Wicklow. The dolmen is famous for its massive capstone, thought to weigh 40 tons (40,640kg) and to be of Neolithic origin.

KINNITTY (Offaly) Ref: F3

Cionn Eitigh. Considered by some to be one of the most attractive villages in Ireland, Kinnitty lies west of the Slieve Bloom Mountains, which rise from the Laois border to 1734ft (528m) Arderin. The attractive glens of the range include Forelacka, a place of outstanding beauty off the Camcor River valley. In many places the heights have been planted with trees. Castle Bernard is prettily placed a mile (1.6km) east and features Kinnitty High Cross, thought to mark the site of a monastery founded by St Finian in the 6th century.

LEIGHLINBRIDGE (Carlow) Ref: G4

Leithglinn an Droichid, the Valley-side of the Bridge. Straddling the River Barrow, this was the site of one of the earliest strongholds of the Anglo-Norman Pale – a castle built in 1181 to command a ford across the river. The remains of Black Castle on the site date from the 14th to 16th centuries. Old Leighlin lies 2 miles (3.2km) west and had a famous monastery founded in the 7th century. The cathedral was founded in the 13th century, but 16th-century restoration left few traces of the original structure. Notable features are the Gothic doorway in the north wall of the chancel, the sedilia, the ancient font, and the 16th-century monument slabs with black letters. West of the cathedral are an ancient cross and the Well of St Laserain.

LONGFORD (Longford) Ref: E3

An Longfort, Fortress. Longford began life in the 15th century as the site of the O'Farrel fortress and a Dominican friary founded by the same powerful family. Traces of these beginnings have been destroyed, but fragments of the Earl of Longford's 17th-century stronghold survive in an old military barracks. The octagonal spire of St John's Church is thought to stand on the site of the friary. St Mel's Cathedral (Roman Catholic) is a classical limestone structure completed in 1893, and the nearby Diocesan College houses an interesting collection of local antiquities. A fine motte-and-bailey construction known as Lissardowlan can be found 3½ miles (5.6km) southeast.

LOUTH (Louth) Ref: E5

Lú. Although it gave its name to a county, Louth is little more than a village. St Mochta, a disciple of St Patrick, founded a monastery here in the 6th century. The small stone church known as St Mochta's House dates from the 12th or 13th centuries, and is a single cell with a croft in the roof. This high, beautifully crafted vaulted roof is reached by a narrow staircase. Little remains of Lough Abbey except wall fragments of the long, narrow church. Just over 2 miles (3.2km) north is a motte-and-bailey construction called Castlering, and a fine pillar stone can be seen 2 miles (3.2km) northeast at Cloghafarmore.

LUCAN (Dublin) Ref: F4

Leamhcán, Place of Elms. Once a famous spa, this small town is situated in a beautiful stretch of the Liffey Valley where the river is spanned by a bridge ascribed to Isambard Brunel. Just west is the demesne of Lucan House, a fine building rebuilt in 1771 and containing noteworthy plasterwork by Michael Stapleton and Angelica Kaufmann. Remains of 16th-century Sarsfield Castle lie southeast of the house. Two miles (3.2km) north is Luttrelstown Castle, a 19th-century castellated mansion which incorporates parts of a medieval castle.

What to see Liffey river; Lucan House (18c); Luttrelstown Castle (19c); Sarsfield Castle (16c).

There are magnificent high crosses at St Buithe Monastery in Monasterboice.

MAYNOOTH (Kildare)
Ref: F4
Maigh Nuad, Nua's Plain. Maynooth is a pretty village with a large seminary for training Catholic priests, called St Patrick's College. This has two large quadrangles, one in the Renaissance style, the other in a 19th-century Gothic style by AW Pugin. Near the College entrance are the ruins of Maynooth Castle, with a 13th-century two-storey keep, and an interesting gatehouse. At the east end of the village is Carton, a magnificent 18th-century house in landscaped grounds.

Several miles southeast of Maynooth is Castletown House, the largest and most architecturally important private house in the country. The layout of the building with its twin pavilions linked to the central block by colonnaded curtain walls, was new to Ireland when it was built between 1719 and 1732. The magnificent 13-bay mansion was designed by Alessandro Galilei. It is now the headquarters of the Irish Georgian Society, and may be visited. There is a tower folly to the north, and the view focus to the east is called Wonderful Barn.

What to see Cartern; Castletown House; Maynooth Castle; St Patrick's College.

MELLIFONT ABBEY
(Louth) Ref: E5
An Mhainistir Mhór, The Big Monastery. Remains of this abbey, founded in 1142, lie in a secluded valley on the banks of the Mattock River. It was Ireland's first Cistercian abbey, and the Order spread quickly from these roots. The abbey was suppressed in 1539 and was fortified by Edward Moore, an ancestor of the Earls of Drogheda. Features of the site include sparse remains of the abbey church, a reconstructed fragment of the 12th-century cloister, and the well preserved Chapter House and Lavabo. North of the abbey are the square towers of the gatehouse, and the remains of a small 15th-century church are on a hill to the northeast.

MOATE (Westmeath)
Ref: F3
An Móta, The Mound. Cattle fairs are held in the wide main street of the village of Moate, which takes its name from a large rath or motte which lies southwest and is known as Moatgrange. This

probably dates from the Norman invasion. On the summit of Knockast Hill, 5 miles (8km) northeast, is a 50ft (15m) diameter cairn measuring only 4ft (1.2km) high. It has no central chamber, but a number of smaller chambers known as cists, and is thought to be the resting place of a pre-Celtic Bronze Age people.

MONASTERBOICE (Louth)
Ref: E5
Mainistir Bhuithe, St Buithe's Abbey. Excellent high crosses can be found amid the ruins of this 5th-century monastery in a small, enclosed churchyard near Timmullen. There are sculptures on every surface of the 17ft 8in (5.3m) Muireadach Cross and the

West (or Tall) Cross, which is 21ft 6in (6.5m) high and has 22 sculptured panels. Scenes include the Crucifixion of Christ and the Last Judgement. The head of the North Cross is held on a modern stem, as the original shaft lies broken nearby. This trio of crosses shares space with two churches, a round tower from the

A WEALTH OF MYTHS AND LEGENDS

Myths and legends are a central element in the character of Ireland, for it is a land steeped in great sagas and the tradition of storytelling survives today. Ireland's mythological heroic age was around the time of the birth of Christ, and its stories centre around the warrior aristocracy of the Red Branch Knights. The greatest of these was Cuchullain, who on his own saw off Queen Maeve and the men of Connaught who

were out to capture the great bull of Cooley. Cuchullain's exploits are many and great, and there is a heroic quality to his death, overcome by sorcery and standing strapped to a stone. Another magnificent warrior was Finn, leader of the Fianna, who has been transformed over the years into a jolly giant called Finn MacCool. During one of his fabled fights with giants in Britain, he threw a clod of earth

into the sea and created the Isle of Man. The hole in the land became Lough Neagh.

A sense of doom hangs over the central figures in many Irish legends. One concerns Deidre, the loveliest woman in Ireland's history, and the sons of Usnach, all destined to die through treachery because of her fatal beauty. Another tells of the Children of Lir who were changed into swans for hundreds of years.

architectural feature is the classical Cathedral of Christ the King, designed by Ralph Byrne. Its twin 140ft (43m) towers make it a conspicuous landmark, and there is some interesting sculpture inside. Mullingar is surrounded by a ring of lakes. Probably the most beautiful is Lough Lene, about 10 miles (16km) northeast. Church Island, 3 miles (4.8km) north in Lough Owel, boasts the interesting remains of a monastic settlement. About 2 miles (3.2km) east is Lough Ennell, where 18th-century Belvedere House stands in fine gardens on the wooded east shore. There is an 18-hole golf course nearby, and all the lakes offer good fishing for brown trout. The large, castellated mansion, Knockdrin Castle, lies 4 miles (6.4km) northeast and adjoins an Anglo-Norman castle – which probably has origins going back to a follower of Hugh de Lacy.

What to see Belvedere House; Cathedral of Christ the King; Church Island; Knockdrin Castle; Lough Ennell; Lough Lene.

NAAS (Kildare) Ref: F4
An Nás, The Assembly Place. This county town of Kildare is now virtually a suburb of Dublin, while its position on the edge of the Curragh makes it a centre for horse-racing (it has its own course, and the fashionable Punchestown course is nearby). The palace that was the seat of the kings of Leinster is on the site of the large North Mote, while St David's Church is said to stand on the site of a camp made by St Patrick during one of his missionary journeys. It has a medieval tower. The Catholic Church of SS Mary and David is a Gothic structure dating from 1827, although the tower and spire were added in 1858. A mile (1.6km) away is Jigginstown Castle, a huge brick mansion begun in 1632 by Thomas Wentworth, Earl of Strafford. Construction ceased after he was beheaded in London. To the southwest of Naas is Droichead Nua (Newbridge) which has rope and cutlery industries, and is southeast of the 676ft (206m) Hill of Allen, supposedly the home of Finn MacCool, leader of the legendary 3rd-century Fianna.

What to see Church of SS Mary and David; Hill of Allen; Jigginstown Castle (17c); Naas racecourse; North Mote; Punchestown racecourse; St David's Church.

9th century, a sundial and two early grave slabs. A modern flight of external steps allows visitors up the incomplete tower.

MOSTRIM or EDGEWORTHSTOWN (Longford) Ref: E3
Meathas Troim, Frontier of the Elder Tree. One family dominates the history of this tidy town: the Edgeworths, who settled here in 1583 and were well known for their interest in social affairs. Maria Edgeworth (1767–1849) became a famous authoress and influenced Sir Walter Scott, William Wordsworth and Turgenev. Among the inventions of her father Richard Lovell Edgeworth was a central heating system for Tullynally Castle (see Castlepollard entry).

MOUNTMELLICK (Laois) Ref: F4
Móinteach Mílic, Bogland of the Place Bordering Water. Originally a Quaker settlement, this small market town still evokes a sense

of its 18th-century prosperity (it was famous for lacework), and several buildings from that period are preserved. One of the county's curious esker ridges, formed by glacial action, passes north to south near the town. About 2 miles (3.2km) northwest is the fine 18th-century house of Summer Grove, and the attractive Cathold Glen lies west at the foot of the Slieve Bloom Mountains.

MOUNTRATH (Laois) Ref: F4
Maighean Rátha, Precinct of the Ringfort. A quiet town southeast of the Slieve Bloom Mountains. About 5 miles (8km) north is Ballyfin House, a 19th-century structure that is now a boarding school, and three miles (4.8km) southwest is a handsome Palladian villa, Roundwood, which dates from the 18th century. Clonenagh Church stands 2 miles (3.2km) east on the site of a 6th-century monastery founded by St Fintan. An unusual sycamore containing a well nearby is named after him.

MUINE BHEAG (Carlow) Ref: G4
Muine Bheag, Small Thicket. Formerly known as Bagenalstown, after its founder Walter Begenal of Dunlecky Manor, this is a small market town laid out on English lines. It hjas a good courthouse, and 2 miles (3.2km) east are the remains of Ballymoon Castle. These remarkably well survived ruins form a square, keepless castle of the 14th century. Features, including doors and fireplaces, have been well preserved.

MULLINGAR (Westmeath) Ref: F4
An Muileann gCearr, Wry Mill. County town of Westmeath and the market centre for Ireland's cattle country, Mullingar sits in the heart of the ancient kingdom of Meath. Henry II granted it to Hugh de Lacy, and during the Middle Ages the town had two religious foundations: an Augustinian house, and a Dominican friary. Its principal

GRAVES OF PREHISTORIC MAN

Newgrange is the most famous of the approximately 1250 megalithic tombs that survive in Ireland. Neolithic colonizers first came to Ireland between 2000 and 3000BC, and were responsible for the earliest megalithic chambered tombs, the court cairns. These are so called because the tombs consist of a covered gallery for burial, with one or more unroofed courts or forecourts for ritual. They are related to more simple monuments called dolmens, which comprise large capstones supported by three or more uprights. These may have been originally dug below ground level, never intended to be seen.

Another variety of megalith is the wedge-shaped gallery, most of which belong to the early Bronze Age (2000 to 1500BC). A good example is at Ballyedmonduff, near Stepaside, Dublin. The most spectacular of the great stone tombs are the passage graves, of which Newgrange is the most famous. It is a grand court grave, in which intriguing examples of megalithic art can be seen and for which there is still no satisfactory interpretation, although they are believed to have had religious meanings. Like many other court graves, it is of an ingenious construction made without the aid of machinery – adding the question of how it was put together to that of why.

NAVAN (Meath) Ref: E4

An Uaimh, The Cave. A town set amid beautiful countryside that sweeps down to the banks of the River Boyne. Although little remains of the fortifications that betray its past strategic importance, there are a number of interesting sites around the town. Perhaps the pick of the bunch is in the southeast outskirts of Navan: Athlumney Castle. This comprises the extensive ruins of a 17th-century house built around a 15th-century tower house. Four floors of this tower are in excellent condition, and there is a secret chamber on the first. In 1690, the owner, Sir Launcelot Dowdall, burned the building down rather than see it occupied by Williamite forces. South of here are the remains of Kilcarn (or Cannistown) church of about 1200. About 1½ miles (2.4km) northeast of Navan is Donaghmore, an intact round 100ft (30m) tower said to stand on the site of a church built by St Patrick. About a mile (1.6km) east of here is the ruined Dunmoe Castle, built in the 13th century and burned in 1798.

What to see Athlumney Castle; Ardbraccan House (18c, 3 miles [4.8km] west); Ardsallagh House (16c, beyond Kilcarn); Donaghmore round tower (and 16c church); Dunmoe Castle (13c); Kilcarn church.

NEWGRANGE (Meath) Ref: E5

Sí an Bhrú, Fairy Mound of the Palace. Newgrange is the major grave in, and often the name used for, the Brugh na Boinne site of some 40 megalithic monuments in the Boyne Valley. The huge Newgrange cairn has been restored to its original

The burial mound at Newgrange has a great sense of mystery.

appearance, and looks very different to the other grass-covered mounds. It took 180,000 tons (182 million kg) of stones to build this passage grave, and inside the 36ft (11m) high mound is a famous decorated stone – many others festoon the magnificent central chamber. Some claim that at 4000 years it is the oldest man-made 'building' in the world. A comprehensive tour of the site is available.

About 2 miles (3.2km) northeast is Dowth, a slightly smaller passage grave which has been plundered many times over the centuries. Knowth is 2 miles (3.2km) northwest and when excavations have been completed it is likely to be recognized as the most interesting and complete of all the Brugh na Boinne monuments.

NEW ROSS (Wexford)
Ref: G4
Rhos Mhic Thriúin, the Wood of Treon's Son. New Ross' narrow, winding streets are sited on a steep hill above the River Barrow that provided its livelihood. This inland port was once a great rival to Waterford, and seagoing barges were manufactured here for many years. St Abban had a 6th-century monastery at New Ross, and the town's secular founder was Isabella de Clare, Strongbow's daughter, who died in 1220. Only a few fragments remain of its mile- (1.6-km) long Norman wall, for the town suffered terribly in the Cromwellian Wars. Indeed, Three Bullet Gate earned its name at this time when three cannonballs were lodged in it. St Mary's Church is a large Anglo-Norman abbey parish church built in about 1200, with an interesting transept and chancel, though the nave was removed to make way for a 19th-century structure. The town in linked with Dublin via the Barrow and Grand Canal, and there is a pleasant water trip to Waterford down the Barrow and up the Suir.

What to see Annagh's Tower (15 or 16c, 2 miles [3.2km] south on the River Barrow); Dunganstown (4 miles [6.4km] south, ancestral home of the Kennedy family, also has John F Kennedy Park nearby); St Mary's Church; Slieve Coilt (630ft [192m] viewpoint which can be reached by car); Three Bullet Gate.

NEWTOWNMOUNT-KENNEDY (Wicklow)
Ref: F5
Baile an Chinnéidigh, Kennedy's Town. The area around Mount Kennedy in the foothills of the Wicklow Mountains, over the

River trips can be made from the characterful town of New Ross.

main road between Bray and Wicklow, is one of the prettiest in Ireland. Almost a mile (1.6km) north is Mount Kennedy house itself, built in 1732 and containing superb plasterwork by Michael Stapleton.

OLDCASTLE (Meath)
Ref: E4
An Seanchaisleán, The Old Castle. An out of the way town which is mainly a fishing base for the Sheelin and the River Inny. Nearby is Loughcrew, a series of about 30 Neolithic passage graves (cairns) scattered over the crests of two hills, the highest being 900ft (274m) Slieve na Calliagh. Here Cairn 'T' has a diameter of 115ft (35m) and is a classic example of a passage grave tomb. Among the tombs is a massive carved rock with a seat-like cavity, known as Ollamh Fodla's Chair, named after a lawgiver who died before 1000BC and is thought to

be buried near here. Over the Cavan border is Virginia, with its golf course and good coarse fishing.

What to see Loughcrew; Virginia.

PORTARLINGTON (Laois)
Ref: F4
Cúil an tSúdaire, The Tanner's Recess. This former Huguenot colony derives its name from its 17th-century owner, Lord Arlington. It still has a 'French' church from its early history, and some lovely Georgian architecture, though the view is rather blighted by the peat-burning power station. The market house dates from about 1800. Four miles (6.4km) north is the 4000-acre (1600-ha) Clonsast Bog, and 2 miles (3.2km) east are the ruins of the 1250 Lea Castle. To the south can be found Emo

Park estate, with a domed Palladian mansion built by James Gandon in 1790. The house was once a Jesuit college, but is now private.

PORT LAOISE (Laois)
Ref: F4
Port Laoise, the Fort of Laois. Batterings by Cromwell's troops have removed traces of the fortifications that marked this as a major Elizabethan town. The town's gaol dates from 1830, and behind it in a burial ground is a former Church of Ireland church. The esker ridge (a ridge of sand and gravel) of Maryborough runs north from here for nearly 20 miles (32km). Four miles (6.4km) east on the Rock of Dunamase are the ruins of Dermot MacMurough, the King of Leinster's 12th-century castle. Five miles (8km) northeast is Coolbanagher with its Church of Ireland church and mausoleum. Beyond the Great Heath of Maryborough to the northeast is Ballybrittas, called the 'Pass of the Plumes' after a battle in the 16th century when Essex's men suffered the indignity of having their feathers cut from their helmets.

What to see Ballybrittas; Coolbanagher (5 miles [8km] northeast, 18c church); Courthouse (19c); Maryborough (esker ridge); Rock of Dunamase.

PORTMARNOCK (Dublin)
Ref: F5
Port Mearnóg, St Earnán's Harbour. The marvellous expanse of sand at this small seaside resort is known as the Velvet Strand, and another attraction is a championship golf course. About 3 miles (4.8km) southwest is St Doolagh's Church, which dates from about 1200 and includes a square tower with living quarters. The church building is divided in two, the western half being for the use of a hermit. Adjacent to this old structure is a modern church, and close by is an ancient holy well covered by an octagonal stone structure.

POULAPHOUCA (Wicklow)
Ref: F4
Poll an Phúca, The Púca's Pool. Puca, or Puck, is a playful water sprite whose home is in one of the pools into which the River Liffey plunges at this point. The cascades are not what they were since a dam and power station were built, but the setting is still beautiful. An excellent view can be enjoyed from a path leading south of the river. One arm of the lake is spanned by Humphrystown Bridge which leads to woodland scenery on the eastern shore.

Avondale House lies in the Avonmore Valley and has a nature trail running through its attractive grounds.

THE MUSIC OF IRELAND

Irish music is a vigorous and living tradition. Many Irish musicians play a variety of instruments, not so much that symbol of the country, the harp, but the fiddle, flute, tin whistle, accordion and guitar. Two distinctively Irish instruments are the uillean pipes (like bagpipes, but inflated by bellows rather than from the player's lungs) and the bodhran, pronounced boe-rawn, which is a goatskin drum. In recent times, a singing style called sean-nos, in solo Gaelic, has regained its old popularity.

Those familiar with American bluegrass music will notice it has much in common with Irish traditional airs. The intricate footwork of step-dancing is usually carried out by girls in national costume, but sometimes in the Gaeltachts a more spontaneous performance can be enjoyed.

Many pubs are venues for live music, and look out for a fleadh, a festival organized by one of the 200 branches of Comhaltas Ceoltoiri Eireann, set up in 1951 to promote traditional music, song, and dance. You may also be invited to a ceilidh, a party with music and dancing.

RATHDRUM (Wicklow)
Ref: G5
Ráth Droma, Ringfort of the Ridge. Rathdrum sits high on the western side of the beautiful valley of the Avonmore, with the wooded Vale of Clara to the north. Three miles (4.8km) into this Vale, Clara Bridge offers especially good views. The town itself boasts a 19th-century parish church by JJ McCarthy with several good features. Patriot Charles Stewart Parnell's old residence (and birthplace, in 1846), Avondale House, is just over a mile (1.6km) to the south.

It is now part of a State forestry estate, and some sections of the 18th-century house can be visited, while there are picnic facilities nearby and a nature trail can be walked.

RATHVILLY (Carlow)
Ref: G4
Ráth Bhile, Ringfort of the Tree. The Wicklow Mountains rise east of this neat village, which lies in the River Slaney valley near the large, Anglo-Norman Rathvilly Moate. This motte is associated with Drimhthann, once a king of Leinster who was baptized by St

Patrick at a nearby holy well. The local Disreali School was designed by Joseph Welland in 1826. About 3½ miles (5.6km) southeast is Haroldstown Dolmen, a portal grave composed of several sidestones supported by two slightly-tilted capstones. It is unusual for, until fairly recently, it served as a dwelling place.

ROBERTSTOWN (Kildare)
Ref: F4
Baile Riobaird, Robert's Homestead. Robertstown stands on the Grand Canal in the vast Bog of Allen, near the Allenwood

turf-burning power station. This is the canal's highest point above sea level, and the Grand Canal Company's Hotel of 1801, built to accommodate 'express' passengers, still stands. The early 19th-century character of the waterfront has been restored, and another local attraction is a large falconry. The waterway itself is no longer used commercially but horse-drawn barge trips can be made. About a mile (1.6km) west, the canal splits into two, with the main branch proceeding to Tullamore and the offshoot extending south to Rathangan and Athy to join the River Barrow.

ROSSLARE (Wexford) Ref: H4
Ros Láir, Middle Headland. A well-known seaside resort with a 6 mile (9.6km) beach, and good angling and golfing. A causeway connects Rosslare to Lady's Island, which has an Anglo-Norman castle with a leaning limestone tower. It stands on the site of a stronghold built by Rudolphe de Lambert, who was killed on the 3rd Crusade. Beside the castle is the site of an Augustinian priory dedicated to St Mary, which is still a place of pilgrimage.

To the west of Rosslare is Tacumshane, with its well-preserved windmill, and just over 6 miles (9.6km) south, Carnsore Point has a number of remains. These include a stone fort, a cross-inscribed stone, and a church and holy well dedicated to St Vogue or Veoc. Three miles (4.8km) from Rosslare is its busy harbour, which prospered after its rival at Wexford silted up. It is the terminal for Welsh and French ports, and has a long pier with a railway crossing the shallows to the embarkation point. The Tuskar Rock Lighthouse can be seen 6 miles (9.6km) out to sea.

What to see Carnsore Point (church, fort); Lady's Island (Augustinian priory site, castle); Rosslare Harbour; Tacumshane; Tuskar Rock Lighthouse.

ROUNDWOOD (Wicklow) Ref: F5
An Tóchar, The Causeway. Wild scenery and good fishing are the main attractions of Roundwood, which lies in the wooded valley of the Vartry River between Lough Dan and the Vartry reservoir. This reservoir covers 400 acres (161ha) and was created last century. The prettiest local lake is Lough Tay, which is overhung by a granite precipice, and has the wooded grounds of Luggals estate nearby. Lough Dan is larger at 1½ miles (2.4km) long, and also has precipitous shores, and sandy

beaches. The hills near here were a refuge for Holt, a leader of the 1798 rebellion. To the south is Laragh, where the Avonmore and Glenmacnass rivers converge, and the road turns for Glendalough. There is a lovely waterfall at the northern end of the Glenmacnass Valley.

What to see Annamoe (village with millrace towards Glendalough); Glenmacnass Valley and waterfall; Laragh; Lough Dan; Lough Tay; Vartry reservoir.

RUSSBOROUGH HOUSE (Wicklow) Ref: F4
Russborough House is a lovely Georgian building close by the Poulaphouca Reservoir and home to many notable paintings. The Palladian mansion was built in 1741 by Richard Cassells and, after his death, Francis Rindon. It features outstanding plasterwork by the Francini brothers, and is

renowned for its furnishings – some with well-preserved Gobelin tapestry coverings. The Beit collection of paintings, begun by an uncle of the house's last owner, Sir Alfred Beit, can be viewed. It includes works by Gainsborough, Goya, Frans Hals, Rubens, Vermeer and Velázquez.

ST MULLIN'S (Carlow) Ref: G4
Tigh Moling, St Moling's House. Northwest of this attractive River Barrow village is 1694ft (516m) Brandon Hill, while the Blackstairs range culminates with 2610ft (795m) Mount Leinster to the northwest. The village itself has early-Christian and medieval remains, including St Mullin's Abbey. This includes a medieval nave-and-chancel church with a spiral staircase. Nearby, there are relics of a round tower, a tiny oratory, and a small granite high

An old cannon gun overlooks the long beach at Rosslare.

cross with a crucifixion scene and various ornamentations. Down the slope is a medieval building with a diamond-shaped window.

SHILLELAGH (Wicklow) Ref: G4
Síol Ealaigh, Descendants of Ealach. Shillelagh lies amid beautiful scenery in the wooded valley of the Shillelagh River, beneath the southern foothills of the Wicklow Mountains. About 1½ miles (2.4km) east is the Fitzwillian estate of Coollatin Park, whose once great oak forest was, it is claimed, the source of the roofing for both Westminster Hall in London and St Patrick's Cathedral in Dublin. The name of this village has become widely known as a synonym for an Irish blackthorn stick.

SKERRIES (Dublin)
Ref: F5

Na Sceirí, The Reefs. This is a
popular resort with a good sandy
beach and excellent bathing and
golfing. The Norse name is
derived from the rock islands just
off the coast: Colt Island, St
Patrick's Island and Shenick Island
(which can be reached on foot at
low tide). St Patrick is said to have
landed on the island that bears his
name at the start of his mission,
and travelled daily to Red Island,
now part of the mainland – his
footprints have been carved into
the rock. St Patrick's Island has
the ruins of an ancient church
with a distinctive roof made of
tufa-stone. Shenick's Island lies to
the south and has a Martello
tower, erected during the
Napoleonic Wars.

At the south end of Skermes is
Holmpatrick, where the church
occupies part of the site of an
Augustinian priory which
transferred from St Patrick's
Island. The fine Anglo-Norman
stronghold of Baldungan Castle
lies 2 miles (3.2km) south, and
has a fine stone tower.

What to see Baldungan Castle;
Colt Island; Holmpatrick; Lusk
(south, has a farm machinery
museum); Man o'War (tiny village
inland); St Patrick's Island;
Shenick's Island.

Above: *The harbour at Skerries.*
Right: *The River Boyne is
particularly beautiful just
upstream of Slane.*

SLANE (Meath) Ref: E4

Baile Shláine. Slane is an
interesting village on the steep
hillsides of the Boyne, famous for
its salmon and trout fishing. At its
centre, the Square features four
excellent Georgian houses
standing at the four corners of the
crossroads. By the river is a
superb mill dating from 1766. St
Patrick is said to have kindled the
first Paschal Fire in Ireland to the
north on 529ft (161m) Slane Hill
in AD433 to celebrate the triumph
of Christianity over paganism.
Near the top of the hill is a ruined
1512 friary and a separate college.
The church features a well-
preserved tower which is worth
the climb for the views. A mile
(1.6km) west is Slane Castle, one
of the best Gothic-revival castles
in Ireland, which is not open to
the public except for special
events. A mile (1.6km) up the
river is Beauparc Houser, built in
1750, standing opposite the
remnants of Castle Dexter.

What to see Beauparc House
(18c, a mile [1.6km] up the river);
Central Square; Mill; St Erc's
Hermitage; Slane Castle; Slane
church; Transport museum.

STRADBALLY (Laois)
Ref: F4

An Sraidbhaile, Street Town. This village is home to a traction engine museum and a collection of vintage cars. Just northeast is Brockley Park, built in 1768 for the Earl of Roden by Davis Ducart. Stradbally Hall has a narrow-gauge railway which operates during the tourist season.

SUMMERHILL (Meath)
Ref: F4

Cnoc an Línsigh, Lynch's Hill. This village was given a tree-lined mall as part of the work by an improving landlord. It leads to the main avenue to Lord Longford's 18th-century mansion, now in ruins. A grove in its grounds contains the remains of a 16th- or 17th-century Lynch stronghold called Knock Castle. A few medieval fragments, including the shaft of a 16th-century Lynch Cross, can be seen on the village green.

SWORDS (Dublin) Ref: F5

Sord, Pure Well. This is a very ancient village whose foundation is linked with St Colmcille, standing on the estuary of the Ward River. Among the old remains is a 75ft (23m) round tower in the Protestant churchyard. This village was one of the major archiepiscopal manors before the Anglo-Norman invasion. At the north end of the main street are the ruins of the archibishop's 13th-century manorial castle, a five-sided edifice which encloses a courtyard of great size. It features porter's and priest's rooms, and the remains of 13th-century windows. About 2 miles (3.2km) west is Brackenstown House, one time home of Robert Molesworth, the 1st Viscount Swords. A large rath is preserved in the grounds of the house.

TAGHMON (Westmeath)
Ref: F4

Teach Munna, Munna's House. In a graveyard here, 1 mile (1.6km) east of Crookedwood are the ruins of the 15th-century fortified church with a four-storey, castle-like residential tower. In the tower are a living room and bedroom. The church and tower room are vaulted. The church has been in almost constant use since its construction, and has been restored several times.

TAGHMON (Wexford)
Ref: G4

Teach Munna, Munna's House. The name of this market town derives from St Munna, who founded an Augustinian monastery here in the 6th century. A massive square tower is all that remains of the town's Anglo-Norman castle. The small 19th-century parish church carries a square tower, and the adjoining churchyard contains remains of an ancient granite cross of rude workmanship. HF Lyte, who wrote 'Abide with me', was curate here in 1815.

TARA (Meath) Ref: F4

Teamhair, Place With a View. Tara has a famous ancient royal site, the Hill of Tara, which was once Ireland's royal acropolis and was the religious, political and cultural capital for more than 2000 years. As Christianity spread, this pagan centre declined in importance, but it was not finally abandoned until 1022. Today the visitor can see a modern statue of St Patrick and some mounds and earthworks. On the hillcrest (at 512ft [156m]) is a pillar stone said to be the coronation stone of the early kings. In the churchyard is Adarnan's Stone with a human figure depicted on it, said to be Cernunnos, horned god of the Celts. There is also a passage grave from 2000BC, called the 'Mound of Hostages', containing the skeleton of a boy wearing a bronze, amber and jet necklace. This stands inside the 'Royal Enclosure', an Iron Age ringfort 950 by 800ft (290 by 244m).

About 3 miles (4.8km) south is Dunsany Castle, dating from the 13th century but much modernized, with the 15th-century St Nicholas' Church in its wooded grounds. A monastery stood on the Hill of Skreen (4

The bland neatness of the Hill of Tara today belies its central place in the ancient history and legends of Ireland.

miles [6.4km] east of Tara) in 875, and the remains of a church with a later tower can be seen.

What to see Banquet hall; Dunsany Castle; Hill of Skreen; Hill of Tara (Adarnan's Stone, coronation stone, 'Mound of Hostages', Rath of the Synods, 'Royal Enclosure', Sloping trenches); St Nicholas' Church.

TERMONFECKIN (Louth)
Ref: E5

Tearmann Féichín, St Féichín's Sanctuary Land. A quaint old village which once housed the summer residence of the Archibishops of Armagh. This has now vanished, but just east of the valley is the well preserved 15th-century Termonfeckin Castle. Probably the home of the Dowdall family, it has interesting conical vaulting and a fine stone spiral stairway connecting the four storeys of its square tower. A high cross in the local protestant cemetery is said to mark the site of a 6th-century church. It stands more than 11ft (3.3m) high and probably dates from the 9th century. The base of a small early cross and a crucifixion slab are also in the church yard while an early gravestone can be seen in the church porch.

IRISH BIRDLIFE

Five miles (8km) out from Wexford are the Saltee Islands, inhabited in great numbers by puffins, razorbills, and many other bird species. Wexford also has a wildfowl reserve on the north side of its harbour, reached by turning off the R742 to Gorey Road. Waders and ducks are abundant but it is for the Greenland white-fronted geese that the area is best known.

This is just one of many places in the country where birdlife can be enjoyed. Ireland has a varied and comparatively unspoilt coastline which supports a wide range of birds. Sea cliffs and offshore islands, especially on the west coast, have some of the best seabird colonies in Europe. Puffins, guillemots, black guillemots, razorbills, kittiwakes, gannets and fulmars are all common in some areas. Seabird colonies are generally deserted after the end of August but the birds can still be seen offshore. Among the best cliff sites are Howth Head (just north of Dublin), Bray Head to the south, Helvick Head south of Dungarvan, Waterford, and Horn Head near Dunfanaghy in Donegal. Estuaries and mudflats are wonderful places for waders and wildfowl, particularly outside the breeding season. Try North Bull Island in Dublin Bay for some superb views.

THOMASTOWN (Kilkenny) Ref: G4

Baile Mhic Andáin, Fitzanthony's Homestead. Thomas Fitzanthony was the Anglo-Norman seneschal (steward) of Leinster, and built a castle here in the 13th century, of which the motte survives. He also founded the parish church, of which the nave, aisles, sacristy, west end, and southwest tower remain. A fine 18th-century bridge of five arches spans the River Nore, and less than half a mile (0.8km) south on the banks of the river are the ruins of the Anglo-Norman fortress of Grainan, also built by Thomas Fitzanthony. The high altar of Jerpoint Abbey (1½ miles [2.4km] southwest, see separate entry) is now in Thomastown Church. Philosopher Bishop George Berkeley was born 2 miles (3.2km) southeast at Dysert Castle in 1685. California's Berkeley University is named after him.

What to see bridge; castle; church; Dysert Castle; Grainan fortress.

TIMAHOE (Laois) Ref: F4

Tigh Mochua, St Mochua's House. Five miles (8km) southwest of Stradbally, Timahoe takes its name from a 6th-century monastery founded by St Mochua, of which a well-preserved 12th-century round tower remains. It is 96ft (29m) high and features a unique Romanesque doorway built of hard sandstone. East of the tower is a small church incorporating a 15th-century arch. The church was converted into a castle two centuries later. About half a mile (0.8km) west of Timahoe is a 12th-century motte-and-bailey castle called the rath of Ballynaclogh.

TINAHELY (Wicklow) Ref: G4

Tigh na hÉille, House of the Thong. Situated among the hills of the valley of the Derry River, this charming little town was rebuilt after being destroyed during the 1798 insurrection. A short walk away at Coolruss are slight remains of an incomplete building known as 'Black Tom's Kitchen'. To the west, on the Wexford border, rises 1987ft (606m) Croghan Kinshela.

TRIM (Meath) Ref: F4

Baile Átha Troim, the Town of the Ford of the Elder Tree. Trim grew up around an ancient ford crossing the river between the present bridges, and was one of

There is a lot to see in Trim, from its well preserved past to its well kept present.

the earliest and largest religious settlements in the country. It sits in a fertile plain and there are abundant horses and cattle grazing in the area. There are a number of substantial relics, the major one being the huge, 16-sided, 75ft- (23-m) high castle, now in disrepair. Once Ireland's biggest, strongest fortress, it was built by 1200, and occupied by King John for five years from 1210.

All that remains of the 13th-century St Mary's Augustinian Priory is the 125ft (38m) Yellow Steeple, dating from 1368. St Patrick's Cathedral opened in 1802, though its 60ft (18m) tower is part of a structure built by Richard of York in 1449 – near the top you can pick out his coat of arms. A number of Anglo-Norman fortified homes can be founded along the valley of the Boyne between Trim and Navan.

What to see castle; Duke of Wellington Monument; St Patrick's Cathedral; Sheep Gate and town walls; Talbot's Castle (once a school attended by the Duke of Wellington); Yellow Steeple.

TULLAMORE (Offaly) Ref: F4

Tulach Mhór, Big Hill. The very wide Patrick Street in this county town owes its proportions to its rebuilding after a disaster in 1785 when a hot air balloon exploded, destroying a hundred houses. Thirteen years later the Grand Canal reached the town, creating good trade links which were exploited by Tullamore's yellow brick manufacturers in the 19th century. Some canal barges can still be seen. Architect Francis Johnston designed the small church on Hop Hill and Charleville House. Half a mile (0.8km) west is a good example of an Elizabethan fortified residence, Shrah Castle, built in 1588.

TYRRELLSPASS (Westmeath) Ref: F4

Bealach an Tirialaigh, Tyrell's Road. The name of this village refers to a road running through bogs where Richard Tyrrell was ambushed by an English force in 1597. It is formally laid out around a semi-circular green, and has several houses of note. The Protestant church has a handsome monument to the Countess of Belvedere.

Selskar Abbey in Wexford: Henry II passed the whole of Lent in penitence here after his words had prompted the murder of Thomas à Becket in Canterbury Cathedral.

WEXFORD (Wexford) Ref: G4

Loch Garman. Once a Viking base, Wexford has a long history of suffering in times of war (particularly at the hands of Cromwell), and the silting up of its harbour has undoubtedly limited its growth. It is a city built on three levels, with a long, narrow, main street at its centre forming a picturesque thoroughfare. Augustinian Selskar Abbey stands in ruins although it has a well-preserved square west tower. The red sandstone West Gate, near the station, is the only survivor of five gates put up in about 1300, and still has its little prison and a short stretch of wall. A beautiful chapel by AW Pugin dating from 1838 stands in St Peter's College. St Doologue's Church has the smallest parish in the world – only 3 acres (1.2ha).

What to see Bullring; John Barry statue; Maritime Museum (in an old lightship); St Doologues' Church; St Patrick's Church; St Peter's College; Selskar Abbey; town walls; West Gate Tower.

WICKLOW (Wicklow) Ref: F5

Cill Mhantáin. A quaint and attractive resort town with a shingle beach and much modernized streets. The Murrough, a long grassy spit of land, formed an excellent refuge for the Vikings, and today has a promenade and a railway along part of it. Some remains of a 13th-century Franciscan friary can be seen near the town entrance on the Dublin-Wexford road, and at the western end of the town are the ruins of Black Castle on a rocky promontory, begun in 1176 by Maurice Fitzgerald. Six miles (9.6km) south is what remains of Dunganstown Castle. The streams of Wicklow offer good trout fishing, and the town also has a nine-hole golf course near Silver Strand to the south.

What to see Black Castle; Dunganstown Castle; Franciscan friary; the Murrough.

WOODENBRIDGE (Wicklow) Ref: G5

Garrán an Ghabhláin, The Grove of the River-fork. A delightful spot which is by the second, and more charming, Meeting of the Waters (the first is at Avoca), where the Aughrim, Avoca and Gold Mine Rivers converge. The discovery of a gold nugget in 1796 led to an Irish gold rush here, and 2600oz (73kg) were found in a few months. Croghan Kinsella rises to 1987ft (606m), 4½ miles (7.2km) south, and about 3 miles (4.8km) southeast are the grounds of Glenart Castle and Shelton Abbey.

CONNACHT

◆

Connacht is a wild and rugged province which has remained largely aloof from invasion and preserves much of its ancient culture. Covering the northwest of Ireland, it forms a natural stronghold bordered to the east by the Shannon, Ireland's greatest river, and to the west by the pounding Atlantic. Connacht is perhaps the least visited of the four provinces, and is predominantly rural in character, despite the presence of some lively towns. It is a region of stones and sheep, mild rain and mountain mists that enhance the brooding qualities of an introspective landscape.

◆

CONNACHT

Sometimes known by its newer name of Connaught, Connacht has been allowed to go its own way for much of Ireland's history, because other areas offered richer pickings to invaders than its vast areas of stone, lakeland and bog. When Oliver Cromwell was forcing dispossessed Catholics from their lands in 1652–4, those who chose to stay in Ireland were banished to Connacht. Most of its land is fairly poor, and less able to support smaller settlements and monasteries than other parts of the country. This also meant that the province bore the brunt of the Great Famine in the middle of last century.

Given Connacht's longstanding isola-tion from, and indifference to, the tribula-tions of the rest of Ireland, it follows that it is home to many of the Gaelic speaking Gaeltacht areas where ancient Irish language and culture are encouraged. Galway in particular is largely Irish-speaking. The Catholic faith is also very strong among the people of the province, which is home to two major religious sites: Knock and the 'holy mountain' of Croagh Patrick.

Galway Galway is a county of two parts: the low lying, fertile east, and the wilder

Mulrany in County Mayo is one of Ireland's most relaxing resorts.

Previous page: *A detail from the Turoe Stone at Loughrea.*

west with its indented coast and the threatening moors, hills, lakes and bogs of the Connemara. Separating these contrasting regions is Lough Corrib, a vast 27-mile (43-km) long lake with an irregular shoreline which pushes its tentacles into the mountains. To its south is the county town, the city of Galway and unofficial capital of the West. This is a vibrant, exciting city which has grown phenomenally in recent years while retaining its own charm, and its love of what the Irish call the 'crack' – a catch-all phrase for having fun.

Galway stands deep within Galway Bay, whose path to the ocean is interrupted by the Aran Islands, an exposed trio on which stand many prehistoric remains, ecclesiastical ruins and the settlements of today's tough, independently-minded inhabitants.

The uncharacteristically straight northern shore of Galway Bay runs west from the city and is bordered by a road which links the coastal villages of a region called Iar Connacht. This is a large and relatively unpopulated area of low granite hills rising treeless among hundreds of tiny lakes. Such an environment forms a natural barrier which has kept outsiders from Iar Connacht for centuries, and most visitors are content to enjoy the picturesque coast. Further northwest is Connemara, one of the most unspoilt and spectacular regions in Ireland, and homeland of the sturdy Connemara pony. Connemara is dominated by the Twelve Bens (or Pins) range and the Maamturk mountains. From the latter, in particular, there are marvellous views of Connemara's lakes, moorland and coastal waters.

Leitrim Leitrim is a small county bounded in the northwest by Donegal Bay and divided, like Galway, by a lake. In this case it is Lough Allen (first of the many Shannon lakes) that forms the barrier, separating the mountainous northern border with Sligo from the prettier south with its plains, lakes and valleys. The scenery aside, there is not much to attract the visitor to the county in comparison with its neighbours.

Mayo County Mayo's name is thought to derive from the first two words in the name of a monastery founded by English monks in the 7th century. Its site was called Maigh Eo na Sacsan, which translates as 'the plain of the yew trees of the English'. Parts of Mayo see few visitors – especially its northern terrain of peat bogs and smooth hills – but there are some major attractions in the county, too. Countless pilgrims make the trek to the Catholic church at Knock, because of the apparition of the Virgin Mary that occurred in 1879. Many tourists also find themselves at Knock, landing at an airport which was built in response to a virtually single-handed campaign by local priest Monsignor Horan.

The simple beauty of this Cong house is typical of Connacht.

The historic town of Westport is another draw, but Mayo is best known for its long, rugged and unspoilt coastline, and particularly for a large island just off it, called Achill. Other Irish islands are visited for their historic monuments: people go to Achill purely for the scenery. It is like a tiny version of the whole province of Connacht, with rocky plains and boglands broken by soaring piles of rock and heather which drop sheer down onto surf-fringed beaches.

South of Achill is Clare Island, which apart from its pleasing environment is known as the one-time base of the O'Malley family. This was one of the most powerful families in the county, and its most famous member is Grace O'Malley. She lived in the 16th century during the reign of Elizabeth I, and proved a major irritation to that redoubtable monarch. Grace O'Malley followed the ways of a piratess on land and sea, and once even stole one of her husband Sir Richard Burke's castles by installing her own guards in it.

Anglers regard Mayo as one of the best fishing counties in Ireland, and many will have heard of Lough Conn, where an unofficial record pike of 53lbs (24kg) was caught on rod and line in 1920. It was weighed after the removal of the 10lb (4.5kg) salmon stuck in its gullet. Visiting anglers often stay at Pontoon, which is between the waters of Loughs Cullin and Conn. Mayo is also home to the youngest lake in Ireland, tiny Lough Achree, which was formed by an earthquake in 1490, and can be found east of Ballina.

Roscommon The only landlocked county in Connacht, Roscommon is a quiet and mainly flat region mostly taken up with bog or pasture. The upper Shannon covers much of its western border, but most visitors will head north, to Boyle, or east, to

Strokestown. Boyle nestles south of the Curlew Mountains and is well worth a visit, and a detour to nearby Lough Key forest park is also rewarding. Roscommon is linked with Longford and Westmeath by the waters of Lough Ree, a 15-mile (24-km) lough fed by the Shannon with many attractive little islands.

Sligo Much is packed into the relatively small county of Sligo, for between its majestic mountains and its long, spindly coastline are a very high number of sites of historic interest, and numerous literary associations. Among the ancient sites are the Neolithic cemetery at Carrowmore and the prehistoric village of Carrowkeel. The links with the written word are chiefly with the Irish poet WB Yeats, who loved this county and is identified particularly with Lough Gill's island of Innisfree and with Lissadell House.

Two beautiful mountains rise in the county: Ben Bulben (part of the Darty range in the north) and Knocknarea. The former is also known as the 'Table Mountain' because of its long, flattened 1722ft (525m) top. Knocknarea is west of Sligo town, and on its 1078ft (329m) summit is a gigantic cairn which tradition holds is the tomb of Queen Maeve. The 1st-century ruler of Connacht, she plunged much of Ireland into war in her attempts to steal Ulster's fabulous Brown Bull of Cooley.

Some 4 miles (6.4km) off the Sligo coast is the island of Inishmurray, reached by boat from Grange. Here are the remains of an early-Irish monastery thought to have been founded in the 6th century. A visit there gives an insight into the rigours of life in an early monastery. As for the way of life in Sligo today, its chief industries are livestock and dairy farming, and consequently the rural population is low and there are few lively settlements apart from the county town.

PLACES *of* INTEREST

ACHILL ISLAND (Mayo)
Ref: E1

Acaill, Access to the Island. At 36,248 acres (14,700ha), this is the largest island off the Irish coast, and is reached over a bridge spanning the narrow channel known as Achill Sound. Some cultivation is possible on the coast and in sheltered valleys, but most of the land is a blend of magnificent cliffs, golden strands, purple moors, precipitous hillsides, and scattered white cottages. In short, this is a resort for the seeker of solitude. The 2-mile (3.2-km) sandy beach at Keel ends at the Menawn Cliffs, which have a sheer 800ft (244m) drop at one point. Two miles (3.2km) on is Dooagh, with a fine sheltered beach, the ideal point to begin an ascent of 2192ft (668m) Croaghaun at the western end of the island. Another resort is Dugort, at the foot of Slievemore's quartzite mass.

What to see Achill Sound; Dooagh; Doogort; Keel; Kildownet.

ANNAGHDOWN (Galway)
Ref: F2

Eanach Dhúin, Marsh of the Fort. Annaghdown is a small village on the eastern shores of Lough Corrib, known as a game and coarse fishing venue. It is the site of a 6th-century monastery founded by St Brendan the Navigator, and probably of a nunnery run by his sister Brigid. All remnants of these origins are gone, but a window in the old parish church is part of a 12th-century church building, as are the side pilasters of a Romanesque doorway. Also in the vicinity are the remains of a Norman castle and a bishop's palace.

ARAN ISLANDS (Galway)
Ref: F2

Oileáin Árann. Three small islands 30 miles (48km) out in the Atlantic, Inishmore (7635 acres [3000ha]), Inishmaan (2253 acres

The sun sets behind Croaghaun, on Achill Island.

[910ha]), and Inisheer (1400 acres [570ha]), form this group which has been inhabited since the earliest times (see box). These are the high peaks of a limestone reef, and the terrain is rocky and unfriendly, enlivened by a wide range of wild flowers. The capital is Kilronan on Inishmore, an island which is also home to Dun Aengus. This is a stone fort near

ISLAND PEOPLE

According to the ancient *Annals of the Four Masters*, the Aran islands were first populated as the result of the first great battle between the Firbolgs and the invading Dedanaans 'in the 303rd year of the world'. The victorious Dedanaans were said to have driven their foes into exile on the islands. During the 5th century, St Enda received the descendants of these refugees into the Christian church, beginning a monastic tradition which has left the Arans with one of the richest collections of early ecclesiastical remains in the country. The islanders pursued a rugged existence in which the struggle for food led to them painstakingly raising crops on pockets of earth built up from sand and seaweed. They also braved the Atlantic ocean to fish in their frail currachs, which are tiny, light vessels made by stretching canvas very tightly over a wooden frame.

The Irish-speaking inhabitants of the Arans have long been considered unique in that they followed a lifestyle largely lost to the rest of Ireland. This interest has inevitably led to intrusive influences from the mainland, changing the way of life and adding a few modern comforts to what is still a tough life. The islands and their people have been accurately portrayed in Pat Mullen's book *Man of Aran*, Tom O'Flaherty's *Aranmen All*, and JM Synge's play *Riders to the Sea*.

The photograph shows women from Inishmaan wearing traditional, brightly coloured shawls. The island has fewer obvious attractions than Inishmore and so remains relatively unaffected by tourism.

Kilmurvy which is considered one of the finest prehistoric structures in western Europe. It stands on the edge of a sheer 300ft (91m) cliff, and once had an outer wall 8ft (2.5m) high and 8ft (2.5m) deep. Its purpose and age remain a mystery. There are other stone forts near Kilronan (called Dun Eoghanacht), Oghil (Dun Oghill), and close by the southern cliffs (Doocaher). Inishmaan also has such a fort, called Dun Conor. Inishmore has a tiny primitive church called Teampall Bheanain at Killeany.

What to see Kilronan; stone forts (Doocaher, Dun Aengus, Dun Conor, Dun Eoghanacht, Dun Oghill); Teampall Bheanain.

ATHENRY (Galway) Ref: F3
Baille Átha an Rí, the Town of the King's Ford. Located between Galway and Ballinsloe, Athenry was the principal town of the Norman de Burgos (later the Burkes) and Bermingham from the end of the 12th century. It still has a market cross, part of a medieval wall, most of a north gate (from 1211) and the keep of the 1238 castle. A Dominican friary was founded in 1241, and the church survives, with well-preserved rows of lancet windows – the east window dates from 1324. There are also a few remains of a 15th-century Franciscan friary. An interesting feature of the town's market place is a ruined 15th-century cross with a representation of the Crucifixion on one side and the Virgin and Child on the other.

What to see Castle keep; Dominican friary (13c); Franciscan friary (15c); market place; town wall.

Athleague (Roscommon) Ref: F3
Áth Liag, Ford of the Standing Stones. This village stands on the River Suck and has the remains of a 13th-century castle called the Fort of the Earls. A ditch dividing the structure in half was, it is said, cut because of an argument between two noblemen. Castle Strange, 1½ miles (2.4km) north, is a ruined house with extensive stables. There is an ancient ritual object known as the Castle Strange Stone in its grounds. This dates from about 200BC and is decorated with ornamentation in the Celtic Iron Age La Tene style.

BALLAGHADERREEN (Roscommon) Ref: E3
Bealach an Doirín, the Road of the Little Grove. The Lung River, near the head of which this little market and cathedral town is sited, flows northeast nearby into Lough Gara. The town includes several charming Georgian houses, and a Gothic-revival cathedral which looks rather out of place.

BALLINA (Mayo) Ref: E2
Béal an Átha, Mouth of the Ford. The largest town in Mayo, Ballina stands near the estuary of the Moy, between the northeast shores of Lough Conn and Killala Bay. This is an excellent centre for salmon and trout fishing, and golf is another attraction. During the 1798 rebellion, General Humbert landed in the bay and conquered the town with 1100 Frenchmen.

The modern cathedral has a beautiful stained glass window, and nearby are the ruins of the 1427 Ardnaree Augustinian friary. Features include an ornamented west doorway, and a window decorated with sculptures of human heads. Half a mile (0.8km) along the Lough Conn road is the Dolmen of the Four Maols. This marks the graves of a quartet of 6th-century foster brothers who killed Ceallach, bishop of Kilmoremoy who was also their tutor. They were hanged by Ceallach's brother across the river at Ardnaree. A mile (1.6km) northwest of the town are the remains of Kilmoremoy, the Great Church of Moy.

What to see Ardnaree Friary (15c); Belleek Manor (wooded grounds on west bank of Moy); Cathedral; Dolmen of the Four Maols; Kilmoremoy.

BALLINAFAD (Sligo) Ref: E3
Béal an Átha Fada, Mouth of the Long Ford. A quiet, small town on the southwest corner of Lough Arrow. Curlieus Castle was built to guard a pass over the Curlew Hills in about 1519, but, unusually, a 13th-century design was chosen for its massive circular towers and squat walls. On the north shores of Lough Arrow is the giant, possibly Bronze Age, Heapstown Stone Cairn. This 20ft (6m) mound of stones may cover a passage grave, but it has never been excavated. Nearly a mile (1.6km) north at Aghanagh are the remains of a small pre-Romanesque church originally founded by St Patrick. Go on a further three miles (4.8km) to 13th-century Castle Baldwin.

What to see Aghanagh church; Castle Baldwin; Curlieus Castle; Heapstown Stone Cairn.

Ballina is set among some lovely walking country, but its major attraction is fishing, especially around Lough Conn.

BALLINASLOE (Galway)
Ref: F3
Béal Átha na Aluaighe, the Ford-mouth of the Host. A horse, cattle and sheep fair is held here for eight days every October. It is the largest livestock market in Ireland – and in the days of cavalry and horse-drawn transport, it was the largest horse fair in Europe. The town stands at the crossing of the River Suck and marks the western terminus of the Grand Canal. Its limestone was once a prized building material and there are many quarries in the area. Four miles (6.4km) southwest is the tiny village of Aughrim, which is surrounded by ecclesiastical remains, and witnessed a disastrous defeat of the Jacobites by the Williamites in 1691.

BALLINROBE (Mayo)
Ref: E2
Baile an Róba, the Homestead of the Robe. Anglers flock to this Plains of Ellerton town on the River Robe, as do golfers and racegoers. Nearby is the largest lough in Mayo, Lough Mask, and on its east shore, 4 miles (6.4km) from the town, is a castle of the same name. This is a 15th-century MacWilliam fortress on the site of an early Fitzgerald stronghold, restored in the 17th century. Nearby is Lough Mask House, once the home of Captain Charles Cunningham Boycott (1832–97). He so annoyed his tenants that they ostracized him – and his name entered the English language. Lough Mask and Lough Carra are divided by a trunk road

and linked via an underground river.

BALLINTOBER (Mayo)
Ref: E3
Bail an Tobair, the Homestead of the Well. The abbey for which this little village is famous is the only church in the English-speaking world to have held Mass continuously for 750 years. This was despite Henry VIII's 1542 suppression (not enforced) and the removal of the roof by Cromwellians in 1653. Restoration began in 1963. The internal stone-vaulted chancel roof remains intact, as does the sacristy and a beautiful chapterhouse door with pointed arch. However, the 15th-century cloisters have been re-instated. The King of Connacht,

Cathal O'Conor, founded the abbey in 1216 on the site of a 5th-century foundation.

BALLYCASTLE (Mayo)
Ref: D2
Baile an Chaisil, the Homestead of the Stone Fort. Ballycastle is a pleasant resort with sand dunes and a small beach where the Ballinglen River flows to join Bunatrahir Bay. There is some spectacular sandstone-cliff scenery 4 miles (6.4km) northeast near Downpatrick Head, where Atlantic storms have eroded rocks into fantastic shapes. There are also a number of blowholes which shoot up spouts of brine during storms. About 2 miles (3.2km) northwest is the splendid Pillar Stone of Doonfeeny, which is 18ft

Irish shops can offer the unusual, as this Ballymoe display suggests.

SPANISH LINKS

In 1588 Philip II of Spain sent a naval invasion force – the Armada – of 129 ships carrying almost 20,000 men towards England. They intended to meet up with a force waiting in the Low Countries, but were defeated in the Channel by the smaller English fleet. The fleeing ships were driven northwards around Scotland before they could head south past Ireland for home. Only half made it through the stormy seas. The largest galleon sank near Belmullet. Others travelled further south but were driven by storms onto the coasts of Galway, Clare and Kerry. Many ships were wrecked at Spanish Point, 2½ miles (4km) east of Miltown Malbay in Clare, and the sailors swam ashore only to face execution by the High Sheriff of Clare. Others were more fortunate, and a number of Spanish sailors settled in Ireland, particularly in Galway which already had strong trade links with their country. That many were accepted into the community is proven by the brown eyes and olive skins that are still associated with Galway surnames, and indeed that city has a number of buildings in the Spanish style.

the east and west walls. Also of interest in Ballymote are the remains of the Franciscan friary where the 14th-century *Book of Ballymote* was written. The book contains valuable historical information and the key to the deciphering of ancient ogham script. It now rests in the Royal Academy, Dublin. Northwest by 3 miles (4.8km) is Temple House, standing on the shores of Lough Templehouse, which was founded by the Knights Templar and expanded in 1560. Temple House is one of the grandest and oldest Anglo-Irish houses in Ireland.

BALLYSADARE (Sligo)
Ref: E3

Baile Easa Dara, the Homestead of the Waterfall of the Oak. A popular town, Ballysadare lies at the head of beautiful Ballysadare Bay, with views of Knocknarea and Benbulben, and the spectacular cascades of Owenmore River. A fish ladder helps migrating salmon over the falls, while anglers do their best to interrupt the fishes' journey. Below the bridge are the remains of a monastery founded in the 7th century by St Fechin of Fore. Remains include a 12th-century church with a later Romanesque doorway, and 300yds (275m) away is a slightly older church, built after the monks accepted Augustinian discipline.

BELMULLET (Mayo)
Ref: D2

Béal an Mhuirthead, Entrance of the Mullet Peninsula. Belmullet stands on the Mullet peninsula, a bleak and sparsely populated area raked by Atlantic winds. But angling is good and there are beaches and sandhills at Elly Bay, between Belmullet and Blacksod Bay. It was in Blacksod Bay that the largest galleon in the Spanish Armada, *La Rata*, sank in 1588. At Doonamo Point, 5 miles (8km) northwest of Belmullet, are the remains of Doonamo Promontory Fort, which was protected by rows of upright stones called *Chevaux de Frise*. The early-Christian site of Kilmore Erris is among the sand dunes 4 miles (6.4km) west, and features a small enclosure, a cross slab, and some small cist-like mounds. About 2 miles (3.2km) west of Binghamstown (which is southwest of Belmullet) are the remains of a small church called Cross Abbey, while what is left of St Derivla's Church can be seen on the south tip of the peninsula at Falmore.

What to see Cross Abbey; Doonamo Promontory Fort; Kilmore Erris; St Derivla's Church.

(5.4m) high and is decorated with two crosses. At Behy, 4 miles (6.4km) west, is one of many prehistoric graves in the area, set in a large blanket bog.

BALLYHAUNIS (Mayo)
Ref: E3

Béal Átha Hamhnais. An attractive town set in a district of small lakes, Ballyhaunis has an Augustinian friary with parts of a church from an earlier foundation. The present structure dates from 1641, but was burnt down nine years later and restored earlier this century. About 2½ miles (4km) west at Lisvaun is the Bracklaghboy Ogham Stone, a 6ft (1.8m) high relic in the centre of a 21-ft (6.4-m) diameter mound. It is

thought to mark the burial place of the person named in the ancient inscription. Ogham is an ancient Celtic alphabet. North by 2 miles (3.2km) is a pillar stone at Coolnaha South, which is inscribed with a ringed cross.

What to see Augustinian friary; Bracklaghboy Ogham Stone; Coolnaha South.

BALLYMOE (Galway)
Ref: E3

Béal Átha Mó, the Ford-mouth of Mó. Ballymoe is a small village on the Roscommon border formed by the River Suck. Four miles (6.4km) southeast are the ruins of

Glinsk Castle, once a fine structure and with well-preserved mullioned windows and chimneys. It was built by the Burke family in about 1647. A mile (1.6km) west is ruined Ballynakill Church, which has a 16th-century effigy of a knight.

BALLYMOTE (Sligo) Ref: E3

Baile an Mhóta, the Homestead of the Mound. Ballymote is a small market town where Richard de Burgo, Earl of Ulster, built a keepless castle of great strength in the 14th century. The stronghold passed into the hands of the O'Conors, then the MacDermots, the MacDonaghs, and, in 1598, the O'Donnells. Red Hugh O'Donnell marched from here to the Battle of Kinsale in 1601. The castle then fell into ruins after it was surrendered to Lord Granard in 1690. The square structure has round towers at each corner of the 10-ft (3-m) thick curtain walls and has D-shaped towers in the middle of

BOYLE (Roscommon)
Ref: E3

Mainistir na Búille, Monastery of the River Boyle. This town rests at the base of the Curlew Hills between Loughs Gara and Key, connected by the River Boyle. Also on the river is a well-preserved Cistercian abbey, considered one of the finest in the country. It was founded by monks moving on from Mellifont in 1161, and the remains that survive allow the visitor to conjure up some idea of life as a monk in the 13th century. There is a gatehouse with a porter's lodge, a cloister, kitchen, sacristy and cellars beneath the refectory. Most impressive is the church, consecrated in 1218, a cruciform structure with a 131ft (40m) nave. It is considered a good example of the Irish transition from Romanesque to Gothic design. The north side features three early, pointed arches, and the south side has eight arches of the Norman style.

Near the south end of Lough Key is the ancient church of Asselyn, and 2 miles (3.2km) west is the Drumanone Portal Grave. This is surrounded by the remains of a circular cairn and about 360 crannogs were discovered when the land was drained in 1952. Excavations have shown the site was inhabited from 3000BC to about AD500.

> **What to see** Asselyn Church; Cistercian abbey (12/13c); Drumanone Portal Grave; Lough Key forest park (picnic area with 18-c estate).

CARRICK-ON-SHANNON
(Leitrim) Ref: E3

Cora Droma Rúisc, Weir of the Ridge of the Crust. This county town of Leitrim stands on a crossing of the River Shannon just below Lough Drumharlow. The river is navigable up to Lough Allen, to the north, and, combined with the River Boyle and local lakes, makes for very good mixed angling. The area is also known for its hunting, gaming and golf. The town, known locally as Carrick, has some fine Georgian houses and shopfronts. One interesting building is Costello Chapel, built in 1877 and thought to be the smallest chapel in the world. Businessman Edward Costello put it up as a memorial to his wife, and is buried next to her in a matching lead coffin, now protected under glass.

CARROWMORE (Sligo)
Ref: D3

An Cheathrú Mhór, The Great Quarter. Southwest of Sligo by 2½ miles (4km), this is the second

Memento-filled Clonaris House.

largest megalithic cemetery in Europe, with 60 tombs spread in a variety of directions – all that remain of perhaps as many as 200 originally built here. Most of the graves are of the small passage type, once covered by stone mounds enclosed by boulder kerbs. The largest is Medb's Cairn, at the summit of Knocknarea, which is best reached from a path leading from a road on the southern slopes. It has been estimated that 40,000 tons (40 million kg) of rock were used to make the 60-ft (18-m) high cairn, which is possibly the tomb of Queen Medb. Off the Sligo road in Tobernaveen is a curious stone with a hole in it.

CASTLEBAR (Mayo) Ref: E2
Caisleán an Bharraigh, Barry's Castle. A plain town, Castlebar was founded early in the 17th century by John Bingham, ancestor of the Earls of Lucan. In 1798, the town's garrison under General Lake made such a rapid exit to escape its (less numerous) French attackers that it was dubbed 'The Races of Castlebar'. There is good fishing in the local lakes, and pleasure flights can be made from an airfield. The town hosts a prestigious international song festival every October. Ballintubber Abbey, founded in 1216 for Austin friars by Cathal O'Conor, King of Connacht, and since restored, is 7 miles (11.2km) south.

CASTLEREA (Roscommon)
Ref: E3

An Caisleán Riabhach, The Striped Castle. Castlerea stands in a large public park amid pleasant woodland scenery, with a sports ground and a swimming pool. Sir William Wilde, father of the wit and dramatist Oscar Wilde, was born here. On the western side of the town is the Victorian Clonalis House, which contains a number of mementoes including the Harp of Carolan, once played by 17th-century blind musician Turlough O'Carolan, known as the last of the Irish bards. Two miles (3.2km) south is the 11th-century Emlagh High Cross with its famous decoration comprising closely-knit geometric patterns and interlacing. Eight miles (12.8km) north, Frenchpark has a few remains of 14th-century Cloonshanville Dominican Abbey, and the shell of an 18th-century Palladian mansion.

> **What to see** Clonalis House; Emlagh High Cross; Frenchpark.

A Castlerea shopfront.

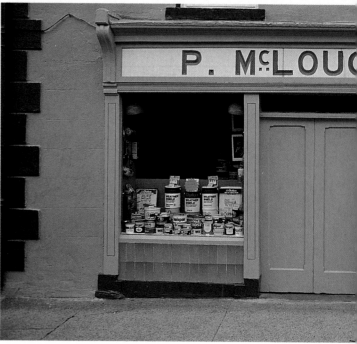

CLARE ISLAND (Mayo)
Ref: E1

Cliara. Clare Island is a small (15sq miles [39km²]) and very pleasant island reached from a ferry that departs from Roonag Quay. Cistercian monks established a cell here in 1220, but the nave-and-chancel church of St Bridget that remains dates from the 16th century. The building includes a sacristy and some medieval frescoes in the chancel, depicting animals, people and the Archangel Michael. It is said that the famous pirate queen Grace O'Malley is buried in the church. Her massive tower castle can be seen near the harbour. It is a three-storeyed building, much altered in 1831 when it became a coastguard station. Grace's exploits are legendary and included stealing the castles of her second husband, Sir Richard Burke of Mayo. Her strong-willed and daunting persona earned the grudging admiration of Elizabeth I. Half a mile (0.8km) northeast is a lintel-roofed holy well, a cashel enclosing a beehive hut and an altar. The island also offers good walking, a climb up 1522ft (464m) Knockmore, pony trekking, and water sports.

CLAREMORRIS (Mayo)
Ref: E2

Once a key railway junction, Claremorris is a good base for exploring the southeastern part of Mayo. Seven miles (11.2km) northeast is Knock, a place of pilgrimage for Catholics around the world. In 1879, an apparition of the Virgin Mary and Saints Joseph and John was seen in the gable of its parish church. As a result of this, a massive church with a capacity of 20,000 was completed in 1976 to accommodate the many visitors the site now attracts.

CLIFDEN (Galway) Ref: F1

An Clochán, The Stepping Stones. Clifden is a popular and busy market town in an attractive setting beneath the Twelve Bens (or Pins) of which Benbaun is the highest at 2593ft (790m). The mountains offer excellent walking and climbing, and Clifden also has sandy beaches and coves within easy reach. To the southwest, a road skirts the bay and leads to the derelict Clifden Castle, built in 1815 by the d'Arcy family, and offering fine marine views from its grounds. In late summer, the town hosts the famous Connemara Pony Show. Five miles (8km) southwest is Derrygimlagh Bog, where John Alcock and Arthur Whitten Brown landed after their pioneering translatlantic flight in

1919. A monument shaped like an aircraft's tail fin commemorates the event, and is sited on high ground just over a mile from this boggy spot. Below the town, the Owenglin River falls steeply over heavy boulders to form the Owenglin cascade.

What to see Clifden Castle; Connemara Pony Show (late summer); Derrygimlagh Bog; Owenglin cascade.

CLONFERT (Galway)
Ref: F1

Cluain Fearta, the Pasture of the Grave. Clonfert is an ancient ecclesiastical settlement 2 miles (3.2km) west of the River Shannon, near the Grand Canal. A

Clonfert Cathedral has a lovely six-arched Romanesque doorway carved with animal heads.

monastery was founded here in 563, and the partly-ruined church dates from the 12th century. Its doorway is a superb example of Irish Romanesque art and has six receding planes decorated with heads, foliage and abstract designs. The 15th-century chancel arch is decorated with angels, rosettes, and a mermaid carrying a mirror. Confert's Catholic church houses an interesting late 13th-century wooden statue of Madonna and Child. The nearby tower house dates back to the 16th century.

COLLOONEY (Sligo)
Ref: E3

Cúil Mhuine, the Recess of the Thicket. Close to this small town 7 miles (11.2km) from Sligo, the Owenmore and Unshin Rivers combine to force their way through the Collooney Gap between the Ox Mountains and Slieve Daeane. The fine Georgian mansion of Markree Castle overlooks the Unshin: its castellations were added in 1801. Some 2 miles (3.2km) southwest are the grounds of Annaghmore, with lovely gardens filled with exotic trees and shrubs. The O'Hara family has lived here since the Middle Ages.

CONG (Mayo) Ref: E2

Conga, Neck. The name of this village beautifully placed between Mask and Corrib Loughs refers to the idyllic isthmus it occupies. The limestone has been worn into

fantastic shapes between the village and Lough Mask. Somewhat unusually, the River Corrib's underground passage can be reached through openings known as Horse's Discovery and Pigeon Hole, but always go accompanied by someone with local knowledge. Cong is a pretty village that welcomes visitors.

The former Guinness family home of Ashford Castle (1870) is now a hotel. Beside it are the ruins of an 1128 Augustinian abbey, and in the village street is a 14th-century inscribed stone cross. Shooting, fishing and boating are all available in the area. To the east is the prehistoric battlefield of Moytura.

What to see Ashford Castle; Ballymacgibbon passage grave (east of Cong); Cong Abbey; Glebe Townland (1 mile [1.6km] northeast, four stone circles, and 15-c castle ruins).

CROAGH PATRICK (Mayo)
Ref: E2

Cruach Phádraigh, St Patrick's Mountain. This is Ireland's Holy Mountain, one of its most sacred sites, a 2510ft (765m) quartzite cone and ridge rising steeply from Clew Bay. St Patrick is said to have fasted and prayed here for 40 days *c*441. The mountain, also known as 'The Reek', is the scene of an annual mass pilgrimage on the last Sunday of July (Garland Sunday). Starting point for an ascent is the lovely, ruined 14th-century Augustinian Murrisk Abbey. The final part of the climb is not easy, but the views are sumptuous. A modern oratory now occupies the site of the old summit shrine. Lough na Corra, near the south base of the mountain, is said to have burst from the earth when St Patrick threw the demon Corra down from the summit of the Holy Mountain.

The ascent of steep Croagh Patrick brings rewarding views. Some pilgrims do it barefoot.

CROSSMOLINA (Mayo)
Ref: E2

Crois Mhaoilíona, Maoilíona's Cross. Fishing and boating in the loughs are the attractions here, with the added bonus of 2646ft (806m) Nephin. On the shore of Lough Conn to the southeast are the remains of Errew Abbey, built in the 15th century for Augustinians, and nearby are the remains of a church built on the site of a 16th-century foundation. Deel Castle stands near the point where the Deel enters Lough Conn, in the grounds of 18th-century Castle Gore. The Bord na Mona and the Electricity Supply Board have efficiently exploited local boglands in this area without harming the countryside.

Dromahair is a pleasant riverside village and home to the impressive ruins of Creevelea Abbey, opposite the Old Hall.

DROMAHAIR (Leitrim) Ref: D3

Drom Dhá thiar, Ridge of the Two Demons. Once the royal seat of Breffni, it was from here that the chain of events leading to the 'Anglo-Norman invasion began, The O'Rourke clan had a palace here (the 1626 Old Hall adjoins its ruins), and from it the 'Helen of Ireland', Dervorgilla O'Rourke, eloped with the King of Leinster, Dermot MacMurrough. Her husband Tiernan had beaten her with a whip and was on a pilgrimage to atone for this.

Apparently the pilgrimage worked, for the pair were reunited, and Dermot was banished. He sought help from Henry II, who agreed to help the invasion which began in 1169. Northwest of the village is Lough Gill, and a flat-topped hill known as O'Rourke's Table rises 3 miles (4.8km) to the north. Over the Bonet River are the considerable remains of Creevelea Abbey, founded by Margaret O'Rourke in 1508, burnt down in 1536 and subsequently rebuilt. There are interesting carvings in the cloister arcades.

DRUMCLIFF (Sligo) Ref: D3

Droim Chliabh, Ridge of Baskets. Dominated by 1730ft (527m)

Benbulben at the head of Drumcliff Bay, this is the site of a 6th-century monastery founded by St Columba. Two relics which may be survivals from it are the stump of a round tower, and a 10th-century high cross, 13ft (4m) high, decorated with Old and New Testament scenes (the only one in the country). In the nearby churchyard is the grave of poet WB Yeats, buried in the parish where his father had been rector in the first half of the 19th century. A short distance west of Cowney Bridge, on the north bank of the river, is a wedge-shaped gallery grave called Giant's Grave. Just to the east is Lough Glencar, famous for the waterfalls (one of 50ft) at its eastern end

and for two crannog lake dwellings. Past Carney, north of the bay, is Lissadell House, a late Georgian mansion with an unusual music room with perfect acoustics and concealed lighting.

What to see Dunfore Castle; Giant's Grave; Glencar; High Cross; Lissadell House; Round Tower.

DRUMSNA, DOON OF (Leitrim and Roscommon) Ref: E3

Droim ar Snámh, Ridge over the Swimming Place. Drumsna is a 'travelling earthwork', 1 mile (1.6km) long which cuts off an area of almost 1sq mile (2.5km^2) between Drumsna and Jamestown, and is thought to have been built to control river crossings. It is said it would take 30,000 men ten years to build it today. In some places, the main rampart is 100ft (30m) wide and 16ft (4.8m) high, and at least six raths lie south of the ramparts. These may have been farmsteads, or could have had some defensive function. The best place to view this mysterious collection of monuments is 3½ miles (5.6km) southeast of Carrick-on-Shannon.

DUNMORE (Galway) Ref: E3

Dún Mór, Big Fort. There is a wool weighouse and weighbridge in this market village, where an Augustinian hermit's friary was founded in 1428. Remains include the Abbey, a church with an interesting perpendicular west doorway and a central tower. Half a mile (0.8km) northwest is 13th-century Dunmore Castle, built by the de Bermingham family on a site once occupied by King Turloch O'Conor's fort. A road divides the ruins, with an upper ward and keep on one side, and a lower ward or bailey on the other. A mound to the west on an esker known as Knomannanan, or Rathcol, is called King Turloch's Grave. There are a number of archeological sites in the area.

*I*RELAND'S *F*INEST *R*IVER

The Shannon is Ireland's finest, longest and most famous river and by the time it loops past Drumsna it has broadened considerably after a long journey which began among the foothills of the Iron Mountains in County Cavan. From there it flows southeast to Lough Allen, the first of three great expansions of the river's

bed. It then escapes its hilly origins and wanders through lake-scattered lowlands and several loughs to Carrick-on-Shannon. South of here, the river widens considerably and passes Drumsna before flowing through Lough Bofin and following the Connacht/Leinster boundary to Ballyclare. Before reaching Athlone, it

joins Lough Ree, second largest of the three main Shannon lakes.

The great river passes right through the centre of Ireland, marking the county borders before entering its longest lake, 25-mile (40-km) Lough Derg. Here the powerful waters are harnessed to the massive Shannon Hydro-Electric

Scheme begun in 1925. The journey ends when the Shannon enters a long estuary at Limerick. Over its course it has helped to form some marvellous scenery, has been spanned by some beautiful bridges, provided excellent fishing for the keen Irish angler, and watered some of Ireland's most fertile land.

DUVILLAUN MORE (Mayo) Ref: F51

Duvillaun More is an uninhabited cliff-guarded castle on an island about 3 miles (4.8km) west of the southern tip of the Mullet Peninsula. People did once live here, and the island, accessible in calm weather, features several reasonably preserved early-Christian monuments. Many are contained within a cashel split by a cross wall. In the eastern half are the foundations of an oratory, and a long cist at the head of which is a cross pillar displaying a Greek cross inside a circle. A Crucifixion scene is also depicted. Several beehive huts can be seen elsewhere on the island.

EASKY (Sligo) Ref: D2

Iascaigh, Abounding with Fish. The abundant River Easky explains this village's Gaelic name, but today there seem to be as many surfers as fish at times, and the village has begun to attract a tourist trade. The Martello towers at each end of the village reveal that Easky was also of some importance in the defence against Napoleon. Opposite the village school is Split Rock, or Fionn MacCool's Finger. Was it formed during the Ice Age, or was it thrown here by Fionn MacCool from the Ox Mountains 14 miles (22.5km) away? Take your pick on the explanations. Almost a mile (1.6km) to the north is 15th-century Roslee Castle, once a MacDonnell stronghold. Prehistoric remains in the area include two court cairns in Fortland, half a mile (0.8km) south, and a gallery grave a further half mile (0.8km) south.

ELPHIN (Roscommon) Ref: E3

Ail Finn, the Rock of the Clear Spring. St Patrick founded the first bishopric here, but nothing remains of its buildings, or those of the Augustinian and Franciscan houses which followed. The local Church of Ireland church was a cathedral until the diocese was amalgamated with Ardagh and Kilmore. Author of *She Stoops to Conquer*, Oliver Goldsmith attended the diocesan school here when he was eight.

ENNISCRONE (Sligo) Ref: D2

Inis Crabhann, Holm of the Esker of the River. There is a 3-mile (4.8km) beach at this resort on the eastern side of Killala Bay, which also offers medicinal baths using hot seawater and seaweed. This is a popular resort for the Irish, and golfing is also available. About 2 miles (3.2km) northeast

Part of the JF Kennedy Memorial Garden in Galway's Eyre Square, frequently a venue for performances during Galway's various festivals.

The River Corrib flows through Galway from the lough that shares its name, and is particularly noted for its salmon.

is Castle Firbis, built in 1560 as a stronghold of the MacFirbis family. One of this clan compiled the 15th-century *Book of Lecan*, a treasure now preserved in the Royal Irish Academy in Dublin. Just northeast are the ruins of a 17th-century 'plantation' castle, with a chamber tomb lying between it and the shore.

FENAGH (Leitrim) Ref: E3

Fíonacha, Wooded Places. St Killian established a monastery here in the 7th century, and the ruins of two ancient churches can be seen. One features a good 14th- to 15th-century east window, carved gable brackets, and a barrel-vaulted west end which would once have included first floor living quarters. The 17th-century mausoleum to the southeast was erected by Torna Duignan, once rector of Fenagh, for his family. The second church also has a barrel-vaulted west end, and includes a corridor along the south side, an unusual feature for this type of building. The village also has a large megalithic tomb.

GALWAY (Galway) Ref: F2

Gaillimh, Stony River. The capital of Connacht, Galway is a thriving and expanding city, which has a busy fishing industry and attracts thousands of visitors with its angling, boating, bathing, and horse racing. The only remnant of the old town walls is Spanish Arch, near the quay, where the fishmarket used to be. Many houses were later built around a courtyard in the Spanish style, and the city's links with that country are also evident in Browne's Gateway (erected in 1627, transferred to Eyre Square in 1905) and Lynch Window in Market Street. Lynch's Castle in Shop Street is now a bank, but was originally a tower house with a staggered line of archery slits.

Nearby is St Nicholas of Myra Church, the oldest parts of which date from 1320, with the tower being from 1500. This is Ireland's second largest ancient parish church, and it has a rare triple nave. It is dedicated to the patron saint of sailors. Down at the river, O'Brien's Bridge is the oldest of the three in Galway, and is said to

contain stones from an earlier bridge built in 1342.

North of this is the Salmon Weir Bridge, which dates from 1818 and offers a good view of salmon and other fish as they travel upriver in season. Over it is Galway's modern Cathedral of St Nicholas and Our Lady Assumed into Heaven (1957–65), a massive limestone and Connemara marble structure, 300ft (91m) long by 158ft (48m) wide with a copper dome. When completed, it received a mixed response, and in particular there has been criticism of the mosaic of JF Kennedy in a side chapel. Also on the west side of the river are St Mary's College, erected in 1911, and University College, which is a handsome Gothic-style building founded as Queen's College in 1849.

On this side of the river, towards the sea, is Claddagh, until recently a fiercely independent and Gaelic speaking area which has now more or less been absorbed into the city. It is probably from here that the Claddagh ring derives its name.

This shows two hands clasping a heart topped by a crown, symbolizing love, friendship and respect. West of it is the resort of Salthill, with a number of typical seaside attractions.

Galway has a busy social and cultural life, with a Gaelic theatre (An Taidhbearc), a hectic race meeting week during August, and a September Oyster Festival.

Some 4 miles (4.8km) northeast is 15th-century Ballindooly Tower, and to the same distance east is a 30-ft (9-m) stump surviving from Roscam Round Tower. Near this is a 14th-century church with two strange carved stones (bullauns) in its graveyard. Ruined Menlough Castle can be seen 2 miles (3.2km) northwest of the tower near the River Corrib.

What to see Ballindooly Tower; Browne's Gateway; Cathedral of St Nicholas and Our Lady Assumed into Heaven (20c); Claddagh; Lynch's Castle (16c); Menlough Castle; O'Brien's Bridge; St Nicholas of Myra Church (14c); Salmon Weir Bridge; Spanish Arch (16c); University College.

A FAST-GROWING CITY

Galway began as a crossing point of the River Corrib, offering a gateway to the Connemara not possible further north because of the Lough. The area was held by the O'Flahertys and O'Hallorans, but was taken over by the de Burgo family after the Anglo-Norman conquest in the 13th century. They fortified the town to withstand repeated attacks from the original rulers, established a Franciscan friary (in 1296), and gradually became Gaelicized themselves (their Irish name lives on as Burke).

Galway was given city status by Richard III in 1484. This was a time of great rebuilding after a huge fire in 1473 and many handsome dwellings were erected for the ruling class,

which comprised 14 families, known as 'the Tribes of Galway'. Under their guidance, Galway expanded its continental trade, particularly with Spain, and the city prospered while remaining loyal to the English crown. This cost it very dear during the Civil War, during which Cromwell ruthlessly beseiged the city for 90 days, and destroyed 14 of its churches and their towers.

After this, the city began a long decline which has only been arrested this century – and now a resurgent Galway is one of the fastest-growing cities in Europe. The fishing village of Claddagh has earlier origins than the city that grew up alongside it, and retained its own character and sense of community.

GRANGE (Sligo) Ref: D3

An Ghráinseach. Grange lies 9 miles (14.4km) north of Sligo and once formed part of the estate of Lord Palmerston, an improving landlord from the first half of the 19th century. West of the village is a beach sheltered by Streedagh Point. Here, three ships from the Spanish Armada were wrecked with the loss of many lives. Some remains of the ancient Church of Staad can still be seen. A boat trip can be made to the island of Inishmurray with its wealth of antiquities. East are the Dartry Mountains including the 1722ft (525m) Benbulben.

HEADFORD (Galway) Ref: F2

Áth Cinn, Ford of Ceann. Headford is a neat little town whose position east of Lough Corrib makes it an excellent angling centre. On its outskirts is Headford Castle and its grounds. About a mile (1.6km) northwest, on the banks of the Black River, are the extensive ruins of the Franciscan friary of Ross Errilly. It was founded by Sir Raymond de Burgo in about 1351, but these ruins date from the 15th century. As in many similar Irish religious establishments, the friars lived within the sacred precincts until long after the Dissolution – these buildings were not abandoned until 1753. The church has a nave with aisles, a choir, a south transept, and a chapel runs parallel to it. The cloisters and their twin pointed arches are in very good condition. Also of interest are the west doorway and the east window. The tall battlemented tower reveals it was used as a fort at one time.

Two miles (3.2km) northwest of Headford are the ruins of Moyne Castle, near an ancient oval church site enclosed by a cashel. The castle's square tower has a spiral staircase connected to a covered passage extended round the walls.

What to see Headford Castle; Moyne Castle; Ross Errilly friary.

INISHBOFIN (Galway) Ref: E1

Inis BóFinne, the island of the White Cow. A pleasant and peaceful island off the Connemara coast with a small harbour and some lovely coastal scenery (including basking seals), Inishbofin is reached by boat from Cleggan. There are traces of a monastery founded by St Colman in about 660, and some remains of a Cromwellian castle. Ruins of clachans (hamlets) can be seen in the sandhills, and on the west shore of the harbour there is a clifftop fort, Doon Grannia. The southeast end of the island is guarded by the promontory fort of Doonmore.

Legend tells how the island got its name. Apparently it lay shrouded in a mist of enchantment until two fishermen chanced upon it. They saw an old woman driving a white cow along the beach, and were terrified when she hit it with a stick and was turned to rock. Thinking her a witch, they struck her, and were themselves turned into stone. A better documented tale from the island is that Cromwell chained a cleric to a rock and let his troops watch as the tide came in and drowned the poor man. The spot is known as Bishop's Rock.

KILCOLGAN (Galway) Ref: F2

Cill Cholgáin, Colga's Church. The derivation of the Irish name for this place supports local tradition that an abbey was founded here in the 6th century. More substantial are the interesting remains of the castle. Drumacoo Church lies about 2 miles (3.2km) southwest and dates from the 13th century. The southwest section of the building is part of an earlier stone church and retains its flat-headed doorway. A north wing was added in about 1830. Two miles (3.2km) southeast of Kilcolgan, at Kilbiernan, is an early monastic site with the ruins of an early church inside a large enclosure, which also has remains of houses and an underground chamber.

KILCONNELL (Galway) Ref: F3

Cill Chonaill, Conall's Church. This is considered to be one of the finest examples of 15th-century Franciscan architecture in Ireland. It was built on the site of an earlier church said to have been founded by St Conall. The church is on the south side of the cloisters, and comprises a nave with south aisle, a transept with an east chapel, and a choir. The groined roof is from a later date. There are a number of interesting tombs recalling the names and arms of influential Galway families, including two with splendid canopies. The cloister courtyard measures only 48 sq ft (4.4m²), and is enclosed by pointed arches supported by columns springing from a low wall – rather like a Spanish or Sicilian monastery. Its excellent condition suggests the friary was occupied well into the 17th century. In the village, there is a 17th-century monument, the Donnell Memorial Cross.

KILLALA (Mayo) Ref: D2

Cill Ala. Killala is a slightly run-down port town which is set among some marvellous scenery. A restored 84ft (26m) round tower is thought to be a relic from a foundation possibly begun by St Patrick in the 5th century. Under the nearby graveyard is an underground network complete with passages and a circular chamber. Killala's cathedral of 1670 includes a Gothic south door from a much earlier building.

Two miles (3.2km) along the shore of Killala Bay are the remains of Moyne Abbey, which dates from 1460 and has superb cloisters and a graceful tower. Beside the River Moy, about 2 miles (3.2km) further away, are the extensive ruins of the Franciscan Rosserk Friary, founded in 1441, with some excellent carvings in its church. The superb craftsmanship of the cloisters has also survived very well. The French invasion to assist the Irish uprising began when Killala was taken in August 1798, but the occupation was short lived.

What to see Carrickanass Castle (1 mile [1.6km] west); Castlereagh (northwest, on the River Rathfran); Killala Cathedral (17c); Moyne Abbey (15c); Rathfran Friary; Rosserk Friary (15c); Round tower.

KYLEMORE ABBEY (Galway) Ref: E2

An Choill Mhóir, The Big Wood. This is a late 19th-century granite and limestone building in the Elizabethan style. It was built by Liverpool merchant Mitchell Henry, and involved reclaiming many acres of bog. Fine gardens and a Gothic chapel are contained within its extensive grounds. It has a restaurant and souvenir shop, but is mainly devoted to its role as a girls' boarding school. It is reached via the Pass of Kylemore, one of the most beautiful places in the wild Connemara district. On the north side of the pass is 1763ft (537m) Doughruagh, and in the south is 1577ft (481m) Benbaun, the northernmost of the Twelve Bens. The road runs alongside Kylemore Lough for its 1 mile (1.6km) length, and the abbey itself is set among some splendid woods.

Kylemore Abbey was originally known as Kylemore Castle, which seems a more fitting name for this elaborate building in its spectacular setting. There is also a Gothic chapel with pillars of Connemara marble. Kylemore has been a convent since 1920, but visitors are welcome.

JOYCE'S COUNTRY

Joyce's Country is a beautiful region of mountains, pasture and lakes which stretches between Leenane in the west to Conbur in the east, and is bounded by the Maamturks to the southwest and the Partrys in the northeast. Confusingly, its name (which is unofficial) has nothing to do with famous Irish writer James Joyce. Rather, the area was colonized by the fierce, proud Joyce clan from Wales who were renowned for their stature and came to the country during the Anglo-Norman invasion of western Ireland in the 13th century. Many local people count these early settlers as their ancestors. Through its heart, Joyce's River runs parallel to the Maam Cross to Leenane road, passing a range of hills in the east rising to 1902ft (580m) in Bunnacunneen.

To the south is Maam Cross on the edge of the Connemara bogland, and scene of an annual three-day horse fair featuring the hardy little Connemara ponies, and which culminates in the big dance at the Bogman's Ball.

LEENANE (Galway) Ref: E2

An Lionan, The Shallow Seabed. This is a small angling and climbing resort in a beautiful setting on Killary Harbour, a 10-mile (16-km) stretch of the sea between steep mountains sometimes called Ireland's only fjord. To the south are the Maamturk Moutains, while east is the splendid viewpoint of 2131ft (650m) Devil's Mother with the Partry range in the background. The Westport road runs northeast to the head of the inlet, passing close to the impressive Aasleagh Falls and the River Erriff salmon fishery. It is worth the trip past Lough Fee and Lough Muck to Salrock on Little Killary Bay. Here there are good views, an ancient church and graveyard and a holy well to which some people still come in pilgrimage.

LOUGH CORRIB (Galway and Mayo) Ref: F2

Loch Coirb. A 27-mile (43-km) long lake, Lough Corrib has a prettily irregular shoreline which offers fine views northwest to the wild Connemara heights. Its shores and islands are rich in ancient remains. One small islet is almost totally covered by the remains of Hen's Castle, or Castle Kirke. This was erected in about 1200 by the sons of Rory O'Conor, the last King of Ireland. The north shores have a number of interesting caves eroded by the running water.

Game fishing is popular on Lough Corrib.

LOUGH GILL (Leitrim and Sligo) Ref: D3

Loch Gile, Lake of Brightness. Lough Gill is a wonderful small lake in a wooded setting, sheltered by hills on its north side. At the west end is Cairns Hill, with its numerous prehistoric remains. The largest island on the lake is Church Island, where there are remnants of a medieval church. Another is Innisfree, celebrated in a poem by WB Yeats. Towards the southwest end of the lake, on Cottage Island, is another old church, near the viewpoint of Dooney Rock. At the west end of the lake is a Richard Cassels' 18th-century house, Hazelwood. Northeast is the large

bawn and two round flanking towers of 17th-century Parke's Castle which has a narrow passage under a wall to let curraghs into the lake.

What to see Cairns Hill; Dooney Rock; Half Moon Bay (picnic site); Hazelwood; Innisfree; Parke's Castle (17c).

LOUGH MASK (Galway and Mayo) Ref: E2

Loch Measca. An underground river links this excellent fishing lake with the larger Lough Corrib through a series of limestone caves. On it is Inishmaine, an island with the remains of an Augustinian monastery founded by St Cormac in the 6th century.

There is a small, early 13th-century cruciform church with good carvings, while the gatehouse is probably 15th-century. The ruins of a typical Irish sweat-house are near the west shore. Inishmaine is an unspoilt island where farming is of more import than an interest in tourism. Lough Mask Castle is a late 15th-century structure altered in 1618.

LOUGHREA (Galway) Ref: F3

Baile Locha Riach, the Red Lough. Sitting on the north bank of the crannog-rich lough from which it gets its name, this was once the home of a 14th-century de Burgh Castle. The same family endowed a Carmelite priory in the 14th century, and some remains survive at the centre of the town. All that is left of the ancient walls is the south-eastern gate tower, which is now a museum with some interesting exhibits, including beautiful 16th-century gold and silver chalices. Beside it is the cathedral, completed in 1903, and featuring some excellent stained glass.

There are many underground passages in the area, and crannogs on the lough. To the east is a crowning dolmen and stone circle at Monument Hill. Four miles (6.4km) north at Bullaun is the Turoe Stone. This squat granite boulder stands 4ft (1.2m) high and has been shaped and carved to form a ritual object whose function is not understood. It is thought to be pre-Christian, and its sculpturing is in a style called La Tene – a distinct Gaelic culture with its origins in Europe 500BC. Similar stones have been found in Brittany and Germany, and there is another example at Castle Strange, Roscommon. Just over a mile (1.6km) east of Loughrea is a megalithic structure known as the Seven Monuments – seven stones set in a low circular bank near the remains of a square chamber tomb. Close by are the ringforts of Rathsonny and Rahannagroagh.

What to see Cathedral; Loughrea Museum; Monument Hill; Seven Monuments; Rahannagroagh; Rathsonny; Turoe Stone.

MANORHAMILTON (Leitrim) Ref: D3

Cluainín, Little Meadow. Charles I granted this town to Sir Frederick Hamilton, which explains the difference between its modern and ancient names. His ruined 1638 mansion is a mile (1.6km) northeast, at Skreen. The town is at the meeting point of four mountain valleys and is surrounded by some striking

YEATS COUNTRY

Lough Gill has close connections with the great Irish poet William Butler Yeats, who spent many boyhood holidays with an uncle in Sligo, and who drew upon the emotions the district inspired in many of his best poems. The tiny island of Innisfree is the subject of 'Lake Isle of Innisfree' which includes the verse:

I will rise and go now, and go
    to Innisfree,
And a small cabin build there,
    of clay and wattles made:
nine bean-rows will I have
    there, a hive for the
        honey-bee,
and live alone in the bee-loud
        glade.

Likewise his 'Fiddler of Dooney' celebrates Dooney Rock, which can be found on the south shore of Lough Gill and offers an excellent view of the lake.

Yeats was strongly influenced by the legends, mysticism and spirit of Ireland, especially in his earlier work. Later, his writings explored Irish politics and his (unreturned) love for actress, patriot and founder of Sinn Fein, Maude Gonne, but he continued to feature the Irish landscape in his work throughout his life. There is a Yeats Memorial Museum in Sligo town with much memorabilia about the man, including his 1923 Nobel Prize and many photographs.

limestone ranges. This forms a beautiful area of steep hillsides, fertile valleys and narrow ravines. The road northwest to the pretty village of Kinlough on the shore of Lough Melvin has some fine views as it rises up the Bonet valley, through a deep glen past Glenade Lough, and passes 2113ft (644m) Truskmore and 2007ft (612m) Cloghcorrach.

MULRANY (Mayo) Ref: E2

An Mhala Raithní, The Hill-brow. A picturesquely-sited resort on the isthmus between the Clew Bay and hook-shaped Bellacagher Bay, Mulrany is noted for its mild climate. This allows rhododendrons, tender fuchsias and Mediterranean heathers to flourish, and provides a lovely environment for bathing, fishing and boating. The sand dunes were dumping grounds in ancient times and have yielded a number of interesting finds. Fine views extend across the island-studded Clew Bay to the holy mountain of 2510ft (765m) Croagh Patrick. Immediately behind the village is the Nephin Beg mountain range.

NEWPORT (Mayo) Ref: E2

Baile Uí Fhiacháin, O'Feehan's Homestead. Newport is a resort and angling centre on the Newport River where tourism has become very important. The numerous drumlins around the town are of scenic as well as geological interest. The fine parish church is from this century, in the Irish-Romanesque style. The east window was by Harry Clarke in 1930. Carrighahooly or Rockfleet Castle lies 3 miles (4.8km) west on the shores of Clew Bay. It was built by the Burke family in the 16th century. Pirate queen Grace O'Malley withstood a siege here in 1574 and lived in the castle from 1583. Ruined 15th-century Burrishoole Abbey lies 2 miles (3.2km) northwest and includes remains of the domestic buildings as well as the church.

What to see Burrishoole Abbey (15c); Carrighahooly Castle; Newport church.

Also known by its older name of Mallaranney, Mulrany is a pleasant resort with a mild climate.

The Normans built Roscommon Castle in 1269, and again in 1280 after the Irish had burnt it down.

OUGHTERARD (Galway) Ref: F2

Uachtar Ard, High Upper Place. This village is an angling centre on the shores of Lough Corrib, near the approach to the wild Connemara Mountains. The little Connemara pony can be seen in the area between here and Clifden, particularly around Maam Cross, Recess and Ballynahinch. The reign of the O'Flaherty family in this area was ended by Elizabeth I, and their 16th-century stronghold can be seen 2½ miles (4km) southeast at Aughnanure. At the northwest end of Lough Corrib is Castlekirke, or Hen's Castle, so called because legend had it that it was built in one night by a witch and her hen. It has the fine remains of a keep built in the 13th century for Rory O'Conor, the last High King.

PORTUMNA (Galway) Ref: F3

Port Omna, Port of the Tree Trunk. Portumna is a traditional market town on the north shore of Lough Derg. On its south side is a Dominican priory begun in 1426 on the foundations of an earlier Cistercian structure. Next to it is Portumna Castle, a derelict mansion from the 17th century which was once the seat of the Burke family. In its grounds is a wildlife sanctuary with a herd of fallow deer and a Japanese sika. On the east shore of the lake is Terryglass, the site of a famous 6th-century monstery which can now offer only the walls of a 15th-century church. Near it is the keep of a 13th-century castle at Old Court. There are plenty of other castle ruins in this area.

What to see Dominican priory (15c); Old Court castle (13c); Portumna Castle (17c); Terryglass church (15c).

RENVYLE (Galway) Ref: E1

Rinn Mhaoile. There are many sandy beaches offering excellent bathing along the northern shore of the Renvyle peninsula and the coast to the east. Renvyle Castle dates from the 14th century, and was successively held by the Joyce, O'Flaherty and Blake families – though it resisted the pirate Grace O'Malley. Near it is a small dolmen with a 7-ft (2.1-m) capstone, a church, and a holy well. There are superb views off Renvyle Hill. Offshore can be seen Crump Island, and the larger Inishbofin (see separate entry) to the west. Inland, the tiny Tully Lough beneath 1172ft (357m) Tully Mountain is one of many very good fishing sites.

ROSCOMMON (Roscommon) Ref: E3

Ros Comáin, St Coman's Wood. This is a colourful county town which derives its name from a 6th-century monastery founded by St Coman, of which no trace remains. What can be seen, however, is Roscommon Castle, which dates from the 13th century and occupies a hillside site and was built by Robert de Ufford, the Lord Justice of Ireland. Also worth visiting is the ruined Dominican friary, founded in 1253 and rebuilt 200 years later. It features a nave, chancel and transept, an effigy of Felim O'Conor and several other interesting sculptures. The town has some lovely Georgian houses, and a plaque on its 18th-century jail (disused after 1822) commemorates 'Lady Betty', Ireland's last hangwoman. She took on the job to avoid her own execution for murder.

What to see Deerabe Abbey (in ruins, to the northeast); Dominican friary; Holywell House (northeast of the town, extensive grounds including St Brigid's Well); Roscommon Castle; Roscommon jail.

Behind Roundstone's quaint stone harbour lurk the twelve Bens of Connemara. The village relies on fishing and a little tourism.

ROUNDSTONE (Galway) Ref: F2
Cloch na Rón, the Stone of the Seals. A small resort on the west side of Bertaghboy Bay, Roundstone was built in the last century by Scottish engineer Alexander Nimmo. One of its main attractions is Dog's Bay, which, with Gorteen Bay forms a long curving shore of a sand spit joining a mile- (1.6-km) long granite island to the mainland. Both bays have sparkling white shell sand which holds many types of whole shell. Just inland, 987ft (300m) Urrisberg overlooks about 300 small lakes. On its slopes can be found the rare heather *Erica mediterrania*. In the village of Roundstone itself, a 19th-century monastery has been redeveloped as a centre for small craft industries such as ceramics. Two miles (3.2km) north on the road to Ballynahinch Lake are a few remains of a Dominican priory founded by the O'Flaherty's in the 15th century.

ST MacDARA'S ISLAND (Galway) Ref: F2
Oileán Mhic Dara, MacDara's Island. This island lies west of Carna on the Galway Coast, and can be viewed from Mweenish Island (reached on foot). On the east shore of the island is the Church of St MacDara, founded in the 6th century. It is a rectangular structure formed with massive slabs, and parts of the original stone roof are intact. St MacDara was venerated by sailors, and passing ships and fishing boats still dip their sails as a mark of respect. Close to the Galway shore of Mason Island is a ruined church, and the tower of ruined Ard Castle stands on the mainland.

SHRULE (Mayo) Ref: F2
Sruthair, Stream. The bridge spanning the Black River here links Mayo to Galway and was the scene of a treacherous ambush in 1641. Almost 100 clergymen and others were retreating from Castlebar under promise of safe conduct by Lord Mayo, when they were attacked and massacred by Edmund Burke and his men. At the northwest end of the village is a 13th-century parish church on the site of a foundation created by St Patrick. The south doorway is beautifully decorated and dates from the 15th century. Close by are the huge towers of a ruined 13th-century castle.

*B*LANKET *B*OGS

One of the best blanket bogs remaining in Ireland is near Roundstone at Errisbeg. Blanket bogs are one of the most outstanding botanical features of the country. They are formed when a thick layer of underlying peat acts as a sponge to retain water, and supports a rich bog flora. Sometimes, mosses even form a blanketing layer across open water, and islands of raised ground support species that prefer drier soils, adding a new dimension to the habitat.

The bog at Errisbeg is, by its nature, largely inaccessible, but visitors should still be able to see a wide range of bog plants and several species of heathers. The presence of Mediterranean heath illustrates the so-called 'Lusitanian' influence on wildlife in south-west Ireland, for here flowers that would be more at home in Portugal and Spain flourish in the mild, wet climate. Sadly, drainage and peat extraction are now threatening the fragile and vulnerable blanket bog habitats which support plants and birdlife.

SLIGO (Sligo) Ref: D3

Sligeach, Shelly Place. The second largest town in Connacht, Sligo is a prosperous seaport and a manufacturing and marketing centre. It grew up around a ford on the River Garavogue where an old bridge still stands. Sligo Abbey is a remnant of a 1252 Dominican friary, and among the ruins of the church is a partly reconstructed rood-screen which once separated choir from nave. Nothing remains of Maurice Fitzgerald's 1245 castle. St John the Baptist church stands on the site of Sligo's first Protestant church, and the square tower dates from this 17th-century structure. The church was rebuilt in the following century, and the Gothic style was added in 1812. The town hall was designed in the Italian Renaissance style in 1865, followed in 1878 by the Venetian Gothic courthouse. Beyond Rosses Point is Coney Island, so-called because of its numerous rabbits, and the inspiration for the naming of New York's Coney Island (which was also infested with rabbits). Near it is a gigantic statue of a seaman known as Metal Man, cast in 1819. On the east bank of the Garavogue River is 18th-century Hazelwood House, a good example of a small country mansion.

What to see Coney Island; courthouse; Hazelwood House; Municipal Art Gallery; St John the Baptist Church (17–19c); St John's Cathedral (19c, Roman Catholic); Sligo Abbey; town hall; Yeats Memorial Museum.

STRANDHILL (Sligo) Ref: D3

An Leathros, The Half-Headland. Strandhill is a well-known Sligo Bay resort with sandy beaches, golfing and fishing. On the shore northwest of the village is Killaspugrone Church, said to be where St Patrick tripped and lost a tooth. The church stands at the end of Sligo Airport airstrip, and you can view the small planes flying in over the top of Medb's Cairn.

STROKESTOWN (Roscommon) Ref: E3

Béal na mBuillí, Ford-mouth of the Strokes. This is a noteworthy planned town laid out in the 18th and 19th centuries by Maurice Mahon, later created Baron Hartland. The town's two main streets intersect at right angles, and at its eastern end a castellated wall with three arches marks the entrance to Strokestown House.

The streets of the market town of Sligo are always busy.

This is a fine Georgian mansion with some 17th-century features, and is particularly remarkable for its well-preserved kitchen and gallery. The house is well worth a visit for its evocation of past lifestyles. Once it stood in 27,000 acres (11,000ha) of grounds, but these have long gone. Nearby, the remains of a medieval church have been turned into a Mahon mausoleum.

SWINFORD (Mayo) Ref: E2

Béal Atha na Muice, Ford-mouth of the Pig. Swinford is a market town surrounded by flat countryside, known for its numerous souterrains. The Round Tower of Meelick rises 3 miles (4.8km) southwest, and has a round-headed, splayed doorway. Although ruined, it still stands 70ft (21m) high, and at its foot is an old gravestone displaying interlacing ornamentation and an Irish inscription. The tower stands on the site of an early monastery attributed to St Broccaidh.

TOBERCURRY (Sligo) Ref: E3

Tobar an Choire, Well of the Cauldron. A busy market centre built along a single long street, Tobercurry lies in an area famous for Irish music and dancing. About 5 miles (8km) west at Banada is the ruin of a 15th-century Augustinian abbey beautifully situated by the River Moy. About 6 miles (9.6km) east at Bunnanadan are the ruins of a castle and church. Southeast of here is Lough Gara, and the one remaining tower of Moygara Castle.

TUAM (Galway) Ref: F2

Tuaim, Grave-mound. Tuam is a small town which has always been an important centre for church affairs. St Jarlath founded a monastery here in the 6th century, and the ruins of Temple Jarlath date from about 1360. In the middle of the town in the market place is the 14ft (4.2m), 12th-century High Cross of Tuam. This sandstone cross was once divided among three owners, and features inscriptions in memory of O'Hoisin the abbot, who became archbishop in 1152, and Turlogh O'Conor, King of Connacht. There is a marvellous 12th-century red sandstone Romanesque chancel arch in St Mary's Cathedral, built in 1878. Also dating back to the 19th century is the Roman Catholic Cathedral of the Assumption, a cruciform building with a square tower. Tuam has an important sugar factory and racecourse. About 4½ miles (7.2km) northwest is the 16th-

century de Burgo stronghold of Castlegrove.
What to see Castlegrove; Cathedral of the Assumption (19c); High Cross (12c); St Mary's Cathedral (19c); Temple Jarlath (14c, northwest of the Catholic Cathedral).

TULSK (Roscommon) Ref: E3

Tuilsce. This village was an incorporated market town and parliamentary borough by charter of Charles II in 1674. In its large cemetery are a few remains of a 15th-century Dominican abbey, including a double-arch doorway divided in the centre by an elegant round pillar. There are some traces of the 15th-century castle of O'Conor Roe, which for many years was the strongest in the whole of Connacht.

TURLOUGH (Mayo) Ref: E2

Turlach, Dry Lake. A well-preserved round tower which is rather lower and fatter than usual can be seen here. The adjoining church was built in the 17th or 18th centuries and features a 16th-century mullioned window.

WESTPORT (Mayo) Ref: E2

Cathair na Mart, the Stone Fort of the Oxen. Westport is set amid some of the most beautiful scenery in Ireland, particularly the island-studded Clew Bay. It was a major distribution centre from about 1780, but declined when the railways and larger ports became established. Today, it is an important fishing centre and hosts an international sea-angling festival every June. In the centre of the town is a granite octagon with a limestone pillar once

topped by a statue. Two malls lined with lime trees flank the Carrowbeg River, evidence of careful town planning by James Wyatt. At the west end of the town is one of Ireland's noblest mansions, Westport House, designed by Richard Cassels in 1731 and added to by Wyatt in about 1788. The dining room is by Wyatt complementing the rest of the house's famous and beautiful interior. Westport House stands in grounds containing a zoo and shopping arcade, plus an attractive modern Church of Ireland church. Along the coast to the west is Louisburgh, a fishing village with sandy beaches. A ferry service to Clare Island runs from nearby Roonagh Quay.

There are many attractions in the grounds of Westport House.

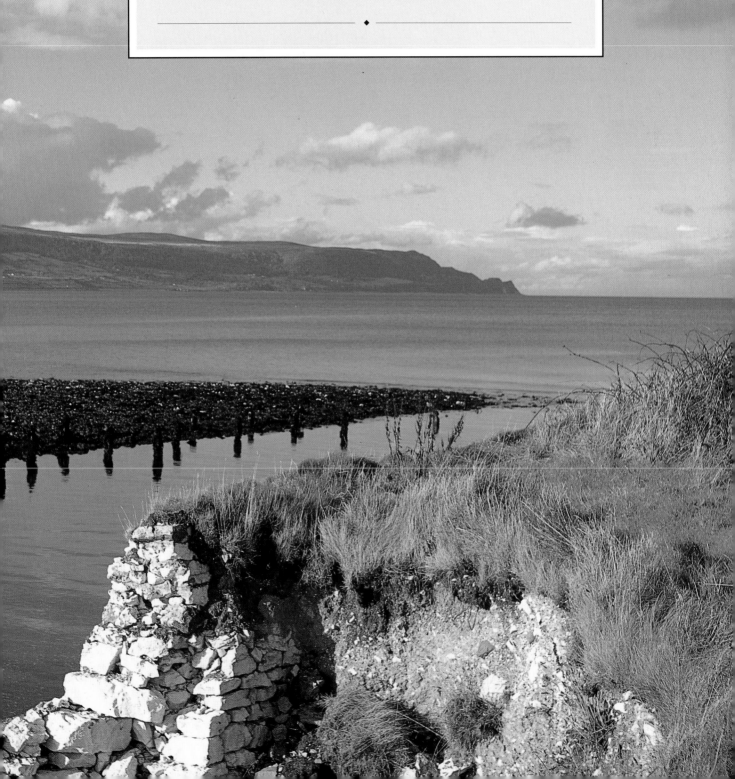

*U*LSTER

◆

From the spectacular Mourne Mountains to the golden strands of Donegal and the placid Fermanagh lakes, Ulster forms a varied landscape of hills and lakes, bogland and wind-dried grasses, which has inspired generations of poets and artists. Its north coast offers some of the most beautiful scenery in the country, and inland from its cliffs Ulster can also boast majestic mountains and exquisite valleys. Its people could be described as being as honest and stubborn as the land which many of them tend.

◆

ULSTER

U lster is the name commonly used for the six counties of Northern Ireland (created in 1921), plus a trio – Cavan, Donegal and Monaghan – now in the Republic. Occupying the northeast quarter of Ireland, Ulster was for centuries the most Gaelic (and Catholic) of lands, with a quite distinct character from the rest of Ireland from which it was so remote. It was this very independence, together with Ulster's proximity to Scotland, that led to the imposition of the 'plantation' policy (giving Presbyterian settlers land) which changed the character of the province and sowed the seeds for many of the troubles which continue to haunt it.

Much of Ulster's landscape was shaped by volcanic lava in the same way that the Inner Hebrides, Faroes and Iceland were forged. The Lough Neagh basin and the lower Bann Valley form a small lowland, where the collapse of a great mass of lava created a 50-mile (80-km) long, 35-mile (56-km) wide depression. Five counties meet in the waters of the Lough, which is fed by thirteen rivers. On the east and west side, the edges of the lava tilted to form some of Ulster's most famous landmarks: the terraced sea cliffs of Antrim; Ben Madigan (or Cavehill) which overlooks Belfast; the high crest of Binevenagh guarding the mouth of Lough Foyle; and the geometric stacks of the Giant's Causeway. Underneath the lava is chalk, and the Antrim coast features white cliffs similar to those at Dover in England. Countless lakes and rivers drain into Lough Erne in south Ulster, and this area is also famous for its abundant small hills (drumlins) formed at the end of the Ice Age, and which characterize County Monaghan in particular.

Antrim No visitor to County Antrim should miss the Antrim coast road, which provides stunning views of the rugged cliffs, amazing rock formations and concealed harbours of the Antrim coast. The fact that the route links Portrush with Belfast is irrelevant: it links glen with glen and passes wonderful spots such as the strange rocks of the Giant's Causeway, Murlough Bay, pretty villages such as Cushendun, the Glenariff Forest Park, and

Previous page: *The coastline at Glenarm.*

110

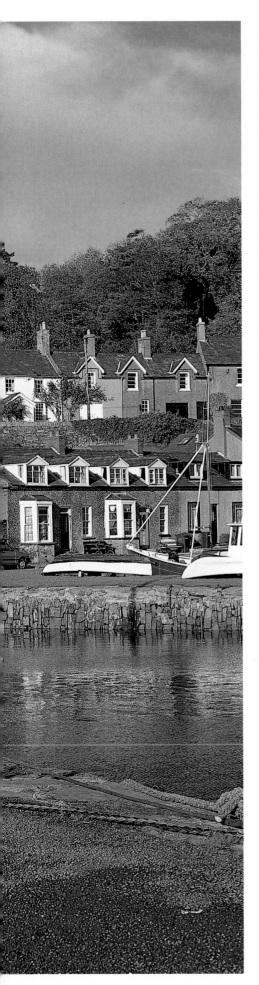

Carrickfergus with its splendid castle. Such a feast of delights leads to congestion during the summer season, and Sundays are notoriously busy on the road most of the year, but there is so much to enjoy that the journey is worth the trouble. Inland is a patchwork of fertile fields, rolling hills, and the nine beautiful valleys known as the Glens of Antrim.

Armagh Armagh is a quiet and rural county with some pleasing scenery, especially near the mysterious mountain Slieve Gullion. Mostly flat in the north, it features extensive bogs, while better drained land elsewhere is used to produce apples, potatoes and flax. Armagh has many associations with early Christianity and St Patrick. Unfortunately, few of these survive in its county town, which is the most interesting settlement in Armagh.

Cavan County Cavan is a boggy and forested region with many lakes, a landscape within which some of the more durable ancient monuments have survived. For example, near Ballyconnell is the principal pagan shrine of the Celts, Magh Sleacht, and there are pagan stone idols at various other lake sites, as well as a number of court cairn tombs. Because it was dominated by the O'Reilly family until the 17th century, when Cromwell was especially ruthless in quelling rebellion and confiscating land, there are few signs of Norman settlement in the county. The soil of Cavan is generally quite poor, and though agriculture has always been important, much of its growth in the 18th and 19th centuries was fostered by the woollen and linen industries.

Donegal Surrounded on three sides by the Atlantic, County Donegal is geologically a continuation of the Scottish Highlands, and so is mostly mountainous. Its 200-mile (320-km) coastline is deeply indented with bays, some with secluded golden beaches, and inland there are uncultivated hills, green glens and clear rivers which form one of the most beautiful regions in Ireland. What population there is in this profoundly Irish (and mainly Irish-speaking) county is scattered thinly over the farms and small villages tucked into sheltered harbours. There is a thriving cottage industry in sweaters, cloth and tweed, which can be purchased quite cheaply. Wherever you are in Donegal there is lovely scenery to enjoy, but points to head for are Slieve League, where you can see the highest cliffs in Europe, and the Donegal Highlands around Errigal mountain, Lough Beagh and Lake Gartan.

Down In the south of County Down are the 48 peaks of the Mourne Mountains,

Main picture: *The small, pretty village of Strangford in County Down.*

Inset: *Grey Abbey was founded in thanksgiving for a sea crossing.*

which glower magnificently over the beautiful Carlingford Lough in their midst. It is a marvellous setting, and contrasts totally with the fertile land and sloping hills in the North of the county, where, incidentally, the climate is the sunniest and driest in Northern Ireland. Apart from the mountains, the main attraction is the coast, best enjoyed at locations such as the Ards Peninsula, Strangford, and Newcastle.

Fermanagh Think of County Fermanagh, and lakes come to mind, for a third of the county is under water, and its greatest attraction is the Lough Erne complex. This comprises an Upper and Lower lake surrounded by wooded hills and scattered with islands, with the pair of lakes separated by the historic county town of Enniskillen. The expansive beauty, together with widely available watersports and fishing, bring many visitors to the county. Keen walkers can cross it along the Ulster Way, which is well signposted and includes some lovely stretches as it passes through Lough Navar Forest.

Londonderry Originally known as Derry, County Londonderry is a beautiful part of Ireland with some lovely beaches and impressive mountains. It has a long and much gentler coastline than that of its neighbour Donegal, and its calm waters are chiefly those of the deep bay formed by Lough Foyle. The river of the same name that feeds the lake passed through the county town, within whose 17th-century walls is much of interest. To the south of this is fertile farming land (though hindered by the wet climate of this area) which eventually rises to the Sperrin Mountains on the border with Tyrone.

Monaghan As the Ice Age came to a close, the glaciers retreated, leaving behind lumpy hills that are known as drumlins. County Monaghan is scattered with drumlins which make it look like a basket of eggs from the air, and between some of the hills are some small lakes. The county attracts plenty of fishermen, but there is more spectacular and interesting scenery elsewhere. There are some megalithic sites in the region, the most notable being Dun Dubh at Tiravera, and the triple ring fort of Tullyrain which is near Shantonagh.

Tyrone Bogs and hilly moorland form most of County Tyrone, but its northern border is formed by the massive Sperrin Mountains. These have a smooth, curved profile despite their maximum height of 2240ft (683m), and are inhabited by a range of wildlife which relishes their wild, empty spaces. There are a few tiny villages in the mountains, but this area, like most of Tyrone is very underpopulated. In the southeast of the range are the Beaghmore stone circles, and there are other prehistoric sites dotted around the county, while visitors to the county are also drawn to the Ulster American Folk Park near Omagh.

*P*LACES
of
*I*NTEREST

ANNALONG (Down) Ref: E5

Áth na Long, the Ford of the Ships. This is a busy fishing town on the coast road between Newcastle and Kilkeel, with strong stone houses set around a deep, double-walled harbour. When the fishing fleet is in it makes a picturesque sight in front of the restored stone mill. Corn is still ground in this mill, which is part of a marine park and is open to the public. Black guillemots nest in holes in Annalong's stone pier. The Mourne Mountains form an awesome backdrop to the town, and much Mourne granite is in evidence in it – there are three granite cutting yards around the harbour. For an excellent walk, begin at Annalong, follow the Annalong River past Glassdrumman to Dunny Water Bridge, and pass the cliff-encircled Blue Lough tarn on the rocky side of the Slieve Lannagan.

ANTRIM (Antrim) Ref: D5

Aontroim. Just northeast of Lough Neagh, Antrim is a busy and expanding town with a number of recent industrial complexes and housing estates. In the Steeple Estate, north of the railway station, is a well-preserved 10th-century round tower which rises to 93ft (28m). The walls are 4ft (1.2m) thick at the base. All Saints Church is a rare example in Ulster of a church which is at least in part 16th-century. It stands at one end of the High Street, while at the other end is the early-Georgian 1726 courthouse, faced by the neo-Tudor Castle Gate. The superb formal landscaped Castle Gardens it leads to probably date from the end of the 16th century, and have been called a 'mini Versailles'. Nearby is the shell of Antrim Castle, built in 1662 and burnt down in 1922.

What to see All Saints Church; Antrim Castle; Castle Gardens;

Clotworthy House (Arts Centre); Courthouse; Shane's Castle (on the Randalstown Road, has a steam railway, nature reserve and other attractions).

ANTRIM COAST ROAD (Antrim) Ref: C5

Hugging the sea from Larne to Cushendall, this road is famed for its magnificent and often startling scenic contrasts. Scottish engineer William Bald blasted through the rock in such a way as to form the foundation for the road when it was constructed in the 1830s. Its purpose was to provide a link with the Glens, and provide famine-stricken workers with employment. The marvellous views continue along the coast all the way to Portrush.

ARDGLASS (Down) Ref: E5

Ard Ghlais, the Green Height. Ardglass is built on gentle slopes running down to a small deep

Annaland is a busy fishing port which is well worth a visit.

harbour which attracted the Vikings to found the village. It was an active trading centre from the 14th century, and from then on many castles were built as storehouses. The one that has survived best is Jordan's Castle on the Low Road. It is considered an excellent example of the Down tower castle, and is thought to commemorate the Norman Jordan de Saukeville, who settled here in 1177. It now houses a museum. Isabella's Tower stands on the lovely Ardglass Downs and offers a splendid view north, over the town to the Ward of Ardtole, a hill crowned by ruined Ardtole Church.

What to see Ardglass Castle (15c); Cowd Castle (16c); Cross of Ardtole (mound of earth and stones of unknown origin near Ardtole Church); King's Castle; Isabella's Tower; Margaret's Castle.

ARMAGH (Armagh) Ref: D4

Ard Mhacha, Macha's Height, or Height of the Plain. Armagh became a centre of learning after St Patrick chose it as the site for his main church in about AD445, and it remains one of Ireland's most venerated cities. Its Gaelic name derives from Queen Macha who, with the Red Branch Knights, founded the capital of Ulster at Emain Macha, 2 miles (3.2km) west, in 300BC. Its circular streets follow the lines of long-gone earthen mounds as they wind up the central hill. The Church of Ireland St Patrick's Cathedral has its origins in 1268, but was virtually rebuilt in the Gothic style in 1834. This houses some strange and interesting carvings and other church monuments. The Roman Catholic Cathedral of the same name has distinctive twin towers and a carillon of 32 bells.

The Bank of Ireland building was originally the courthouse, built by Francis Johnston who was born here in 1760 and was the most celebrated architect of his generation. Opposite it is the Mall, where tranquil Georgian buildings and lines of oaks and limes make a wonderful setting for cricket during the summer. The Mall is one of many gifts to the city by Archbishop Robinson, who held the post for 30 years to 1795. The city also has some lovely Georgian houses and streets, and numbers collections of books, manuscripts

and paintings as well as a Planetarium among its many attractions. Near the city is a farmyard museum with pleasant walks at Ardress.
What to see Archbishop's Palace; Ardress (farmer's house and museum near Loughgall); The Argory (interesting 19-c house at Moy); County Museum; Planetarium; St Patrick's Cathedrals (13 and 19c).

AUGHER (Tyrone) Ref: D4

Eochair, Border. At the west end of this Clogher Valley village set on the River Blackwater is Augher Castle, also known as Spur Royal Castle. This three-storey structure was built in 1611 by Lord Ridgeway as a 'plantation' stronghold on the site of an earlier fortress. About 4 miles (6.4km) northeast is Errigal Keeroge, thought to have been a

St Patrick's Roman Catholic Cathedral, Armagh.

15th-century Franciscan foundation. Here can be seen the fragments of St Kiernan's Church and the 6ft (1.8m) high Errifal Keeroge Cross.

BALLINTOY (Antrim) Ref: C5

Baile an Tuaighe. This is a little village with a tiny harbour on a magnificent section of coast. Its one-time landlord was Downing Fullerton, who endowed the Cambridge College which now bears his name – and, indeed, it has oak panelling and a staircase taken from a castle on the west side of the village. To the east is a disused lime quarry, Larrybane, which gives good views of the coast and of Sheep Island, where many birds, including puffins and cormorants, stay. Further on is the famous Carrick-a-Rede rope bridge, spanning a 60ft (18m) chasm to the rock stack of the same name. The 80ft (24m) high bridge was first put up about 300 years ago and is used for fishing when it is in place between spring and autumn. It offers a hair-raising but safe crossing. West of the village is White Park Bay, with its excellent beach reached only on foot.
What to see Carrick-a-Rede; Larrybane; Portbradden (with what is claimed as Ireland's smallest church); White Park Bay.

*T*HE *L*INEN *I*NDUSTRY

Ireland is famous for its linen, which is mainly associated with the county of Armagh and the Lagan Valley area, although its production has spread to many rural parts of Ulster and Connacht. The Irish have been making linen since the Bronze Age, but the industry really began to grow after the arrival of Huguenot refugees towards

the close of the 17th century. They worked with damask cloth, which has a figured pattern and was strong enough to receive elaborations such as embroidery, crochet edging and hand painting.

Linen is made from flax, whose seeds are used to make linseed oil, while the stems are steeped in warm, stagnant

water. This separates out the long fibres, which are then dried, and spun into linen thread. The result is a material twice as strong as cotton, but with superior delicacy, making it ideal for lace making, although other uses are from tough sailcloth, canvas and sacking to delicate cambric and lawn. The process of making

linen was gradually mechanized, and small, water-powered mills began to play a part in its production, while larger mills appeared in the towns. Although it has suffered in competition with man-made fibres, linen is still recognized as a top quality material and is made by factories and small-scale cottage industries.

BALLYBOFEY (Donegal)
Ref: D3

Bealach Féich, the Homestead of Fiach's Castle. Ballybofey is a small market town connected by a many-arched bridge across the River Finn to Stranorlar. It lies in very scenic country and is noted for its game fishing. The two roads into Ballybofey offer superb views. One runs up the Finn Valley to Fintown and then along the shores of Lough Finn to Glenties. The other climbs through the Barnesmore Gap to views of the Blue Stack Mountains and Lough Eask.

BALLYCARRY (Antrim)
Ref: D5

Baile Cora, Weir Homestead. The (now ruined) first Presbyterian church built in Ireland and dating

Ballyclare hosts an annual fair which has made it famous, though it is not as big an event as the Lammas Fair at Ballycastle, held in late August.

from the 17th century stands in this small industrial town. In the graveyard is the grave of James Orr (1770–1816), a weaver and United Irishman poet, alongside the graves of other supporters of the 1798 uprising.

BALLYCASTLE (Antrim)
Ref: D2

Baile an Chaistil, the Town of the Castle. Ballycastle is a major coastal resort in the middle of a wide bay. The town divides into two distinctive parts. Old Upper Town is spacious and dignified, and includes The Diamond, where the ancient and very lively Lammas Fair is held every August Bank Holiday weekend. Lower Town has some fine buildings grouped around the harbour, including the Antrim Arms Hotel. Here also is Bonamargy Friary, founded in 1500 and restored this century. Its church features 17th-century family vaults of the Earls and Marquesses of Antrim. West of the town are the ruins of

Dunaney Castle, one of the first strongholds of the MacDonnell family. Along the coast is the spectacular Fair Head (see separate entry).

What to see Antrim Arms Hotel; Bonamargy Friary; The Diamond; Dunaney Castle; the harbour; Lammas Fair (August Bank Holiday weekend).

BALLYCLARE (Antrim)
Ref: D5

Bealach Cláir, Road of the Plain. Ballyclare stands on the Six Mile Water river and was once the centre of a thriving linen industry. Numerous forts, some incorporating natural caves, indicate extensive pre-Christian settlements around the town, which is famous today for its annual fair held at the beginning of May. The War Memorial Park has a motte without ditch or bailey, plus a 15-ft (4.5-m) high, 54-ft (16.4-m) long earthwork which may have been a sepulchral mound. About 2 miles (3.2km)

southeast is Lisnalinchy Fort, a circular structure rising 25ft (7.5m) above its surrounding ditch, and whose saucer-shaped top measures 146ft (44.5m) across.

BALLYHALBERT (Down)
Ref: D5

Baile Thalbóid, Talbot's Homestead. Here is a village with an attractive small harbour set in a rocky shoreline. About 1½ miles (2.4km) southeast is Burial Island, the easternmost point of Ireland and a place of special scientific interest. The rocks which form it date from the Silurian era and are a breeding ground for seabirds and seals. There are many small, sandy bays on the mainland to the south where soft rock has been eaten away. South of the village are the ruins of an old parish church, a tumulus, and a standing stone. To the north is The Moat, a ditch cut into the centre of a natural ridge running parallel to the sea.

BALLYJAMESDUFF (Cavan)
Ref: E4

Baile Shéamais Dhuibh, James Duff Town. This small town with its unusually wide streets takes its name from an English officer who fought in Ireland during the 1798 uprising. The market house of 1813 carries a plaque recording Wellington's victories. The town was made famous by the Percy French song 'Come Back Paddy Reilly to Ballyjamesduff'. To the northeast are the twin loughs of Nadreegeel.

BALLYMENA (Antrim)
Ref: D5

An Baile Meánach, The Middle Town. A busy town whose prosperity was founded on the linen industry, today Ballymena is a favourite among anglers attracted by the salmon and trout in the Rivers Main, Braid, Clough and the Kells Water. Three major churches were built here within 60 years last century. First came the First Presbyterian, completed in 1812 and featuring an interesting interior with pine galleries and cast iron lotus flower columns. St Patrick's Church (Church of Ireland) was built in 1855, and again in 1881 after suffering a fire. Its Gothic exterior houses two art nouveau windows and other interesting features. The Roman Catholic All Saints' Church with its square, buttressed tower was finished in 1860. Other fine 19th-century buildings can be seen in Church Street and Mill Street. Nearby in the Braid Valley is Slemish, an extinct, grass-sloped volcano said to be one of the hills where St Patrick wandered with his flock. West by 1½ miles (2.4km) is Gracehill, built by Protestants who kept the sexes apart even after death, as can be seen in the segregated graveyard.

What to see All Saints' church (19c); Bank of Ireland (19c); First Presbyterian Church (19c); Gracehill; St Patrick's Church (19c); Slemish; Town Hall (19c).

BALLYMONEY (Antrim)
Ref: C4

Baile Monaidh, the Homestead of the Moor. Ballymoney is an attractive town said to have developed from a huddle of houses around two medieval castles. One site was near Castle Street, the other was north of the modern town. A street known as Cockpit Brae includes some terraces of small Georgian houses, and is said to have taken its name from cockfighting, a sport beloved of local carters who drove stage coaches between here and Belfast. Much of the rest of the town was built in the last century, including

the 1866 red and yellow brick town hall. Ballymoney is within easy reach of the excellent fishing offered by the Rivers Bann, Ballymoney and Bush. Near the River Bush to the north is the Garry Bog, one of the largest in Ireland.

What to see Castle Street; Cockpit Brae; Garry Bog; town hall.

BALLYNAHINCH (Down)
Ref: D5

Baile na hinse, the Homestead of the Holm. This is a town of great character set among many low, rounded drumlins. It was laid out in the first half of the 17th century by the Rawdon family, who later built Montalto House. This fine mansion stands in magnificent grounds filled with shrubs, plants, trees, and red deer. The town benefitted from improving landlords, the Ker family, in the 18th century. They are responsible for the town's pleasant terraces of houses and the large shops with good façades. Two miles (3.2km) south is The Spa, two springs of chalybeate and sulphurous waters once used for their medicinal properties. On the south slopes of Cratlieve Mountain is Legananny Dolmen,

one of the most famous prehistoric sites in Ireland. Its tapering capstone is supported by two 6ft (1.8m) portal stones at the front, and a smaller stone at the rear. Southwest of the town is the earthen fort of Dunbeg.

Most of the pretty town of Ballymoney dates from the last century.

What to see Dunbeg fort; Legananny Dolmen; Montalto House; The Spa.

PLACE NAMES

As the Gaelic names listed in this book show, most placenames in the Republic are Anglicized versions of the original Irish name. The prefix 'bally' comes from the Gaelic word for home. It was first used in a domestic, rather than administrative sense, and generally refers to smaller places. Other common prefixes and their meanings are: ard (height); ath (a ford); carrick (rock); dram or drum (height or hillock); dun (fort); inis – which became Ennis – or inch (island); knock (hill); rath (an earth-banked ring fort); and slieve (mountain).

Other names are physical descriptions, for example Carlow means 'a fourfold lake',

Cork 'a marshy place', Dublin means 'black pool', Limerick means 'bare spot', Sligo 'a shelly river', and Youghal 'a yew wood'. Some names derive from individuals or groups. For instance, Donegal means 'a fort of foreigners', Kilkenny 'church of (St) Canice', and Slievenamon 'mountain of the women'.

The Norse influence is also evident in some names, for example Waterford was Vatnfjordhr, and Wexford Waesfjord (both meaning 'sea-washed town'). However, not all names ending in ford are of Norse origin – Longford, for example, is derived from the Gaelic word for fortress, Longphort.

BALLYSHANNON (Donegal) Ref: D3

Béal Átha Seanaidh, the Ford-mouth of the Hillside. This is a busy town sitting on a hill overlooking the River Earne, which feeds a 900-acre (364-ha) lake reservoir and a large hydroelectric power station at Cathleen's Fall. In its estuary is the islet of Inis Saimer, said to be where Partholan landed from Scythia in about 1500BC and began the colonization of Ireland. Just north of the market place is the 1423 O'Donnell castle where 80 men held out for three days against an army of 5000 in 1597. Northwest by almost a mile (1.6m) is the ruined 12th-century Cistercian Abbey of Assaroe and St Patrick's Well. Further north on the coast by about 3 miles (4.8km) the ruins of Kilbarron Castle mark a one-time fortress of the O'Clery family – one of whom, Michael, was among the authors of a history of Ireland and its major families up to his own times in the 17th century.

BALLYWALTER (Down) Ref: D5

Baile Bháltair, Walter's Homestead. A pleasant village grouped around a wide main street and a small harbour, Ballywalter hosts a music festival in May and another festival in June. Somewhat in contrast, power boat races are held in the off-shore waters during the summer. Close by is Ballywalter Park, which stands around a mansion begun in 1846 by Sir Charles Lanyon. Near the Church of Ireland Holy Trinity Church are the remains of Templefinn – the White Church. These include some Anglo Norman grave slabs attached to the north end of the east gable. A mile (1.6km) northwest is Dunover Motte, a 36ft (11m) high mound considered a good example of a minor Anglo-Norman castle without a bailey.

BANBRIDGE (Down) Ref: D5

Droichead na Banna. Banbridge was once an important linen centre, and is famous for its main street: the central part of this wide road is at a lower level than its two sides, which are connected by a bridge, so creating an underpass. In Church Square is Crozier House, 18th-century home of Captain Francis Crozier, who was a deputy to Sir John Franklin during his voyage in search of the Arctic North West.

Bangor's seafront is more than 4 miles (6.4km) long.

Passage. The Unitarian Church was Presbyterian when it was built in 1846 and is considered to be one of the last and best of the classical Presbyterian structures in Ulster. Its interior is equally well worth seeing. The River Bann, together with Corbet Lake (3 miles [4.8km] east) and Lough Brickland (3 miles [4.8km] southwest) offer excellent coarse and game fishing.

BANGOR (Down) Ref: D5
Beannchar. This is a very popular and large seaside resort with a front extending more than 4 miles (6.4km) round the bays of Smelt Mill, Bangor and Ballyholme. Part of its attraction is the way it has grown on steeply rising ground over the waters and quays of its bay. Its expansion dates from the age of rail and the steamship, as shown by its many Victorian and Edwardian villas and its excellent Victorian parks. One of these, Ward park, has two large ponds supporting a range of wildfowl and with a resident flock of barnacle geese.

Bangor was an international centre of learning and home to 3000 monks when St Comgall founded a monastery here in the 6th century. An imaginary reconstruction of it can be seen in the Heritage Centre, housed in the old laundry of Bangor Castle. The rest of the building is now Council offices. Nearby is Bangor Abbey parish church, built around a 15th-century tower in 1616. The imposing Custom tower opposite the harbour is only 21 years younger than the church.

What to see Abbey Church; Ballymacormick Point; Bangor Castle (with Heritage Centre); Custom Tower House; Pickie Pool and Marine Gardens.

BEAGHMORE (Tyrone) Ref: D4
Turf cutters discovered this set of prehistoric monuments in the middle of this century, and the peat they were extracting has preserved its collection of stone circles and cairns remarkably well. Lying northwest of Cookstown, the site covers 1½ acres (0.6ha). It has three pairs of stone circles, and a single circle, all with associated stone rows. There are also a number of cairns. These five monuments have been dated to the Early Bronze Age, but the finding of a stone axe suggests that neolithic people may have used the site before then.

BELFAST Ref: D5
Bealfeirste, Mouth of the Sandy Ford. The capital of Northern Ireland, Belfast is a largely Victorian city with a wealth of interesting sites, good shopping, and a friendly population. At its centre stands City Hall, a late Victorian structure of Portland stone into which architect Sir Brumwell Thomson incorporated many features of London buildings – it even has a whispering gallery like St Paul's Cathedral. There are regular guided tours of it taking in the palatial marble entrance hall, robing room, and the council chamber.

Behind City Hall is the 18th-century Linenhall Library, which

Belfast City Hall by night.

houses a massive collection of early Belfast printed books and a 40,000-strong 'Political Collection' covering relevant publications since 1968. The main shopping area including the pedestrianized Cornmarket is to the northeast of the library, and if you venture there have a look at the series of alleys (or 'Entries') between High Street and Ann Street, where some of the city's best bars can be found.

Meanwhile, back in Donegall Square, to one side down Chichester Street are a few early 19th-century houses, and the Law Courts. In the other direction is the Royal Belfast Academic Institution, locally known simply as 'Inst', dating from 1814. Close by is Christ Church, which has some delicate cast-iron columns inside, along with a three-decker pulpit in pitch pine, erected in 1878.

On the other side of Grosvenor Road is the Grand Opera House, which opened in 1895. It boasts an exotic and lavishly decorated interior which draws on images of the Orient and was restored in 1980. Across Great Victoria Street (also known as 'The Golden Mile') is the extraordinary Crown Liquor Saloon. This is a fine gin palace, owned by the National Trust but still serving drinks in a highly decorated room with a long, elaborate bar on one side and a row of wooden snugs on the other – note the mounted gun-metal plates which are for striking matches on.

Moving south along the Golden Mile takes the visitor to the University Quarter. This area around the superb Queens University building (1845) in Georgian University Square has been called a 'perfect Victorian suburb', and its churches and terraced houses are bursting with little details. Next to the mock-Tudor Union Theological College are the Botanic Gardens. These were opened in 1829 and offer well sheltered walks, with the highlight being the Palm House, one of the earliest curvilinear glass and iron structures in the world, and resplendent with exotic plants.

Still in the Botanic Gardens is the Ulster Museum, a huge collection with exhibits covering everything from dinosaurs to modern transport (with vehicles shared with the Ulster Folk and Transport Museum, see separate entry). Notable among the innumerable displays is the treasure reclaimed from the *Girona*, a galleon of the Spanish Armada which sank off the Giant's Causeway.

Heading back towards the city, Saint Malachy's church (1848) in Alfred Street has an unusual exterior with many turrets and battlements, and inside, the most sumptuous church interior in Belfast. In the centre of the city are a number of other interesting churches. St George's Church in High Street stands on a site once occupied by the ancient Chapel-of-the-Ford-of-Belfast. The present structure dates from 1819 and is considered a fine example of Georgian stonework. Its portico of Corinthian columns was transferred from the front of a palace being built at Ballyscullion by the eccentric Frederick Hervey, Bishop of Derry.

Nearby, in Rosemary Street, is the Old Presbyterian Church, completed in 1783. This has an overall elliptical shape, and the oval pattern is repeated in the box pews and the gallery. When John Wesley preached here in 1789 he pronounced it 'the completest place of worship I have ever seen'. A little to the north, in Donegall Street, is Saint Anne's Cathedral, a simple neo-Romanesque basilica begun in 1899. There are some fine mosaics by Gertrude Stein in its baptistry. A detour further north up Donegall Street until it becomes Clifton Street is worthwhile to enjoy Clifton House, or the Old Charitable Institute. This is a marvellous Georgian house which functioned

Belfast's Palm House predates the hothouse at Kew, London.

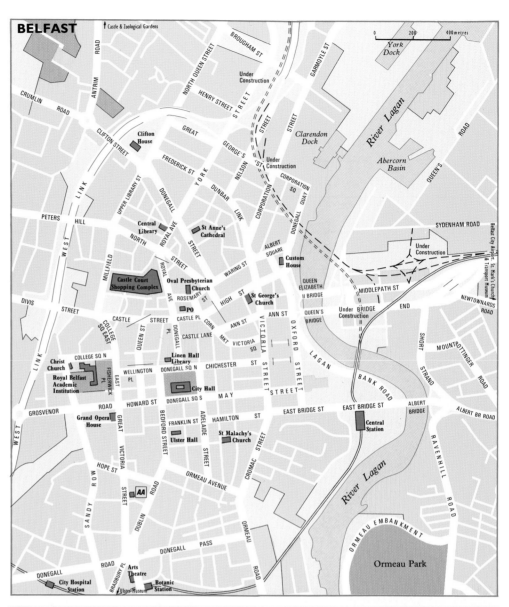

118

as a Poor House and was designed by an amateur architect, paper merchant Robert Joy. It features a pedimented brick façade with an octagonal-based stone spire, and the wings were added in 1821 and 1829, about 50 years from the date of construction.

Towards the river, Corporation Square is home to the Sinclair Seaman's church, which has an unmistakably maritime atmosphere. The presence of such a church is evidence of the importance of the sea to Belfast, and outside there is a good view of the Harland & Wolff shipyard. Rising up to the sky are Goliath and Sampson, the world's second and third largest cranes, and by them is its largest dry dock. Countless ships have been built here, including the *Titanic*.

The Crown Liquor Saloon is owned by the National Trust, but it still serves a fine drink.

Stormont Castle, 4 miles (6.4km) outside Belfast, was the seat of the Northern Ireland parliament until 1974.

Staying on the west side of the river and moving down to Albert Square, there stands the Albert Memorial Clock Tower, built between 1867 and 1869. This is tipped a little to one side, for its foundations are in the estuarine clay. Close by is the 1857 Custom House, a Corinthian-style structure of mainly golden stone which has been called Belfast's finest public building. It was designed by Sir Charles Lanyon in the 'Italian style after Palladio'. Another of this architect's designs is the Belfast Banking Company building in Waring Street, where he transformed the 18th-century Assembly Rooms into a Renaissance-revival style structure.

A visitor to Belfast should also try to see some of the attractions that ring the city on its outskirts. Among the hills to the north is Cave Hill, whose profile is known as Napoleon's Nose. From its heights, the whole of Belfast and its lough are laid out. This site was once dotted with Iron Age forts, and was mined for flint to be used in tools and weapons. The 1182ft (360m) hill is named after its five caves, and at its top is the earthwork of MacArt's Fort. On the lower slopes is Belfast Castle, built in about 1870 although the striking Italianate stairway was added in 1894. Also close by is Belfast zoo.

Five miles (8km) to the east of the city centre are the Parliament Buildings at Stormont, the administrative centre of the province, set in 300 acres (120ha) of gardens. To the south by a few miles is the Giant's Ring, a massive ceremonial burial ground with a huge dolmen at its centre, set within a 20-ft (6-m) high earthen rim. During the 18th century, the circuit formed by the site was used as a horse racing track.

What to see Albert Memorial Clock Tower (Victoria Street); Christ Church (18c, Church of Ireland, College Square); City Hall (20c, Donegall Square); Clifton House or Old Charitable Institute (18c, North Queen Street); Custom House (19c, High Street); Linenhall Library (Donegall Square North); Old Museum (19c, College Square North); Old Presbyterian Oval Church (18c, Rosemary Street); Royal Belfast Academic Institution (College Square North); St Anne's Cathedral (20c, Church of Ireland, Donegall Street); St George's Church (19c, Church of Ireland, High Street); St Malachy's Church (19c, Roman Catholic, Alfred Street); St Patrick's Church (Roman Catholic, Donegall Street).

A CITY GROWN FROM CLOTH AND SHIPS

Belfast was a settlement of little consequence until the 17th century. It began life as a group of forts along the River Farset, which today runs under the High Street. A Norman castle built in 1177 only wrested control of the area from the O'Neills for a century or so. In 1604, James I 'planted' Sir Arthur Chichester in the area but it was the arrival of French Huguenots later in that century that boosted the local linen industry and fostered major development. Belfast had a liberal reputation and indeed the 1798 rebellion had its origins here, although it was more successful in the south.

By the 19th century, Belfast was firmly Presbyterian and much less tolerant, and in 1888 was granted city status by Queen Victoria. Shipbuilding and textiles were by now long established in Belfast, and this was a time of massive expansion and development – most of the major public buildings in the city date from the Victorian era. In this century, most of the decaying Victorian housing has been replaced, some of the demolition work being done by bombs dropped during World War II. More recently, the city has been the focus for much of the country's troubled history – a look at the number of P for parking signs on the map is a reminder that today no vehicle can be left unattended on the streets for fear of car bombings. That said, Belfast remains a hard-working and friendly city which is fighting for its own revitalization after the decline of the industries which founded it.

BELLEEK (Fermanagh) Ref: D3
Béal Leice, the Ford-mouth of the Flagstone. The most westerly village in Northern Ireland, Belleek rests on the pretty far tip of Lower Lough Erne. The River Erne has been deepened by rock extraction, and giant sluice gates have been fitted to regulate the flow of water and prevent flooding. Belleek is known throughout the world for its pottery. Its creamy lustre porcelain is made from felspar, a mineral once mined locally and now imported from Norway. Visitors can tour the pottery where the china is made in an 1858 three-storey factory. A road running along the south side of Lough Erne and near the edge of a limestone plateau is dominated by the sheer cliff of Magho rising in front of the Lough Navar forest park.

BENBURB (Tyrone) Ref: D4
An Bhinn Bhorb, The Rough Peak. High above the Blackwater River near this village stands O'Neill's Castle, a 'plantation' castle dating from about 1615. Once the home of the Longfield family, it consists of a large enclosure, and two rectangular corner towers. On the cliff edge to the southeast is a small circular tower. The site on which this structure stands was once occupied by an ancient O'Neill stronghold. A modern mansion in the grounds of the castle was opened in 1949 as the Priory of Our Lady of Benburb by the Servite Order. The Protestant church dates from 1618 but has some medieval stonework.

BUNCRANA (Donegal) Ref: C4
Bun Cranncha, Mouth of the River Crannach. Buncrana is sheltered on three sides by hills in its cosy spot on the east shores of Lough Swilly – also known as the Lough of Shadows – and is a popular resort. Near Castle Bridge is O'Doherty's keep, the 14th–15th-century tower of a castle built for the family who were Lords of Inishowen. The structure was rebuilt in the 17th century. Beyond the bridge is the decaying Buncrana Castle, a handsome building when it went up in 1716. To the south, is the 3-mile (4.8-km) Lisfannon Strand, and to the northwest the road to the lighthouse at Dunree Head offers lovely views over the lough. There are a number of megalithic monuments within a 3-mile

This is the home of famous Belleek pottery, an imposing 1858 factory.

(4.8-km) radius of Buncrana, including a Bronze Age burial cairn a mile (1.6km) north at Crockcashel and two pairs of pillar stones a mile (1.6km) southeast.

BUNDORAN (Donegal)
Ref: D3
Bun Dobhráin, Mouth of the River Dobhrán. A 300yd (275m) beach with promenade, good fishing, an excellent golf course, and its superb location on the shores of Donegal Bay have made Bundoran a successful resort. Erosion has caused some strange rock formations along the cliffs beyond Aughrus Head, including the 24ft (7m) natural arch Fairy Bridge, and the Puffing Hole, which ejects water impressively,

especially during rough weather. The cliffs to the west also feature the Lion's Paw Cave fissures and other odd rock shapes. To the north is the 1½ mile (2.4km) Tullan Strand, which continues as far as the mouth of the River Erne. Between it and Fairy Bridge are the ruins of 15th-century Finner Church, while there is a chambered cairn on Finner Hill.

BUSHMILLS (Antrim)
Ref: C4
Muileann na Buaise, the Mill of the River Bush. Bushmills is a small and prosperous town noted for its game fishing and distillery, which can be toured (see page 19). Bushmills stands on the River Bush southwest of the famous huge, geometric basalt columns of

the Giant's Causeway. A pair of the mills which gave the town its name stand on the River Bush, which is full of trout and salmon. This water once provided the power for flour, paper and spade mills, and for the world's first hydroelectric tramway (running to Portrush) between 1883 and 1949. About 2½ miles (4.2km) west of the town is ruined Dunluce Castle, a formidable structure built in about 1300 by Richard de Burgh, earl of Ulster. The castle is separated from the mainland by a deep, 20ft (6m) wide chasm. It has five circular towers and a strong curtain wall. A platform on the inside of the wall allowed archers to fire through openings in the battlements.

CALEDON (Tyrone)
Ref: D4
Cionn Aird, High Head. This historic village on the Blackwater takes its name from the Earls of Caledon. It has one of the finest Georgian mansions in the country, Caledon House, built by Thomas Cooley in 1779, with the colonnade and domed pavilions added by John Nash in 1812. A feature of the park is Bone House, which has pillars and arches faced with ox bones and is the only survivor of Ireland's earliest rococo gardens.

Founded in 1608, Old Bushmills Distillery is the oldest (licit) distillery in the world. The free tour (recommended) takes in extensive views of casks.

CARRICKFERGUS (Antrim) Ref: D5

Carraig Fhearghais, Fergus' Rock. Once an important port, Carrickfergus is today part seaside resort and part industrial centre, but its real claim to fame is its magnificent castle, which may have been the first true castle to have been built in the country. The Norman John de Courcy built it sometime after 1180 on a rocky peninsula enclosed by curtain walls. It was altered in Elizabethan times to accommodate artillery, and now houses a museum. Off Market Square is the Church of St Nicholas, which dates from the 12th century but was rebuilt in 1614. There is a leper's window in the chancel, and one stained glass represents St Nicholas as Santa Claus. A medieval fair is held in the town in early August every year.

> **What to see** Carrickfergus Castle; Church of St Nicholas (12c and 17c); medieval fair (early August); North Gate; Town Hall (incorporates County Court House frontage of 1779); town wall remains.

CARRICKMACROSS (Monaghan) Ref: E4

Carraig Mhachaire Rois, the Rock of the Plain of Ross. This is a handsome Georgian town with spacious streets and traditional shop fronts and is famous for its lace, some of which is still produced. In the grounds of St Loius Convent are a few remains of a castle built by the Earl of Essex, to whom Elizabeth I granted the town. In the Roman Catholic church are some interesting stations of the cross. To the southwest and standing among picturesque oaks and beeches is Lough Fea House close by the lake itself, while about $1\frac{1}{2}$ miles (2.4km) west are the interesting limestone caverns of Tiragarvan. Northeast by 7 miles (11.2km) is Inishkeen, where in the 6th century St Deagh founded a monastery. Sadly all that remains now is a round tower. A mile (1.6km) away is Channon Rock, which was once a boundary mark for the Pale.

> **What to see** Channon Rock; Inishkeen; Lough Fea House; Tiragarvan.

CARRIGART (Donegal) Ref: C3

Carrigart is the gateway to the Rosguill Peninsula, and is situated where a winding road passes an inlet of Mulroy Bay. The town has a fine beach and superb golfing facilities. It can also boast several sandhill prehistoric buildings, which have yielded a number of

interesting finds. Mulroy Bay has many wooded ridges and its high ground offers superb views of the many tiny wooded islands and the indented shoreline. A circuit of the Rosguill Peninsula, taking in the golf links and Tranrossan Bay, also provides lovely views, and is known as the Atlantic Drive. There is an early Christian cross at Meevagh church.

CASTLEROCK (Londonderry) Ref: C4

This is a peaceful resort with a long sandy beach on Londonderry's north-east coast west of the mouth of the River Bann. A mile south is Hezlet House, a low thatched cottage made in 1690 using wood frames bought in by settlers, filled in with clay and rubble. To the west are the remnants of a great demesne

Left: *The streets of Carrickfergus host a fair in early August.*

planted by Frederick Hervey, Bishop of Derry and 4th Earl of Bristol. Among the interesting features is the domed rotunda Musenden Temple, built as a library on a site perilously close to the cliff edge. This Anglican bishop allowed a Catholic mass to be said here as there was no other suitable venue. There are marvellous views down to the 6-mile (9.6km) strand of Magilligan from Gortmore on the Bishop's Road.

CASTLEWELLAN (Down) Ref: E5
Caisleán Uidhilín, Uidhilin's Castle. This is a charming village surrounded by wooded countryside and featuring broad, tree-lined streets and squares which were laid out from 1750 onwards by the Annesley family. William Annesley built the market house in the 18th century, and its main block comprises five bays

and two storeys. Access is by four arched openings, and the tower is a later addition. The family built a Scottish Baronial-style castle in the 1850s and founded an interesting arboretum. This has a wide range of chamaecyparis and abies and many other southern hemisphere species, and now forms part of the national forest park. At the east end of nearby Lough Island Reavey, are Dromena cashel and underground passage.

CAVAN (Cavan) Ref: E4
An Cabhán, The Hollow. Cavan lies in a pleasant district of low-lying hills and numerous lakes. These offer good game and coarse fishing, while there is also a golf course near the town. The interior of the 1942 Roman Catholic cathedral is worth seeing, especially for its

Part of the lovely grounds of Castlewellan Castle.

STONES WITH MESSAGES FROM THE PAST

Finn MacCool's Fingers, the line of standing stones on Shantemon Hill near Cavan, seems to have had a ritual significance, but what this was is not known. There are many standing stones, or gallans, in Ireland, and their purpose seems to have varied. Size varies, too, from a barely-discernible 3ft (90cms) to a towering 20ft (6m). Some record notable events, others mark boundaries. The great stone of Turoe is probably a fertility symbol, while a tall stone at Punchestown in Kildare marks the site of a grave, and where stones are placed at known religious sites their purpose seems clearer.

However, the Christian carvings on some of the stones at other sites could have been added long after the monument was erected, possibly for a quite un-Christian purpose.

Early stones feature Ogham writing, in which groups of up to five lines are used instead of letters. This may have been a code, or a sign language, but where they have been translated into our alphabet the meanings are still obscure, often giving the name of a person followed by that of an ancestor. A good example can be seen at Ballycrovane in the Beran peninsula, Cork. Other stones in the southwest also feature Ogham writing.

sculptures. Off Bridge Street is Abbey Street, where the belfry tower of a Franciscan friary founded by Giolla Iosa Rua O'Reilly stands. On its wall is a plaque commemorating Owen Roe O'Neill, who defeated Monro in the Battle of Benburgh in 1646. O'Neill later died in Cloughoughter Castle, which now stands in ruins to the west on an islet in Lough Oughter. The O'Reilly's ancient inauguration place was Shantemon Hill, 3 miles (4.8km) northeast, where the prehistoric standing stones called Finn MacCool's Fingers stand. Three miles (4.8km) northwest of Cavan is Farnham House and its 3000 acres (1200ha) of woodland. The house was built in 1700, and enlarged in 1801.
    What to see Belfry tower; Cavan Cathedral (20c); Cloughoughter Castle (part 13c); Farnham House; Shantemon Hill.

CLOGHER (Tyrone) Ref: D4
Clochar, Stony Place. Clogher sits in the heart of the Clogher Valley, which used to have a railway running along it – the red brick stations are still visible. The village itself was once a cathedral town and had a bishop's palace. The Church of Ireland cathedral (built early in the 18th century, reconstructed in 1818) stands on the site of an ancient monastery, whose sole remains are two 9th or 10th century high crosses. Also

of interest is Park House, sometimes called the Old Palace, dating from c.1800. About 2½ miles (4km) away is the Daisy Hill demesne, which boasts one of the two stone 'chairs' found on Ashban Mountain, and the Findermore Abbey Stone, a cross-incized pillar. To the southwest, is Fardross Forest, which has plenty of wildlife and a bathing pool among its attractions.

COOKSTOWN (Tyrone) Ref: D4
An Chorr Chríochach, the Boundary Hill. Cookstown boasts what is thought to be the longest main street in Ireland, and was laid out and built by an early 17th-century Protestant settler (a 'planter') named Alan Cook. An important family in the history of the town were the Stewarts, who lived in the fine mansion of Killymoon to the north, on the south-east bank of the Ballinderry River. This was designed by John Nash in 1803, and he also built Lissan Rectory, an Italianate villa some 2 miles (3.2km) northeast. An 18th-century water-powered beetling mill can be seen 3 miles (4.8km) west at Wellbrook. Situated as it is on the Dungannon to Maghera road, west of Lough Neagh, Cookstown makes a good base from which to explore the Sperrin Mountains, a range which is very rich in megalithic remains.
    What to see Beetling mill; Lissan Rectory; Sperrin Mountains.

COOLEY (Donegal) Ref: C4

Cuaille. The graveyard at Cooley is well known for its extensive archaeological remains. These include an ancient ruined church, and an unusual slender stone cross, which stands 10ft (3m) high just outside the entrance. There is also a small building known as Skull House, which is a curious form of tomb associated with one of Ireland's many saints. Also of interest in the area are a number of underground passages and a sweat house at Leckeny. Many ringforts, standing stones and megalithic tomb remains can be seen in this area.

COOTEHILL (Cavan) Ref: E4

Muinchille, Sleeve. This prosperous town was founded by the Coote family after they gained possession of confiscated O'Reilly lands in the 17th century. Some of the land acquired north of the town was known as Bellamont Forest, and the house of Bellamont is considered one of the finest Palladian structures in Ireland. It stands in extensive lake-watered and wooded grounds. Dating from 1730, Bellamont House has suffered very little change in its history. The area surrounding Cootehill is dotted with prehistoric remains, one of the most notable being the Cohaw dual-court grave. The cairn of this monument is 85ft (26m) long, with forecourts leading to two pairs of chambers, in which the remains of two young people were found during excavations.

CRAIGAVON (Armagh) Ref: D5

This was the first New Town to be created in Northern Ireland, and is named after Viscount Craigavon, the first prime minister. It is set in wooded countryside and offers a wide range of leisure facilities, including water sports and an artificial ski-slope. It has many public parks including the Lord Lurgan Memorial Park, where the grave of famous greyhound Master McGrath can be seen.

East of the city – which includes the earlier towns of Lurgan and Portadown – is Loughgall, an apple-growing area which has earned Armagh the title 'the orchard county of Ireland'. Also east are two picturesque villages. Moira has a lovely 18th-century church and handsome houses along its wide main street, while Waringstown features some fine 'plantation' buildings and a 17th-century church. It also has Waringstown House, whose assured classical appearance belies its construction in clay and rubble in the 17th century.

CRAWFORDSBURN (Down) Ref: D5

Sruth Chrafard, Crawford's Stream. This village is sited 1 mile (1.6km) from the sea at the head of the glen from which it takes its name, and is considered by many to be one of the most attractive villages close to Belfast. Its little thatched inn dates from 1614 when it was built as a staging post. North of the village is Crawfordsburn Country Park,

which has attractive bays and beaches as well as woods and parkland, and is a major tourist site. There is a 10-mile (16-km) coastal footpath bordering the southern side of Belfast Lough, which passes Holywood, Cultra, Helen's Bay and Crawfordsburn on its way to Bangor.

CREESLOUGH (Donegal) Ref: C3

An Craoslach, The Gullet. Standing on high ground overlooking an inlet of Sheep Haven, Creeslough is a good base from which to climb 2197ft (670m) Muckish Mountain to the west. Favourite stopping places for tourists are the Duntally Bridge and waterfall, and the mountain-shadowed Glen Lough, which is 4 miles (6.4km) away. Two miles (3.2km) from the village, along a landstrip running into the sea, is Doe Castle. Once the chief stronghold of the MacSwyney family, it dates from the 15th century but has been extensively modernized. The sea protects it on three sides, and an artificial ditch covers the fourth, while the 55ft (16m) high keep is rounded by a bawn protected by a high curtain wall carrying round towers. A graveyard adjoining the castle on a Franciscan monastic site contains a tombstone to the memory of the MacSwyneys. Nearby, Ards House sits on a superbly-wooded peninsula and is occupied by the Capuchin order.

On scenic Red Bay, Cushendall is an ideal base for exploring the Glens of Antrim.

CROSSMAGLEN (Armagh) Ref: E4

Crois Mhic Lionnáin, MacLionnáin's Cross. Crossmaglen is a border town with a huge market square which was once a venue for fairs that became notorious for attracting undesirables. It is surrounded by many small lakes which, together with the River Fane, offer excellent boating and fishing. About a mile (1.6km) south at Lissaraw is a fine ringfort with an open souterrain, and a similar complex can be seen 2 miles (3.2km) northwest at Corliss. Annaghmare, 1½ miles (2.4km) north of Crossmaglen, has a well-preserved prehistoric grave with a horseshoe-shaped court from which leads a 23ft (7m) gallery divided into three chambers. The monument features some fine drystone walling in the court. Further north is Lisleitrim Trivallate Rath, which has an underground passage, while there is a crannog at nearby Lisleitrim Lake.

CULDAFF (Donegal) Ref: C4

Cúil Dabhcha. Culdaff is a secluded village offering safe sea-bathing and some very good fishing both in the Culdaff River and in its coastal waters. The cliffs rise to 800ft (244m) and there is plenty of pleasing scenery around the village. On the way to Carrowmore is Clonca where there is a ruined church with a beautifully carved sepulchral slab bearing an Irish inscription. This translates as: 'Fergus MacAllen made this stone; Magnus MacOrriston of the Isles lies under this mound'. Carrowmore itself is the site of an ancient monastery and has a group of stone crosses. Close to Culdaff, at Bocan, is a church containing St Buadan's Bell, which dates from the 9th or 10th century. Close to Bocan church, Black Hill rises, surmounted by a horned cairn known as the Temple of Deen.

CUSHENDALL (Antrim) Ref: C5

Bun Abhann Dalla, Mouth of the River Dall. This is a delightful and unspoilt village on a spectacular stretch of coastline. Four pleasant streets of late-Georgian and Regency houses meet at the Curfew, on Turnley's Tower, built by the landlord Francis Turnley in 1809 as a place of confinement for idiots and idlers. When the Red Bay tunnel was being built last century the removed sandstone was used to construct the courthouse. The tunnel itself is entered 1½ miles (2.4km) south

How Towns were Shaped

Most of Ulster's towns bear the stamp of 17th- or 18th-century market communities, being laid out around a broad street, or diamond, which served as a market place. Crossmaglen's large market square is a particularly ambitious example of this type of development. In such towns, as a general rule, at least three denominations would each have a church, with the Episcopalian building being put in a fairly central position in the market place or high street. Nonconformist meeting houses and Roman Catholic chapels were generally placed some distance away on roads leading to the centre, and it has been suggested that this arrangement prevented the devil from entering the town.

The most important secular buildings in the town would be the court and market houses (which were united under one roof in smaller settlements). Usually erected between 1750 and 1850, these buildings have an austere, neo-classical dignity, and can be found throughout urban Ulster. Perhaps the most outstanding are Francis Johnson's graceful structure of 1809 in Armagh, and the charming, much later court house at Hillsborough, Down.

from the Coast Road. Cushendall's location at the head of a trio of the nine Glens of Antrim makes it an excellent base for exploring these beautiful valleys. On the cliffs north of Red Bay are the remains of a 16th-century O'Donnell fortress; and two miles (3.2km) northwest of the village is Ossian's Grave, which dates from the neolothic era. On the minor coast road leading to the village is the ruined 13th-century church of Layd. It was used until 1790, and is the resting place for many of the MacDonnells.

What to see Layd Church; Ossian's Grave; Red Bay; Turnley's Tower.

CUSHENDUN (Antrim) Ref: C5

Bun Abhann Duinne, Mouth of the River Dunn. This is a very pretty village at the foot of Glendun, one of the nine glens of Antrim. In its middle are some whitewashed and slated cottages

with the look of Cornwall about them. Lord Cushendun (Robert MacNeill) had them built in memory of his wife, Maud, who came from that county. Their designer was Clough Williams-Ellis, who also created Portmeirion village in Wales. A sandy beach runs to the north, and in the opposite direction, behind the hotels, are some interesting caves. There are two megalithic tombs near the village, of which the most notable is Carnamore, 4 miles (6.4km) northwest. This is the best preserved of a group of Antrim passage graves. West, by 1½ miles (2.4km) at Innispollan are an underground passage and Mass Rock, an altar of the Penal times also known as the Altar in the Woods.

The houses of Cushendun look like something out of a picture book with their slate roofs above whitewashed walls.

BYAM·SHAW.

Thought to be buried in Downpatrick, St Patrick is the patron saint of Ireland but was born in South Wales in AD389. As a boy he was carried off by pirates and sold into slavery as a shepherd in Antrim. He escaped, probably to Britain (it may have been France, then Gaul) and trained as a missionary. He returned in either 432 or 456, landing near Downpatrick, and his subsequent work was a vital factor in the spread of Christianity in Ireland.

It is said he began his mission by lighting a fire on Slane Hill, Meath, challenging the druids of High King Leary at Tara. He is credited with founding the diocese of Armagh, of which he became bishop, but this may have been achieved by an earlier missionary called Palladius or Secondinus. Such was the reverence with which he was regarded, the name Patrick was shunned for centuries, even after the Anglo-Normans brought it over. It began to be used in the late 17th century, and is now the fourth most common male name in Ireland. In similar vein, 17 March, St Patrick's Day, was an ecclesiastical feast until the last few decades when it has become a more social occasion.

DERRYGONNELLY (Fermanagh) Ref: D3

Doire Ó gConaile, the Oak Grove of the Connollys. Close to this small village are the Knockmore Caves, which have strange figure markings and designs known as rock scribing on their walls. Nearby are the ruins of a 17th-century 'plantation' church built by Sir John Dunbar. Not far away, Lough Navar Forest offers angling, picnic sites and a 7-mile (11.2-km) forest drive leading to the top of the Magho Cliffs. From these can be seen a spectacular panorama of Lough Erne. On the shores of Carrick Lough, 2 miles (3.2km) northwest, are the remains of Aghamore Church.

DONAGHADEE (Down) Ref: D5

Domhnach Daoi. Donaghadee is a pleasant port town which is only 20 miles (32km) from Portpatrick in Scotland – a ferry crossed between the two until 1849 when the Larne-Stranraer route took over. A pleasure boat takes visitors round the Copeland Islands which shelter the harbour. When this harbour was being constructed in 1821, a castellated powder house for storing explosives was built on top of a prehistoric rath known as the

An unusual feature of Downpatrick Cathedral is its private box pews.

Moat. The restored parish church includes a Jacobean tower of 1641, and shares its grounds with a holy well. To the south, is a coastal walk known as the Commons, and west of Millisle is Ballycopel and Windmill, which is open to the public. Parts of the foreshore at Coalpit Bay are of scientific interest because of the rock successions they display.

DONEGAL (Donegal) Ref: D3

Dún na nGall, the Fort of the Foreigners. Until the 17th century, Donegal was the chief seat of the O'Donnell family, and on the seashore, south of the town, are some remains of a Franciscan friary founded by Red Hugh O'Donnell and his wife Finola in 1474. Donegal Castle has stood above the quay since 1505, and was enlarged by Sir Basil Brooke in 1610. Of particular note is its massive Jacobean fireplace, incorporating the arms of Brooke and Leicester. At the heart of this pleasant town is a wide triangular space called The Diamond. Here an obelisk commemorates the four local friars who compiled the

17th-century *Annals of the Four Masters*, one of the most important sources of early-Irish church history.

What to see The Diamond; Donegal Castle; Franciscan friary.

DOWNPATRICK (Down) Ref: D5

Dún Pádraig, St Patrick's Fort. Downpatrick is a charming collection of late-Georgian and early Victorian buildings on twin hills, and is best known for its links with St Patrick. He is said to have landed 1½ miles (2.6km) to the north of here on the Slaney

River when he returned to Ireland in AD432. A modern church now stands on high ground near the spot, and across the valley, on Slieve Patrick, is a 35ft (10.6m) high granite statue of the Saint. Downpatrick Cathedral is reputed to be his resting place, along with the bones of St Brigid and St Columba. A large slab of granite protects his grave. The present cathedral dates from the 18th century, but a church has stood on this site since 520. Down Museum on English Street was once a gaol, and is surrounded by other interesting 19th-century

buildings. A beautiful stretch of water called Quoile pondage ideal for walking, picnics and angling can be found to the northwest. Further on is Inch Abbey, founded in 1180, although the well and bakehouse are 15th century.

What to see Down museum; Downpatrick Castle; Inch Abbey; Quoile pondage.

DROMORE (Down) Ref: D5

Droim Mór, Big Ridge. Under the altar of the diocesan cathedral dating from about 1661 is the body of its builder Bishop Jeremy Taylor. The structure was restored in the last century. A cross-inscribed stone in the south wall, known as St Colman's Pillow, is thought to be a relic of a monastic foundation created here in about 600. Near Regent Bridge is a restored 9th- or 10th-century high cross, and the parish stocks still stand in the Market Square. A splendid 12th-century motte-and-bailey called The Mount rises just to the northeast of the town. Its mound is about 200ft (60m) in diameter, and is linked to the banks of the River Lagan by a sunken way.

DUNDRUM (Down) Ref: E5

Dún Droma, Fort of the Ridge. Dundrum is a picturesque fishing village which boasts a magnificent ruined castle. Built in the 12th and 13th centuries, it features a great circular keep which is well preserved, partly because of the funnel-shaped pit in its basement where subsoil water percolated. Among its other points of interest are a latrine in the outer wall, and an Elizabethan gateway with pointed arch and towers. It was built by John de Courcy, and taken by King John in 1210. The Murlough National Nature Reserve nearby was the first of its kind in Ireland, and offers dunes, a beach, beautiful heathland and the estuary. There is an excellent signposted nature trail and a good information centre. Opposite the main entrance at Slidderyford is an 8ft (2.4m) high, 4000-year-old dolmen.

DUNFANAGHY (Donegal) Ref: C3

Dún Fionnachaidh, Fort of the White Field. Dunfanaghy is a 'plantation' town built by Protestant settlers, and is set among some spectacular coastal scenery. To the north is 600ft (183m) high Horn Head, where dramatic cliffs are topped with heather and inhabited by a variety of seabirds. This magnificent headland is perhaps best viewed from the sea. West of the Head is the natural feature of Templebreaga Arch, and 2 miles (3.2km) west of the town is a blowhole called MacSwiney's Gun. Good sands and cliff scenery are offered by Port-na-Blagh Cove, 2 miles (3.2km) east, while Collumbkille's Lake is a holy well 2 miles (3.2km) south.

DUNGANNON (Tyrone) Ref: D4

Dún Geanainn, Geanann's Fort. This town was one of the chief seats of the O'Neill family until 1602, when it and its castle were burnt down to prevent them falling to English forces. Confusingly, O'Neill's Castle has nothing to do with the family apart from standing on the site of their fortress, for it was built in 1790 by Thomas Knox Hanyngton. A number of impressive 18th- and 19th-century

Dundrum Castle is said to be the most impenetrable fortress in the land.

buildings can be seen, including the courthouse, and the frontage of Tyrone Courier House.

DUNGIVEN (Derry) Ref: C4

Dún Geimhin, the Fort of the Hide. This is a small market town lying at the foot of 1535ft (468m) Ben Bradagh and close to several other mountains. It was once an O'Cahan stronghold, and some of their fortifications were incorporated into the 1839 castle. Only the bawn walls remain from a 17th-century 'plantation' castle built by the Skinners Company. Almost a mile (1.6km) south on a cliff above the River Roe are the remnants of an Augustinian priory founded by the O'Cahans in 1100. These include a ruined church which houses the beautiful 15th-century tomb of Cooey-na-Gall O'Cahan, who died in 1385. About 2½ miles (4km) east, on the picturesque Maghera Road, is the Boviel wedge grave known locally as Cloghnagalla, which means Hag's Stone.

THE RURAL HOUSE

The scarcity of good local stone in Ireland encouraged the builders of rural dwellings to use other materials close at hand, which meant that the house fitted naturally into its landscape. Walls would be made of clay, rubble and what local stone there was, and held together with earth, sand or lime. Surfaces would then be protected with limewash, the many layers of which now hide the true construction of these houses. Almost all the roofs were thatched, again made from whatever could be found in the neighbourhood (wheat straw, rye, flax, marram grass) and placed on an underthatch of sods of earth.

Many houses in the northwest had a back door immediately opposite the main entrance. This, combined with the use of additional half-doors on the outside, facilitated control of the draught which fed the ever-alight turf fire, the heart of the home. This open hearth at one end was the hub of the house, a source of warmth and light and, of course, the place where meals were cooked.

A slightly different form of house was built south of the line between Glenarm and Enniskillen. It followed the Irish model of a rectangular plan and single storey, but the roofing thatch was pegged down, and the hearth was in the middle of the home. separating the kitchen from the bedroom.

DUNGLOE (Donegal) Ref: C3

An Clochan Liath, The Grey Stepping Stones. This is the only town in the Rosses (meaning headlands), an area of rocky terrain, lakes and streams covering 60,000 acres (24,000ha). The fishing village of Burtonport can be reached from a side road. Southwest by about 5 miles (8km) is a geological oddity called Talamh Briste, a quarter mile (400m), 12ft (3.6m) wide chasm. Close to this feature are the impressive cliffs of Crohy Head under which are interesting caves which can only be visited by boat.

From here can be seen the excellent beach of Maghery Bay. North of the town is the ancient church of Templecrone, and northeast by 4½ miles (7.2km) is the glacially-formed Lough Anure.

ENNISKILLEN (Fermanagh) Ref: D4

Inis Ceithleann, Ceithle's Island. This town is beautifully sited on an island between the upper and lower sections of Lough Erne. Enniskillen Castle, which is also known as Watergate, commands the old ford (now replaced by the West Bridge), and is much changed since it was built in the 15th century. It has a three-storey keep, and a square that looks like a military barracks, and which houses the county and regimental museums. St MacCartan's Cathedral stands on a hill in the town and dates mainly from 1841, although its tower carries the date 1637. On the northwest edge of Enniskillen is Portura Royal School, founded by Charles I in 1626, and whose pupils included Oscar Wilde and Samuel Beckett. About 1½ miles (2.4km) southeast is Castle Coole, a neo-classical house built in the 1790s by James Wyatt, standing in wooded parkland.

What to see Castle Coole; Fermanagh County Museum; St MacCartan's Cathedral; Watergate (Enniskillen Castle).

FAIR HEAD (Antrim) Ref: C5

An Bhinn Mhór, The Big Peak. Fair Head is a barren and forbidding, but beautiful, headland which marks the northeastern tip of Ireland. A herd of wild goats can sometimes be seen moving about on the face of its 400ft (120m) cliffs past the nesting birds, and visitors can walk down Grey Man's Path with care. At the top of the head is a trio of small loughs. Of these, Lough-na-Cranagh is the site of a crannog-type lake dwelling, oval in shape. Half a mile (0.8km) west is Doon Fort, a motte-and-bailey structure dating from about 1180. Opposite Fair Head is Rathlin Island which can be reached by boat, and to which some of Marconi's early experimental broadcasts were made from Ballycastle. Below Fair Head, and in complete contrast, are the numerous trees of Murlough Bay.

FIVEMILETOWN (Tyrone) Ref: D4

Baile na Lorgan, Town of the Shank. This town's strange name derives from the popular misconception that it is 5 miles (8km) away from Clabby, Clogher

and Colebrooke. Sir William Stewart built a 'plantation' castle here during the reign of James I, and its remains can be seen on the north side of the main street. The border between Fermanagh and Monaghan is marked by Slieve Beagh, which rises 1221ft (372m) to the southeast.

GIANT'S CAUSEWAY (Antrim) Ref: C4

Clochán an Aifir, the Giant's Stepping Stones. The Giant's Causeway is a strange formation of basalt columns which was formed by the slow cooling of lava which had erupted through the earth's crust some 60 million years ago. It solidified on white chalk into about 37,000 columns, all with between four and eight sides, and some with ball and

The Giant's Causeway, formed 60 million years ago.

sprocket joints. Between eruptions, the surface of the lava decayed, leaving a red bank of iron ore which can be seen halfway up the cliffs. Various formations form the causeway, and these are known by such fanciful names as The Giant's Organ. The Giant's Grandmother, The Amphitheatre, The Harp, Chimney Point, and The Wishing Chair. Its overall name stems from the story that Ulster warrior Finn McCool built it so that he could reach a giantess on the island of Staffa, where the causeway resurfaces off the Scottish coast. The tales, as much as the weird formations, have long made this site a major tourist attraction.

GLENARM (Antrim) Ref: C5
Gleann Arma. Glenarm is a
delightful village sitting on the
south bank of Glenarm River near
a cliff-bound bay on the Antrim
Coast Road. Its pretty cottages
stand on streets whose names –
Toberwine, The Vennel – suggest
that its layout has changed little
since medieval times. The site of
St Patrick's Church was formerly
occupied by a 15th-century
Franciscan friary, and in its
graveyard is the decapitated body
of the 16th-century Gaelic chief
of Ulster, Shane O'Neill. Glenarm
Castle on the west bank displays a
bizarre mixture of styles, for its
mid-18th-century body stands on
the foundations of an Elizabethan
keep and it has Tudor-style
chimneys and Jacobean dripstones
above the windows.

**GLENCOLUMBKILLE
(Donegal) Ref: D3**
Gleann Cholm Cille, St Columba's
Valley. This is one of the most
inaccessible villages in Donegal,
lying as it does in a deep,
secluded valley north of 1972ft
(600m) Slieve League. It is famous
for its rural co-operative
movement, founded by a local
priest to limit emigration from the
area. Irish rural life through the
ages is represented in its folk
village. St Columba (Colmille) has
many associations with the village,
which was said to be his retreat,
and there are many early Christian
remains bearing his name, some of
which attract pilgrims. There is an
enjoyable walk to Glen Head, a
sheer 700ft (213m) high
precipice to the north.

**GLENS OF ANTRIM
(Antrim) Ref: C5**
The series of narrow valleys
which mark the paths of streams
and rivers flowing from the
Antrim Plateau is known as the
nine Glens of Antrim. Most can be
seen and visited from the Antrim
Coast Road, though some are far
off the beaten track. The first is
Glenarm, which leads to the
village of the same name (see
separate entry). Next is Glencoy,
which leads to the limestone
harbour village of Carnlough. The
finest valley is said to be
Glenariff, where a Forest Park
offers good walks as the valley
leads down to Red Bay. The
village of Cushendall (see separate
entry) welcomes a trio of valleys:
Glenballyemon, Glenaan and
Glencorp, while Glendun runs to
Cushendun, and Glenshesk and
Glentaise converge at Ballycastle.

*In addition to lush greenery,
Glenariff features a series of
beautiful waterfalls.*

Greyabbey is surrounded by fertile land and sloping hills.

GREENCASTLE (Donegal) Ref: C4

An Caisleán Nua, The New Castle. This is a small Inishtown resort offering good bathing and pleasant views, and featuring the remains of a castle built in 1305 by Richard de Burgo. The fortress is dominated by a great gatehouse fronted by polygonal towers, and served as a port of supply for English armies in Scotland. The village itself was once a meeting point for emigrants bound west across the Atlantic. The cliffs of Inishowen rise more than 300ft (91m) northeast of the village and offer views east and north to Derry and Antrim. A well-preserved Armada warship was discovered 3 miles (4.8km) north, at Kimagoe in 1971.

GREYABBEY (Down) Ref: D5

An Mhainistir Liath, The Grey Monastery. Greyabbey takes its name from the Cistercian monastery founded in 1193 on this site on the east shore of Strangford Lough. A remarkable portion of the beautiful abbey remains, despite the burning of the site in 1572 by the O'Neills to prevent English colonists from sheltering here. On the north of the site is the church with its elaborately-carved west door and its short chancel with tall lancet windows (probably added later). There is also a cloister, refectory and chapter house, plus several other monuments of interest. To

The roofless remains of the Cistercian church at Greyabbey.

the north, is the fine 18th-century house of Mount Stewart, set among some exquisite themed gardens which benefit from the mild climate of the area. They were laid out in the 1920s by Edith, the 7th Marchioness of Londonderry, whose family have always owned the house – which is itself also worth a visit for the many treasures on display.

GRIANAN OF AILEACH (Donegal) Ref: C4

Grainán Ailigh, Sun-palace of Aileach. On the top of an 800ft (244m) hill at Carroreagh, the Grianan of Aileach (now called Greenan Fort) was the royal seat and stronghold of the O'Neills, Kings of Ulster. Its building pre-dates that clan, for the circular stone fort dates from about 1700BC, when it was probably being used by druids worshipping the sun. Three delapidated concentric ramparts encircle a strong stone cashel with a 17ft (5m) high wall which is 13ft (4m) thick at the base. The entrance doorway is narrow and easily defended. The fort was occupied until the 12th century, and restored in the 1870s. It offers excellent views over Loughs Swilly and Foyle.

HILLSBOROUGH (Down) Ref: D5

Cromghlinn, Crooked Valley. Hillsborough is a charming village with an abundance of Georgian town houses, other major buildings, shops and bars. It is named after Sir Arthur Hill, whose family obtained land here in 1611. Most of its development took place in the 18th century, a good example being the 1760 Market House in the Square. In the centre of the village is Hillsborough Castle, once the Governor's residence and now used by visiting royalty and for state occasions. Hillsborough Fort, just off the Square, was probably built in the 1650s and was refurbished in the mid-18th century. This massive building is defended by four quadrangular bastions, and has a pointed arched gateway. The church was rebuilt over a period of 14 years to 1774, and is an important example of the Georgian Gothic style.

What to see church; Hillsborough Castle; Hillsborough Fort; Market House.

INISHOWEN PENINSULA (Donegal) Ref: C4

Inis Eoghain, Eoghan's Island. This stretch of land separating the two large inlets of Loughs Swilly and Foyle includes Ireland's most northerly point and, more

importantly, some of its most beautiful scenery. The best of this is along the northern and western seaboards. The chief town is Buncrana (see separate entry) and the major attraction is Grianan of Aileach (see separate entry). Also worth visiting are Carndonagh which has what is thought to be the oldest cross standing in Ireland, the Donagh Cross. Said to date from the 7th century, it can be found about half a mile (0.8km) west of the town. In the north of the peninsula, is Malin Head, where cliffs rise more than 200ft (60m) as they guard Ireland's northern extremity. Towards Glengad in the east they reach 800ft (244m).

ISLAND MAGEE (Antrim) Ref: D5

Oileán Mhic Aodha, Magee's Island. This is a low, undulating peninsula extending northwest from the area of Whitehead, with the almost entirely enclosed Larne Lough on its west side. Its name is said to derive from a Scottish family to whom it once belonged. Close to the lough is Ballyharry townland, whose small parish

church is one of the best early-Jacobean churches in Ulster. The cliff scenery along the east side of Island Magee is very fine, particularly at the Gobbins, which are basalt cliffs almost 250ft (76m) high.

KILLYBEGS (Donegal) Ref: D3

Na Cealla Beaga, the Small Monastic Cells. Excellent river trout and sea fishing, fine scenery, and a good nearby beach, make this small fishing port particularly attractive to visitors. It is not dependent on tourists, however, for Killybegs is also famous for its hand-woven carpets and its fishing industries. One of the walls in its Roman Catholic church incorporates a sculptured memorial slab to Niall Mor MacSweeney. It was found to the south near St John's Point, and there is only one similar slab in the whole of Ireland (in the cemetery at Creeslough, Donegal). The town also has some slight remains of a castle and a church, and two miles (3.2km) away is the splendid sandy beach of Fintragh Strand.

It may look quiet, but Killybegs harbour welcomes some of the biggest fish catches in the country.

KILLYLEAGH (Down) Ref: D5

Cill O Laoch, the Church of Uí Laoch. An interesting feature of this little 'plantation' town is the way it has been formally arranged on a grid pattern. Its impressive hilltop castle fringed by trees has 13th- or 14th-century origins, but these can hardly be detected because it was rebuilt in 1666 and again in 1850. It now features soaring turrets, strong battlements, a bawn wall and a pretty gatehouse. Sir Hans Sloane, whose immense collection was the basis for the British Museum, was born in Killyleagh's Frederick Street in 1666. A stone before the castle gates commemorates his achievements. Remains of a 15th-century church can be seen in low marsh a little to the north. At Ringahaddy, 4 miles (6.4km) north, are the remnants of a 12th-century motte, a 13th-century church, and a 15th- to 17th-century castle.

What to see Castle (17 and 19c); church (15c); Ringahaddy (castle, church, motte).

KILMORE (Cavan) Ref: E4

Chill Mhór, Big Church. William Bedell, who translated the Bible into Irish and was bishop of this ancient bishopric in the 17th century, is buried in the old Church of Ireland churchyard. The modern cathedral incorporates a richly-carved, 12th-century Romanesque doorway removed from the church on Trinity Island in Lough Oughter.

LAGAN VALLEY (Down and Antrim) Ref: D5

This valley was cleared and developed during the plantations by Protestant settlers, and subsequently benefitted from the linen and damask weaving introduced by the Huguenots. When the bleaching industry arrived in the 18th century, further settlement transformed the area into what one 1812 visitor called 'one continued garden, shadowed with trees, interspersed with thickets and neat whitewashed houses'. Eventually, the Lagan Navigation Canal ran along it linking Belfast with Lough Neagh. Its towpath makes a good walk through some fine parks with the grand houses of the linen magnates in the distance. There is a lovely little suspension bridge at Lambeg, and the section of canal from Shaw's Bridge is particularly attractive.

LARNE (Antrim) Ref: D5

Latharna. This is a port and holiday resort at the mouth of Larne Lough at the southern end of the Antrim Coast Road (see separate entry). There is a passenger ferry to Island Magee (see separate entry), and Larne offers the shortest ferry crossing to Scotland – indeed, the Scottish coast can often be seen from the Promenade and the Curran. This is a long, bending gravel spit curving south from the town at 10–20ft (3–6m) above the high water mark. At its end is the ruined 16th-century Olderfleet Castle. Larne's only real landmark is a modern replica of a round tower, 92ft (28m) high, overlooking the harbour. This commemorates James Chaine, who founded the crossing to Scotland and at his own request was buried standing up in a niche in the cliffs.

What to see Antrim Coast Road; Chaine Memorial Tower; the Curran; Olderfleet Castle (Curran Castle).

LETTERKENNY (Donegal) Ref: C3

Leitir Ceanainn. Letterkenny is a very busy town near the head of the River Swilly estuary. The commercial centre of Donegal, and famous for its salmon angling, it also boasts one of Ireland's longest main streets. St Eunan's Cathedral, built at the end of the last century, is neo-Gothic in style and has many Celtic carvings and a tall spire. It is mainly built in sandstone from Mount Charles, on Donegal Bay, and features decorated ceilings by Amici of Rome. Nearby, is St Eunan's College, a castellated, stone-built boarding school with a small cloistered courtyard. To the north is Killydonnell with its ruined 16th-century friary. About 2 miles (3.2km) west of the town are the scant remains of Conwal monstery, and the cemetery here has numerous ancient tombstones. Northwest of the town is Glenveagh National Park with a castle, lough and gardens.

What to see Conwal monastery and graveyard; Glenveagh National Park; Killydonnell friary; St Eunan's Cathedral.

LIMAVADY (Derry) Ref: C4

Léim an Mhadaidh, Dog's Leap. Limavady is a small town in the River Roe valley, with mountains on every horizon, including 1260ft (384m) Binevenagh above Lough Foyle, and 1318ft (400m)

St Eunan's Cathedral at Letterkenny has an intricate stone roped ceiling.

A VULNERABLE CITY

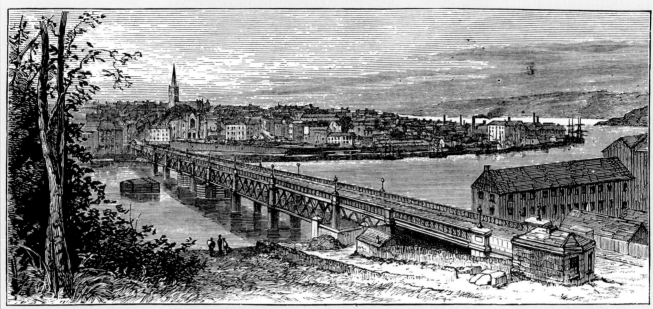

In 546, St Columba founded a monastery at Londonderry among the oak trees sitting on a mound overlooking marshy land known as the Bogside. It was an idyllic setting, but highly vulnerable to attacks from the sea, which duly followed, courtesy of the Vikings, the Anglo-Norman barons de Courcy and Peyton, and, in the late 16th century, the English, who built a fort to attack the Prince of Hy-Neill.

In 1613, James I granted the now-destroyed town to the Twelve Companies of the Corporation of London (hence the addition of 'London' to its name) and settlers (planters) from England and Scotland moved in. The massive protective walls they built withstood attacks in 1641, 1649 and 1688–9, the latter including a 105-day seige by the Jacobites. During this, 7000 of the town's 30,000 inhabitants died, and many of the survivors emigrated to America. The seige was ended when the ship 'Mountjoy' broke the boom across the river, but Derry survived, earning the nickname 'the Maiden City'.

The city grew rich in the 19th century on the back of a booming linen industry and its value as a seaport. It has been the scene of some terrible events in Ireland's recent troubled history, but in the last few years it has witnessed little violence and has prospered.

Donald's Hill to the southeast. In the broad main street is the home of Jane Moss, who made her name by noting down the tune 'Londonderry Air' (better known as 'Danny Boy') being played by a passing fiddler. The 'Dog's Leap' name derives from the tale of a mighty bound made by a dog carrying a message from a beseiged castle. To the south is Roe Valley Country Park, where there is a small weaving museum and Roe Mill, Ireland's first hydroelectric power station, built in 1896. Just over 5 miles (8km) northeast are a number of standing stones and cairns at Largantees. Some chambered tombs can be found 4½ miles (7.2km) southeast, close by Donald's Hill. A mile (1.6km) west of the town is Royal Fort, a prehistoric ringfort in an enclosure of trees.

What to see Donald's Hill; Langantees monuments; Roe Valley Country Park; Royal Fort.

LISBURN (Antrim) Ref: D5

Lios na gCearrbhach, the Ringfort of the Gamblers. Once an important linen town, Lisburn has been largely assimilated into the suburbs of Belfast which is downstream on the River Lagan. During the 17th century, under its original name of Lisangarvey, it was colonized by English and Welsh settlers. The castle that protected them was destroyed in 1707, but its remains can be found in Castle Gardens. The cathedral in the centre of the town dates from 1623 but was largely rebuilt last century.

LONDONDERRY (Londonderry) Ref: C4

Doire, Oak Grove. Often known simply as 'Derry', this is Northern Ireland's second largest city, and a major manufacturing centre and port. Its most notable feature is the remarkably well-preserved walls, which are the most complete city fortifications of their kind in Ireland or Britain. Varying in width from 14 to 30ft (4 to 9m), and with a maximum height of 25ft (7.5m), the walls form an excellent walk within which most of the city's shops and business centres are enclosed.

Their one mile (1.6km) circumference was originally pierced only by four gates. None remain, but the Shipquay Gate of 1805 at the bottom of Ship Quay Street is worth seeing. This street ascends steeply to the Diamond where it becomes Bishop Street and leads to Bishop Gate, a triumphal arch from 1789. Nearby, at Church Bastion, is the 17th-century cannon Roaring Meg, which fired 18-pound cannon balls. Also close by is St Columb's Cathedral, completed in 1833 along the lines of an English parish church. In its chapter house (1910) are relics of the city's history. Its near-neighbour is the courthouse, which was built using Dungiven sandstone in 1817 and features a pedimented portico.

Outside the walls to the north is the Roman Catholic cathedral, St Eugene's, designed in a 19th-century Irish Gothic style by JJ McCarthy. Not far away is the 19th-century Foyle College building, part of an institution founded in the 17th century.

The River Foyle was crossed by ferry until a wooden bridge was built in 1790, and the present Craigavon Bridge dates from 1933.

On this side of the city is a modern bronze sculpture of Princess Macha by FE McWilliam. Legend has it that she founded the first Irish hospital, so it is fitting that she now stands in front of the modern Altnagelvin Hospital.

St Columba's stone is a 6ft (1.8m) square block lying 2 miles (3.2km) north of the city in the grounds of Belmond demesne. It features the impression of two feet and is thought to be the inauguration stone of the Tir-Owen chiefs. Close by is Elagh Castle, a one time O'Doherty stronghold. On the mouth of the Foyle northeast of the city is Culmore Fort, first built as a triangular artillery fort in 1610. About 2½ miles (4km) northeast of the city in Lough Enagh is Rough Island, which has a crannog and is the site of neolithic and later finds.

What to see Bishop Gate; Boom House (18c); courthouse; Culmore Fort; Elagh Castle; Foyle College; Rough Island; St Columb's Cathedral; St Columba's Stone; St Eugene's Cathedral; Shipquay Gate; town walls.

LOUGH ERNE (Fermanagh) Ref: D4 and E4

Loch Éirne. Lough Erne offers scenic waterways and islands, and some fascinating ancient religious settlements and monuments. It comprises the Upper and Lower Loughs, either side of Enniskillen, which are linked by a 10-mile (16-km) river, and together form 50 miles (80km) of water scattered with 154 islands. By far the best way to see it is from the water, and there are many cruises available throughout the summer. Several of the islands have a special ecclesiastical interest, including Devenish which houses the remains of a monastery founded in 564 or 571 by St Molaise. This has an 81ft (25m) high, 10th- to 12th-century round tower with a cornice carved with faces whose beards and moustaches intertwine. White Island has eight strange figures carved in stone, some of them Christian while others are pagan – the area's complex system of waterways is almost impenetrable to outsiders and obviously resisted the advance of Christianity for some time. Set back from the Lough at Monea is a fine castle, which survives from the 17th century. The Lower Lough has fewer interesting sites but is rich in birdlife.

LOUGH NEAGH (Antrim, Armagh, Derry) Ref: D4 and D5

Loch nEathach, Eocha's Lake. At 153 sq miles (396km²), Lough Neagh is the largest inland lake in the British Isles, but unfortunately because it is surrounded by relatively flat countryside it lacks the picturesque qualities of smaller lakes. However, there are marinas at Ballyronan, Maghery, Sixmilewater and Oxford Island. On a rocky height at Arboe is a fine high cross which marks the site of a monastery. The shores of the lough offer very good walking, and are rich in wildfowl, especially duck. There is a wildfowl refuge in the northeast section, and several nature reserves. (See Randalstown entry for information on Shane's Castle.)

MALIN MORE (Donegal) Ref: D3

Málain Mhóir, Big Malin. This is a remote resort with a fine strand and some good cliff scenery nearby. Silver Strand can only be reached on foot and is considered one of the loveliest in Ireland. South at Cloghanmore is a wedge-shaped court grave with a full court to the east and associated graves in a long cairn to the west. A site known as Dermot and

In the superbly lit chambers of the Marble Arch Caves you can marvel at delicate veils of minerals as well as massive stalactites and stalagmites.

Grania's Bed has six chambered graves arranged in a straight line stretching over 100yds (91m). The massive west grave has pillars more than 10ft (3m) high, and two capstones. There is a lighthouse on Rathlin O'Birne Island 1½ miles (2.4km) off the coast. The island's older features include an early church, penitential stations and a holy well.

MARBLE ARCH CAVES (Fermanagh) Ref: D3

This is the largest and most famous set of caves of many which have formed in the limestone of Fermanagh. Unlike many of the others, it can be safely visited. The 'Arch' is a lofty underground bridge, surrounded by lakes, stalactites (which hang down) and stalagmites (which rise like spikes), and the whole series of chambers is brilliantly lit. Five miles (8km) away is Florence Court, a magnificent three-storey mansion linked to small pavilions by long arcades. It dates from 1764, and features wonderful rococo plasterwork and much exuberant external detail. It was home to the Earls of Enniskillen and is set in attractive Forest Park, which offers some challenging walks in the foothills of Cuilcagh Mountain.

MONAGHAN (Monaghan) Ref: E4

Muineachán, Place of Thickets. There is much fine Victorian architecture in Monaghan, but of more dubious taste is a highly ornate drinking fountain in the main square (the Diamond). It commemorates a Baron Rossmore, who died in 1874. The town has an excellent county museum housed in the 1829 courthouse which displays the Cross of Clogher, a processional cross from about 1400. St Macartan's Cathedral stands on a high site in Castleblaney Road and was designed by JJ McCarthy, being completed in 1882 after his death. Its interior is dignified and uncluttered. Three miles (4.8km) south is Rossmore Park which includes a golf course and hosts a festival of Irish music each June.

What to see County museum; the Diamond; Rossmore Park; St Macartan's Cathedral (19c).

The civic buildings of Monaghan seem to swell with pride as they evoke their Victorian origins.

MONEYMORE (Derry)
Ref: D4

Muine Mór, Big Thicket.
Moneymore is a handsome and
graceful 'plantation' town which
owes its existence and
development to the London
Drapers' Company. This group
completed a distinguished series
of buildings in 1819 including the
market house, a hotel, a coach
arch and a dispensary which
became a bank. The town was
already notable for having been
the first in Ulster to have piped
water, in 1615. Half a mile
(0.8km) southeast is Springhill, an
example of the fortified,
stonewashed dwellings built by
17th-century settlers, and which
now houses a costume museum
and a cottar's kitchen.

NAVAN FORT (Armagh)
Ref: D4

A few miles west of Armagh, a
massive earthworks is all that
remains of what was once a great
palace, built by Queen Macha in
300BC. It became the home of the
warrior kings of Ulster, and the
court of the Knights of the Red
Branch – the Irish equivalent of
the Knights of the Round Table.
The feats of these genuine
historical figures and particularly
their greatest champion,
Cuchullain, have passed into, and
been embellished in, legend, and
are told in the songs and stories of
the Ulster cycle. The entire
complex of Navan Fort was razed
to the ground by the three Cullas
brothers in AD330. When the site
was excavated in the 1960s, a
strange structure unique in the
Celtic world was discovered with
a diameter of 36yds (33m), which
may have been a temple, or a
huge funeral pyre.

NEWCASTLE (Down)
Ref: E5

An Caisleán Nua, The New
Castle. This is a popular seaside
resort with a 3-mile (4.8-km)
crescent-shaped sandy beach. It
takes its name from a castle built
in 1433 where the River Shimna
flows into Dundrum Bay. This was
destroyed early last century to
make way for a hotel to serve
visitors attracted by the town's
spa. South, along the coast, is a 6ft
(1.8m) chasm with a 90ft (27m)
drop called Maggie's Leap, named
after a girl fleeing an admirer who
jumped across it and landed with
all the eggs in her basket intact.
To the north, the beach runs to
Dundrum, passing the
championship golf course of
Royal County Down. To the west
is Tollymore, a Forest Park with
many Gothic gates and follies, and
a good range of walks.

THE MOURNE MOUNTAINS

The Mournes are a set of
'young' mountains, comprising
relatively un-weathered granite
which is almost sheer in places,
and in others leaves a raw,
jagged outline in the sky.
Newcastle is the best base from
which to explore them, and
guidance on walks can be
obtained from the Mourne
Countryside Centre in the town.
The range includes ten peaks of
more than 2000ft (610m). The
highest, at 2796ft (852m), is
Slieve Donard, which being
only 1½ miles (2.4km) from the
coast is a particularly
spectacular sight. It is fairly easy
to climb the well-marked path
to its summit, where there is a
large hermit cell. Another spot
worth reaching is Hare's Gap,
where precious and semi-
precious stones have been
formed by minerals seeping
through the rock, landing in the
recesses of the Diamond Rocks.
A ribbon of drystone wall
surrounds 10,000 acres
(4050ha) of the mountains and
marks Belfast's water catchment
area. The higher lands are
inhabited by ravens, kestrels
and sparrowhawks, while
meadow pipits, skylarks and
red grouse share space with the
sheep on the lower slopes. The
Mournes are only crossed by
one road, from Hilltown to
Kilkeel, so there are plenty of
remote spots for walkers to
seek out.

135

NEWRY (Down) Ref: E5

An tIúr, The Yew. This is a handsome port and town which is connected by a canal to Carlingford Lough, 6 miles (9.6km) away. The waterway opened in 1741 and accelerated Newry's development as a distribution centre – it was known as the Gap of the North because it was situated at the main crossing between hills from the south into Ulster. St Patrick founded a monastery here and planted a yew tree at the head of the strand of Carlingford Lough. After the Dissolution, Nicholas Bagenal played a major role in Newry's growth, rebuilding its castle and, in 1578, erecting the parish church of St Patrick, of which part of the tower survives. His tombstone can be seen in the church porch. Newry is a good

The Ulster American Folk Park effectively re-creates the past.

base for exploring the Mourne Mountains and Carlingford Lough.
What to see Bank of Ireland (Georgian); Cathedral of SS Patrick and Colman (19c); St Mary's Church (19c); St Patrick's Church (part 16c).

NEWTOWNARDS (Down) Ref: D5

Baile Nua na hArda, New Town of the Promontory. This is a busy town which was founded early in the 17th century by Scottish Laird Hugh Montgomery, on the site of a 13th-century Dominican friary. The ruins include a nave and north aisle, separated by an arcade of arches. The north tower dates from the 17th century. The octagonal market cross was first erected in 1635, and its interior served as the town gaol. A mile (1.6km) south, on Scrabo Hill, is Scrabo Tower, which commemorates the 3rd Marquess of Londonderry and is near the

wooded property of Killynether. A mile (1.6km) east is the site of Movilla Abbey, where a monastery was founded in the 6th century by St Finnian. The church is 13th to 15th century, and arranged along the north wall are a number of coffin lids from early in its history.
What to see Colville mansion (17c); Dominican Friary (13c); Market Cross (17c); Movilla Abbey (13 and 15c, 1 mile [1.6km] east); Scrabo Hill and Tower (19c, 1 mile [1.6km] south); town hall (18c).

NEWTOWN BUTLER (Fermanagh) Ref: E4

An Baile Nua, The New Town. The forces of James II were forced to retreat to this village when they were attacking Crom Castle, 4 miles (6.4km) west, in 1689. They lost 2000 men in a major victory for the settlers of Enniskillen. Fire destroyed the

castle in 1764 but its picturesque ruins remain, alongside the present-day Crom Castle, which dates from 1829. In its fine grounds is what is claimed as the largest yew tree in Ireland. Surrounding it are some beautiful wooded islands and peninsulas. About 3½ miles (5.6km) southwest is an enormous circle of stones called Druid's Temple, which once surrounded a large burial mound.

OMAGH (Tyrone) Ref: D4

An Omaigh. This prosperous county town is a good base for visiting the Sperrin Mountains, and is encircled by some very good Forest Parks. North is Gortin Glen, which has a 5-mile (8-km) forest drive with splendid views, plus wildlife enclosures and other attractions. Northwest is Barons Court Forest Park, where Bessy Bell hill has marvellous views of Donegal, the Sperrins and Lough

Erne. South is Seskimore with its collection of ornamental birds and domestic fowl. Five miles (8km) to the north, at Camphill, is the excellent Ulster American Folk Park, which authentically evokes life in Ireland, on the boats to the New World, and on arrival. There are also displays of traditional crafts (see separate entry).

What to see Barons Court Forest Park; Church of the Sacred Heart; Courthouse (19c); Giant's Cave (burial chamber 1½ miles [2.4km] west); Gortin Glen; Inniskilling Fusiliers Regimental Museum; St Columba's Church; Seskimore; Ulster American Folk Park.

PORTADOWN (Armagh)
Ref: D4
Port an Dúnain, the Bank of the Small Fort. This is a manufacturing, linen and fruit farming centre which is also famous for its roses. In ancient times, Portadown was a major

settlement near a strategic fort across the River Bann. At its centre is St Mark's Church, built in 1826 and much enlarged since – the pinnacled tower dates from about 1930. Carnegie Library houses an interesting museum.

PORTAFERRY (Down)
Ref: D5
Port an Phiere, the Harbour of the Ferry. This is a seaside town with a long shore front overlooking the Strangford Lough's narrow link with the sea. A Norman family, the Savages, were great castle builders in this area and they constructed Portaferry Castle, a tower house in the middle of the town, in the 16th century. The town hotels offer good locally caught fish, probably brought in by the fishing fleet of Portavogie across the Ards peninsula. About 1½ miles (2.4km) northeast are the Derry Churches, two small churches standing where a monastery founded

before the 8th century once stood. Southeast by 2½ miles (4km) is Millin Bay and its complex neolithic burial site, while close by is a fine beach at Ballyquintin.

What to see Derry Churches; Market House (c.1800); Millin Bay; Portaferry Castle; Strangford Lough.

PORTRUSH (Antrim)
Ref: C4
Port Rois, Harbour of the Headland. Portrush sits around three beaches at the north end of the Antrim Coast road, and is a popular holiday resort. The town is built on a basalt peninsula, and its elevated position offers views to the Donegal Mountains, Rathlin Island and even as far as Scotland's Mull of Kintyre. Below the Recreation Grounds, off Lansdowne Crescent, is Portandoo Countryside Centre. The shore nearby is noted for its fossils of ammonites and is a geological

nature reserve. Two miles (3.2km) east at White Rocks are some beautiful caves, and the handsome house of Beariville lies 4 miles (6.4km) southeast. A heraldic plaque above its door is dated 1713.

PORTSTEWART (Derry)
Ref: C4
Port Stíobhaird, Stewart's Harbour. This is a very pleasant resort with an excellent 2-mile (3.2-km) beach backed by dunes and extending to the mouth of the Bann. It also has rock pools, a dinghy pool and a children's pool. Portstewart was developed in the early 19th century and is dominated by the 1834 Low Rock Castle which stands high on the edge of a cliff. Thackeray disliked its Gothic style and called it 'a hideous new castle'. It is now St Mary's Dominican Convent School.

Part of the harbour at Portrush.

RANDALSTOWN (Antrim)
Ref: D5

Baile Raghnaill, Randal's Town. There are many fine buildings in Randalstown, but one of its most fascinating structures is the 19th-century viaduct, which uses seven stone piers to carry brick-vaulted arches across the River Main. The 18th-century market house is a five-bay, two-storey building which is now the library. Between here and Antrim is Shane's Castle, beautifully sited on the north shore of Lough Neagh. The west entrance to this 19th-century structure has a Tudor-style entrance arch. Steam locomotives remained in use here long after disappearing in the rest of Ireland. A 2-mile (3.2-km) strip of land is managed as a nature reserve, and there is interesting woodland and plant life all around.

What to see First Presbyterian Church (19c); library (18c); Methodist Church (19c); Presbyterian (Old Congregational) Church (18c); St Macanisuis' Church (19c); Shane's Castle; viaduct.

RASHARKIN (Antrim)
Ref: C4

Ros Earcain, Earcáin's Wood. Sited on the edge of the lovely Bann Valley, this village sits below high ground to its west. About 100yds (91m) south of the parish church of Rasharkin Old Church, which has well-preserved 17th-century walls. The building was mentioned in the Taxation Roll of about 1300, and was still in use until a new church was built last century.

RATHFRILAND (Down)
Ref: E5

Ráth Fraoileann, Fraoile's Ringfort. This village shares its 506ft (154m) hilltop with an ancient castle dominating the plain of Iveagh. Rathfriland Castle was the chief stronghold of the Magennis family, who were Lords of Iveagh. All that remains of it is a 20ft (6m) fragment of the south front and traces of the east and west walls. This tall, narrow castle dates from 1611, when James divided the baronies of Upper and Lower Iveagh among the main Magennis families.

RATHLIN ISLAND (Antrim)
Ref: C5

Reachlainn. Also known as Raghery, this L-shaped island is the largest to be found off the coast of Northern Ireland, measuring 4½ miles (7.2km) long by up to 3 miles (4.9km) in width. Inhabited by about 100 people, it lies about 7 miles (11.2km) from Ballycastle from where it can be

THE PLANTATION OF ULSTER

Once the most Gaelic of provinces, Ulster was transformed by the 'plantation' policy adopted by James I which entailed bringing in English and Scottish 'settlers'. The newcomers were given land and property, and proceeded to stamp their identity on the north of Ireland. Previously, England had attempted to keep control through its army. This time the rationale was to replace the rebellious Catholics with loyal Presbyterian Scots and Anglican English, ending the problematic independence of this strategically important corner of Ireland.

The Scottish proved more ready to take over larger and more hostile tracts of land. The English preferred the more secure lands such as the Lagan Valley and the lower portions of Armagh, Tyrone and Fermanagh. The indigent Irish became tenants, paying rent to the outsiders, or left the country altogether. Either way, they resented the enforced change of life. A rebellion in 1641 failed, and more waves of settlers came in the later 17th century. A new culture was established based on the Protestant religion and eagerness for economic success.

reached by boat. It is said to have more in common with Scotland than Ireland, and indeed Robert the Bruce's famous encounter with a determined, web-spinning spider which showed him how to 'try, try and try again' occurred here after his defeat at Perth in 1306. The spot is now known as Bruce's Cave. Many birds stay on the island, including guillemots, razorbills, shearwaters, fulmars, kittiwakes and puffins, and are best studied from Bull Point. Doon Point, on the east side, has geological formations similar to those at the Giant's Causeway, and the eastern corner of the island has a great variety of unusual fauna.

RATHMULLAN (Donegal)
Ref: C4

Ráth Maoláin, Maolan's Ringfort. This attractive town stands on the western shore of Lough Swilly, and has some well-preserved remains of its 15th-century Carmelite Friary. In 1595, the friary was raided for its valuable properties, and in 1618, Bishop Knox extended it into a fortified castle. It continued to serve as a church until it was abandoned 200 years later. In 1587, Red Hugh O'Donnell was tricked onto a ship here, and taken to Dublin Castle, from where he escaped after four years. It was from Rathmullan that the earls of Tyrone and Tyrconnell fled to France in 1607, marking the end of the Gaelic nation, and freeing up their estates for the 'plantation' of Ulster by Scottish and English settlers. Today, Lough Swilly offers good salmon fishing, and there are brown trout in the local lakes. Eight miles (12.8km) north is the 10th-century Drumhallach Cross Slab, which has lovely carvings of two figures sucking their thumbs.

ROSTREVOR (Down)
Ref: E5

Ros Treabhair, Trevor's Wood. This is a very pretty resort with many pleasant Victorian houses built round broad squares. The village is sheltered by ancient woodland and modern forest, and sited as it is on south-facing slopes of the Mourne Mountains, it enjoys an almost tropical climate. A steep drive from the back of the town up Slievemartin is rewarded by superb views of the Cooley mountains. Southeast by 2½ miles (4km) and beside the lough is a fine house in the Scottish baronial style which is now a hotel. In its grounds is the Ballyedmond single-court grave.

Rathmullan Museum's Flight of the Earls.

SAINTFIELD (Down)
Ref: D5

Tamhnach Naómh, Field of the Saints. Saintfield is a delightful village in a district where linen is still made. Its Market House was built in 1802 by the landlord Nicholas Price. Just south are the Rowallane Gardens, 50 acres (20ha) of rough ground punctuated by granite outcrops. The area was transformed into a series of gardens by Hugh Armytage Moore in the 1920s.

SCARVA (Down) Ref: D5

Scarbhach, Shallow. This 18th-century village is famed for its July celebrations commemorating the day in 1689 when Williamite forces rallied here on their advance south. A 1½-mile (2.4-km) length of the ancient defensive boundary known as the Dane's Cast lies south of Lough Shark, in the Scarva demesne. It is thought to have been built by Ulster's rulers who were forced to retreat east from Navan in about 330. The Rath of Lisnagade is a pear-shaped fortress measuring 300 by 200yds (274 by 183m), and can be found in the avenue leading to Lisnagade House. To the north is Terryhoogan, whose Ballynahack Church is the resting place of 17th-century highwayman Redmond O'Hanlon.

SILENT VALLEY (Down)
Ref: E5

Once known as Happy Valley, this is a deep trough in the heart of the Mourne Mountains and provides the only vehicle access to the inner Mournes. It is surrounded by a rough stone wall stretching for more than 20 miles (32km) as it covers at least 15 mountains. Between 1012ft (308m) Slievenagore and Slieve Bignian, the river was dammed in 1933 to form a 240-acre (97-ha) reservoir. Together with Ben Crom reservoir, this supplies Belfast with 30 million gallons of water a day. During its construction, its 600-strong workforce lived in a village called Watertown, since dismantled. Near the dam is a park laid out with shrubs, lawns, borders and ponds.

Silent Valley provides a channel for cars into the Mournes, but exploration on foot is worthwhile.

Being a haven for watersports, Strangford has a harbour for leisure craft.

3 miles (4.8km) south, dated about 1440; the late 16th-century Walshestown Castle 3 miles (4.8km) west; and the 15th-century stronghold, Audley's Castle, a mile (1.6km) northwest in the grounds of Castle Ward. This latter was built in the 18th century by Lord Bangor, half to suit himself (in Classical style) and half according to his wife's wishes (Gothic), and there are many attractions in its grounds.

What to see Audley's Castle (15c); Castle Ward; de Ros family estate; Kilclief Castle; Old Quay (17c); Strangford Castle (18c); Walshestown Castle; The Watch House (19c, at the edge of Ferry Quarter Point).

STRANGFORD LOUGH (Down) Ref: D5

Loch Cuan. Twenty miles (32km) long and up to 3 miles (4.9km) wide, Strangford Lough is a beautiful and almost landlocked inlet studded with islands. There are several nature reserves around it, and it supports a colony of seals and many birds, including two thirds of the world's population of Brent geese during the winter. There are good viewing points at Ballyreagh and Castle Espie. Mahee Island was inhabited by monks who left three cashels and a church with a carved sundial at Nendrum.

TEMPLEPATRICK (Antrim) Ref: D5

Teampall Phádraig, St Patrick's Church. This village surrounds the stronghold of Upton Castle, which was known as Norton Castle when it was begun in the late 16th century. Later rebuilding involved commissions for Robert Adam, including the corner and archway towers, and the stables. Two miles (3.2km) southeast is Lyles Hill, a prehistoric site discovered through aerial photography in 1927. The summit of this 753ft (230m) hill is ringed by a low earthwork thought to be of neolithic date. Within it is a low and complex cairn which yielded thousands of neolithic pot sherds and flints, and in its centre, the cremated remains of a child.

STEWARTSTOWN (Tyrone) Ref: D4

An Chraobh, The Mansion. Hilly countryside surrounds this village west of Lough Neagh. Just outside it, on the road to Cookstown, is an attractive early 19th-century house called Annie Hill. About a mile (1.6km) east is Drumcairne House, a Georgian mansion which is the seat of the Earls of Charlemont. Near Lough Neagh is Mountjoy Castle, built in 1602 to a star-shaped plan by Hugh O'Neil. Much of it lies in ruins, but the remains include a square stone and brick building with four projecting rectangular towers, each well supplied with loopholes. Close to Newmills village is Roughan Castle, a small, square, three-storeyed castle with towers built in 1618.

STRABANE (Tyrone) Ref: D4

An Srath Bán, The White Holm. Strabane is a large market town in a farming area just across the River Mourne from Lifford in Donegal. It has many links with America. The American Declaration of Independence of 1776 was printed by John Dunlop, who had been an apprentice at Gray's Printing Shop in Strabane (still in place in Main Street, now housing a museum). A fellow trainee printer was James Wilson, whose grandson became President Woodrow Wilson. The Wilson family lived in Dergalt, 2 miles (3.2km) east, and their home has been well restored and furnished for the Ulster Historical Trust. The modern Roman Catholic St Teresa's Church has a slate sculpture of The Last Supper on its façade. Sion Mills, a model village above a fine mill in a valley, can be found a few miles south.

STRANGFORD (Down) Ref: D5

Baile Loch Cuan. The Vikings arrived here in the 9th century and set up a base on the narrowest part of the strait, linking Strangford Lough with the sea. This strategic position explains its four castles: 16th-century Strangford Castle guarding the quays; Kilclief Castle

TOBERMORE (Derry) Ref: D4

An Tobar Mór, The Big Well. The parish church in this village was rebuilt in 1816, but a fine

A sheltered position gives Strangford Lough a mirror-like calm surface.

One of the impressively detailed rooms in the Ulster Folk Museum.

Norman-style niche survives from an earlier structure. The local Presbyterian meeting house was built in 1728, and a nearby earthen fortification is known as William's Fort. The Moyola River flows a little to the north.

TORY ISLAND (Donegal) Ref: C3

Toraigh, Place of Towers. Eight miles (12.8km) off the Donegal Coast, this 3 by 1 miles (4.8 by 1.6km) island is inaccessible for several months of the year due to its rocky coast and the pounding ocean. Saint Columba is said to have founded a monastery here in the 6th century, of which one relic may be the Tau Cross. This is a small, undecorated T-shaped cross made of thick mica slate. There is also an unusual 57ft (17m) high round tower made with beach stones and granite. There are no trees on the island and farmers struggle to grow crops on the barren soil. Near the centre is a wishing stone, which was apparently used to stop the gunboat 'Wasp' which was coming to collect taxes in 1884. It sank, and the islanders still pay no tax.

ULSTER FOLK AND TRANSPORT MUSEUM (Antrim) Ref: D5

This museum at Cultra has collected typical buildings from around Ulster and reassembled them on one site to give an impression of the different ways of life in the north. The authentically furnished exhibits include a church, water-powered mills, a market house, and a range of dwellings from tiny cottages to a 1717 rectory, including a terrace of street houses from Belfast. There are also displays of folklore and craft. Across the bridge is a transport museum with examples of every mode of transport, including a three-masted schooner which was built across the Lough at Carrickfergus.

WARRENPOINT (Down) Ref: E5

An Pointe, The Point. In 1780, Warrenpoint comprised two houses and a few fishermen's huts. It developed as a watering place and packet station with a service to Liverpool early last century, and is now a popular seaside resort. It has a pleasant quay facing a large central square, and a half-mile (0.8km) long promenade lined with trees. A mile (1.6km) to the east is 16th-century Narrow Water Castle.

COTTAGE INDUSTRIES

Wherever you go in Ireland, you are likely to come across craft shops offering goods made by local craftsmen. They are usually worth a visit. The rural nature of much of Irish life has helped to encourage and preserve many of the crafts that generations have practised in their own homes, and some of which are on show at the Ulster Folk and Transport Museum.

Different areas had different specialities. Carrickmacross is noted for a certain style of lace, in which the solid areas are of muslin or cambric (later cotton or nylon net), and is also famous for its lawn appliqué on a net background. Four Irish nuns travelled to Paris to learn crochet in the 18th century, and

returned to teach their skills to poverty-stricken families. Irish hand crochet is still famous today. Other crafts around the whole of Ireland include the famous Aran jerseys, first hand-knitted on the Aran Islands with patterns which may have been used to identify bodies of drowned fishermen from the area. The wool of rough grazing sheep is transformed into high quality tweed by the hand-spinning and weaving cottage industries of Donegal. The crafts of tapestry, rugmaking and embroidery are being encouraged by the Kilkenny Design Centre in the Republic and the Local Enterprise Development Unit in Northern Ireland.

*I*NDEX

ACKNOWLEDGEMENTS

The Automobile Association would like to thank the following photographers, libraries and associations for their assistance in the preparation of this book.

BORD FAILTE 15 Traditional music, 17 Signpost, 38 Ennis, 48 Parknasilla, 60 L. Gur, 76 Monasterboice, 79 New Ross, 81 Rosslare, 90 Aran Islands, 95 Clonfert cathedral, 106 Sligo Town, 131 Killybegs, 132 Letterkenny, 134 Monaghan Town.

DEREK FORSS 56 Wicklow Head, 61 Baltinglass, 88 and 103 Mulrany.

INTERNATIONAL PHOTOBANK Front Cover Bundoragha River, Back Cover Timoleague Abbey.

MARY EVANS PICTURE LIBRARY 20 Viking Raiders, 22 Battle of the Boyne, 23 *Gulliver's Travels*, 35 Cork Harbour, 45 Limerick, 69 Dublin, 101 James Joyce, 113 Spinning Yarn, 133 Londonderry.

MUSEUM OF IRELAND 63 Kells Mosaic.

NORTHERN IRELAND TOURIST BOARD 112 Annalong harbour, 114 Bally-clare fair, 115 Ballymoney, 116 Bangor, 124 Cushendan, 129 Glenariff, 134 Marble Arch Caves, 137 Portrush harbour, 139 Silent Valley.

THE MANSELL COLLECTION LTD Front and back endpapers Upper Lake Killarney, 43 Old Weir Bridge, Killarney, 49 St Brendan's voyage, 99 Thomas Lynch's house, 102 Yeats, 120 Belfast, 126 Baptism at Tara, 142 Lace making.

THE SLIDE FILE 13 Colliemore harbour, 16 Oysters and Guinness.

WATERFORD CRYSTAL 52 Jug maker.

All remaining transparencies are from the Association's own photo library (**AA PHOTO LIBRARY**) with contributions from:

L Blake, J Blandford, D Forss, G Munday, The Slide File, P Zoeller.